Developing AI Literacy in Students

Jitendra Pandey
Middle East College, Oman

IGI Global
Scientific Publishing
Publishing Tomorrow's Research Today

Vice President of Editorial Melissa Wagner
Director of Acquisitions Mikaela Felty
Director of Book Development Jocelynn Hessler
Production Manager Mike Brehm
Cover Design Jose Rosado

Published in the United States of America by
IGI Global Scientific Publishing
701 East Chocolate Avenue
Hershey, PA, 17033, USA
Tel: 717-533-8845 | Fax: 717-533-7115
Website: https://www.igi-global.com E-mail: cust@igi-global.com

Library of Congress Cataloging-in-Publication Data

LCCN: 2025017884 (CIP Data Pending)
ISBN13: 979-8-3373-2297-1
Isbn13Softcover: 979-8-3373-2298-8
EISBN13: 979-8-3373-2299-5

British Cataloguing in Publication Data
A Cataloguing in Publication record for this book is available from the British Library.

Table of Contents

Detailed Table of Contents

This chapter studies the integration of artificial intelligence (AI) in various educational curricula, highlighting the importance of adapting AI concepts to different subjects and grades. It demonstrates the potential for AI to improve individual learning, promote critical thinking, and provide students with problem-solving experiences in the real world. Through research into successful case studies, this paper demonstrates topics such as science, mathematics, humanities, and arts and how AI can be seamlessly included in its role in professional and technical training. There are also challenges, such as access to AI resources, teacher training, and digital gaps. This chapter contains recommendations for educators, curriculum developers, and political decision-makers. We will wisely integrate AI into the curriculum to ensure students develop technical skills and ethical awareness. The research highlights the need for an interdisciplinary approach and future-oriented curriculum development to prepare for the rapidly developing world of AI control.

The impact of AI tools has brought incredible development to all sectors of the global arena. AI is a software technology that aims to create artificial general intelligence (AGI) to add comfort to humanity. For the past few years, the growth of AI tools has been massive, and the development of technology is inexorable. Though AI tools are helpful for alluring students in education, there are a few drawbacks faced by educators and learners in this field. There are many e-contents created by AI tools that reduce the necessity of acquiring knowledge from the faculty. This paper is going to examine the drawbacks of AI tools in the education sector and contribute to the development of originality by enhancing the creative thinking skills of educators and students. The research is going to conduct a survey among the educators and the learners about the dependency of AI tools. From the study, the research is bringing forth the drawbacks of AI writing tools and the need for originality in the education field.

Preface

SHAPING THE FUTURE OF LEARNING

The beginning of the 21st century has been characterised by an unprecedented technological revolution, with artificial intelligence (AI) emerging as one of its most transformative influences. From the algorithms that curate our social media feeds and suggest our next purchase to the sophisticated systems guiding medical diagnoses and autonomous vehicles, AI is no longer a futuristic idea but an undeniable part of our daily lives. As AI continues its rapid integration into every possible sector, shaping industries, economies, and societies, the necessity to develop AI literacy among the next generation has become essential. This book, Developing AI Literacy in Students, serves as a vital resource in this mission, designed to provide educators, policymakers, and learners with the basic knowledge and practical strategies needed to navigate, influence, and engage with an AI-driven world.

AN OVERVIEW OF THE SUBJECT MATTER: UNPACKING AI LITERACY

At its core, AI literacy goes beyond just technical skill or the ability to use AI tools. It provides a broad framework that enables people to understand the key ideas behind artificial intelligence, critically assess its uses, recognise its ethical issues, and engage responsibly with its social effects. Just as reading and writing are vital skills for navigating the written world, AI literacy is becoming equally essential for succeeding in our increasingly connected, data-rich society.

This book explores the many aspects of AI literacy, dividing it into several essential parts:

- Conceptual Understanding: This involves grasping the fundamental principles of AI, including machine learning (supervised, unsupervised, reinforcement learning), deep learning, natural language processing (NLP), computer vision, and robotics. It focuses on understanding how AI functions, not just what it can do.
- Critical Evaluation: AI systems are not infallible. AI literacy requires the ability to critically assess AI applications, spot potential biases, understand limitations, and scrutinise the data and reasoning behind AI decisions. This includes distinguishing credible information generated by AI from misinformation.
- Ethical and societal awareness: Perhaps the most vital aspect, this involves understanding the ethical challenges posed by AI, such as data privacy, algorithmic bias, job displacement, and the implications for human autonomy and societal equity. It encourages a responsible attitude towards AI development and deployment.
- Application and Creation: While not every student will become an AI developer, AI literacy encourages practical engagement. This might include interacting with AI tools intelligently, basic programming, data analysis, or even designing conceptual AI solutions. It fosters an understanding of AI's real-world applications and creative possibilities.
- Future Preparedness: AI literacy is mainly about getting students ready for a future workforce where AI collaboration becomes standard, and for civic life where AI will impact policy, public discussion, and personal freedoms.

This publication provides a comprehensive overview of these components, utilising current research and best practices to create a solid guide for developing AI literacy from early education to higher education. It acknowledges that AI literacy is not a single skill but a range of competencies that develop alongside technological progress and societal needs.

WHERE OUR TOPIC FITS IN THE WORLD TODAY: AI AS A GLOBAL CATALYST

The modern world is undergoing a significant transformation, primarily driven by the widespread influence of artificial intelligence. AI is no longer limited to research laboratories; it is integrated into everyday life, transforming industries from healthcare and finance to entertainment and transport. Consider the personalised learning platforms that tailor educational content to individual students, the feedback systems offering real-time insights into academic performance, or the advanced diagnostic tools in medicine powered by machine learning—all exemplify AI's expanding presence.

This omnipresence makes developing AI literacy not just beneficial but essential. Without a basic understanding of AI, individuals risk becoming passive recipients of technology rather than informed participants capable of guiding its development. The digital divide, once defined by access to hardware and internet connectivity, is now widening to include a knowledge gap in AI. Those lacking AI literacy risk being excluded from future economic opportunities and civic discussions. Conversely, equipping students with this knowledge enables them to:

- Get involved in the future workforce: jobs are evolving. Automation and AI are transforming roles, creating new demands for skills in human-AI collaboration, data interpretation, and ethical reasoning. AI literacy prepares students for these emerging roles and encourages innovation.
- Engage as informed citizens: AI influences everything from political campaigns to news dissemination. An AI-literate citizenry can critically evaluate information, understand algorithmic impacts on society, and advocate for responsible AI governance.
- Promote fair innovation: By understanding how AI functions, students from diverse backgrounds can help develop AI systems that are fair, inclusive, and reflect a wider range of human experiences. This contributes to reducing biases and supporting equitable access to technology's benefits.

The urgency of this subject is emphasised by global initiatives aimed at incorporating AI education into curricula across the world. Countries recognise that fostering AI literacy is a strategic necessity for economic competitiveness, social cohesion, and technological sovereignty. This book adds to this international discussion by offering practical insights and comprehensive guidance for embedding AI literacy in various educational contexts, ensuring that education systems respond effectively to the demands of a swiftly changing technological landscape.

OUR TARGET AUDIENCE: EMPOWERING THE EDUCATIONAL ECOSYSTEM

Developing AI Literacy in Students is specifically designed for a wide but highly engaged audience within the educational ecosystem. Our principal readers include:

- Educators and Classroom Teachers: From elementary school teachers introducing computational thinking to high school instructors incorporating AI concepts into STEM subjects, and university faculty designing specialised courses, this book offers practical pedagogical approaches and curriculum development insights.

- Curriculum developers: Those responsible for designing educational programmes will find comprehensive guidance on structuring AI literacy curricula, selecting suitable content, and aligning learning outcomes with the needs of an AI-driven future.
- Researchers: Academics and researchers in educational technology, AI in education, and learning sciences will find a comprehensive collection of current ideas, theoretical frameworks, and empirical results that can guide future research and policy advice.
- Teacher Educators: Those training the next generation of teachers will benefit from insights on preparing educators to teach AI concepts effectively and ethically.
- Policymakers: Decision-makers at local, national, and international levels involved in education policy, technology integration, and workforce development will develop a deeper understanding of the urgent need for AI literacy and practical strategies for its widespread adoption.
- School administrators: Leaders responsible for the overall vision and resource distribution in schools will discover persuasive arguments and practical models for embedding AI literacy throughout their institutions.
- EdTech Innovators and Developers: Those creating educational tools and platforms can gain insights into the specific needs and challenges of promoting AI literacy, guiding the design of more effective and ethical solutions.

Ultimately, this book is intended for anyone committed to preparing students not just to survive but to thrive and lead in a world increasingly influenced by artificial intelligence. It acts as a comprehensive guide for promoting informed awareness, critical thinking, and responsible interaction with emerging technologies.

THE IMPORTANCE OF EACH CHAPTER SUBMISSION: A JOURNEY TOWARDS AI LITERACY

This book is organised as a progressive journey, with each chapter contributing an essential piece to the mosaic of AI literacy. By bringing together diverse perspectives and expertise, the authors highlight the many facets of this important subject, offering both theoretical basis and practical applications. The following paragraphs offer a glimpse into the indispensable contributions of each chapter.

1. AI's Role in Promoting Mental Wellness in Higher Education

From Chatbots to Predictive Analytics: Introduction, AI-Powered Crisis Hotlines, Ethical and Practical Issues for AI, Digital Literacy – the chapter explores how AI-powered tools have the potential to transform mental health care in academia by offering scalable, accessible, and personalised support to both students and staff at an affordable cost. Emerging technologies, including chatbots, early-warning systems, and VR therapies, enable students to navigate mental barriers that affect academic performance and overall wellbeing.

2. Foundations of AI Literacy

Summarises how various Artificial Intelligence (AI) methodologies enable unique approaches to address complex real-world issues. Understanding different classifications—such as expert systems, machine learning, rule-based systems, and evolutionary algorithms—provides a structured basis for distinguishing between various AI models and their applications. In fields like fraud detection, rule-based systems offer transparency and control by depending on predefined logic rules. Expert systems are widely used in sectors like healthcare and law, mimicking human expertise while providing reliable advice.

3. History of AI: Key Milestones and Figures

Highlighting the evolution of AI from its early beginnings to its present state, also underscores the importance of AI in all fields, from healthcare to banking. AI has driven acceleration and improvements, while also raising ethical and societal concerns. The goal of AI research soon will include achieving Artificial General Intelligence (AGI), along with enhancing interpretations and reducing biases in AI systems, thereby creating a future where human and AI intelligence are seamlessly integrated. Future developments also consider quantum AI and autonomous systems, with an emphasis on sustainable AI.

4. Impact of Using ChatGPT on Students

This study offers valuable insights into how ChatGPT influences students' academic experiences. The findings indicate that while ChatGPT can be a powerful tool for enhancing learning methods, time management, and problem-solving, it also poses challenges related to over-reliance, critical thinking, and academic integrity. The cross-cultural aspect of the study highlights significant regional differences in ChatGPT usage, with students from resource-rich countries using it as a supplementary tool and those from resource-limited environments relying on it as a primary academic resource.

5. Integrating AI Across Curricula - Adapting AI Concepts for Various Subjects and Grade Levels

The key findings from integrating AI curricula show that including AI in education requires careful planning, thoughtful implementation, and a balance between technical skills and broader interdisciplinary ideas. Best practices highlight the importance of integrating AI with existing curricula to ensure equal access to AI tools and to support the professional development of educators. These practices help promote AI integration whilst ensuring students gain a comprehensive understanding of AI applications and their effectiveness. The introduction of AI concepts should not be limited to high schools or universities but should start at earlier educational stages. This can be achieved by including diverse themes in social sciences and ethics, as well as age-appropriate AI topics in mathematics and natural sciences.

6. Mind the Gap - Examining the Disadvantages of AI Writing Tools in Education, Focusing on Originality

The study advocates for a collaborative effort among educators, students, and educational technology developers to bridge the gap between the advantages and disadvantages of AI writing tools. By fostering a culture that values originality, institutions can harness the benefits of AI while ensuring that students retain their unique voices and perspectives. The evolving educational landscape requires a mindful integration of technology that aligns with the overarching goal of cultivating independent thinkers and creative contributors to academia.

7. Pedagogical approaches in project-based learning, inquiry-driven methods, computational thinking, and design thinking for AI education

The future of AI literacy depends on fostering curiosity, agency, and resilience among students. They should be encouraged to explore AI not just as users, but as creators, collaborators, and ethical leaders. By embracing inquiry, experimentation, and reflection, students can become active participants in the digital age, empowered to shape technology in ways aligned with human values and societal good.

8. Towards an integrated artificial intelligence literacy framework in education

concludes with the idea that research on AI literacy in general and AI literacy in education in particular has generated evidence. According to this review, there are no significant differences in AI literacy across various domains. The most common domains of AI literacy include understanding AI, applying AI, assessing and developing AI, and AI ethics. However, this research has broadened the scope of AI literacy to cover computational thinking, data literacy, digital literacy, algorithm literacy, and transdisciplinary and interdisciplinary knowledge.

Each chapter, through its thorough examination of specific aspects of AI literacy, provides a rich tapestry of knowledge and practical advice, making this book an invaluable resource for anyone invested in the future of education.

CONCLUSION: IMPACTING THE FIELD AND CONTRIBUTING TO THE SUBJECT MATTER

Developing AI literacy in students is more than just a collection of chapters; it is a rallying cry for action and a comprehensive blueprint for transforming education into the age of artificial intelligence. This book makes a significant contribution to the growing field of AI in education by presenting a multifaceted and practical approach to a concept that is often discussed but rarely fully explained: AI literacy.

Its impact is felt in several key areas:

- Defining and Demystifying AI Literacy: By providing a clear and practical definition of AI literacy and breaking it into its essential parts, the book makes complex ideas more accessible, establishing a shared language for educators and policymakers.
- Offering a Pedagogical Roadmap: Emphasising diverse pedagogical approaches, practical learning experiences, and ethical considerations creates a much-needed guide for educators facing challenges in teaching AI effectively and responsibly. It moves beyond theoretical discussions to include tangible strategies.
- Highlighting the Interdisciplinary Nature of AI: By advocating for the integration of AI concepts across the curriculum, the book emphasises that AI literacy is not solely for computer scientists but is essential for all students, reflecting AI's broad influence across various areas of life.
- Promoting equity and inclusion: The dedicated focus on addressing digital divides and ensuring fair access guarantees that the conversation around AI

literacy remains inclusive, aimed at empowering all learners and preventing the deepening of existing inequalities.

- Shaping Future Policy and Practice: By underscoring the crucial roles of policymakers and ongoing professional development, the book calls for systemic changes to firmly embed AI literacy within educational frameworks, shaping future policies and best practices.

In a rapidly changing world where AI is not merely a tool but a fundamental part of innovation and societal progress, Developing AI Literacy in Students acts as an essential guide. It enables educators to nurture a generation of informed, critical, and ethical citizens who can not only adapt to technological shifts but also actively shape a future where AI advances human highest aspirations. This book exemplifies the belief that by fostering strong AI literacy, we are not just preparing students for a technological future, but also investing in a fairer, smarter, and more responsible world for everyone.

Chapter 1
AI's Role in Promoting Mental Wellness in Higher Education:
From Chatbots to Predictive Analytics

Kaushalya Thopate
https://orcid.org/0000-0001-7163-1262
Vishwakarma Institute of Technology, Pune, India

Mayuri Gawade
https://orcid.org/0009-0009-7431-6992
Vishwakarma Institute of Technology, Pune, India

Shweta Anand Joshi
Trinity Academy of Engineering Yewalewadi, Pune, India

Amruta Amol Bhawarthi
Vishwakarma Institute of Technology, Pune, India

Madhumati Nilesh Pol
Vishwakarm Institute of Technology, Pune, India

Deepika Lalit Falak
PES Modern College of Engineering, Pune, India

ABSTRACT

We address the implementation of AI-based approaches in mental health services with an emphasis on their contribution to alleviate growing mental health crises in student and faculty populations of higher education settings. The AI-powered tools such as chatbots, early-warning systems and VR-based therapies scale personalized and accessible solutions for mental health care and disrupt ways to manage support and intervene on that level. These tools have the ability to radically improve care by making timely and effective mental health assistance possible, thus benefiting the individual as well as society. Nonetheless the essay also makes the points to be very

DOI: 10.4018/979-8-3373-2297-1.ch001

mindful of ethical issues so that these tools are not just implemented responsible but also fair. It mainly encourages the development of health supportive and enabling Academic Institution Environments to increase resilience to promote academic success. The chapter stresses that although AI has the potential to improve mental health care, it will only be well implemented if the problems with AI in care avoid getting worse.

I. INTRODUCTION

Mental health needs to be a paramount topic in higher education, leaving no time for the old school solutions. Beyond the stressors in the academic culture for students and faculty, it is no wonder that anxiety depression and burnout are epidemic. It feels like a student's first big independence, but with school work and peer pressures just compounded in all it overwhelming nature often leaves many students feeling overwhelmed. The added financial burdens, add one of the many components forcing many into an anxious and borderline schizophrenic state (Zhai et al., 2024).

Stressors to faculty are just as complicated. Teaching, research and administrative responsibilities add up into a load that can feel almost impossible(Zawacki-Richter et al., 2019). Academic environments frequently prioritize productivity and performance (restorative processes are sadly non existent in the culture (Xie et al., 2023)). Such compounding stressors can lead to chronic stress, reduced job satisfaction and finally burnout (Shahzad et al., 2024).

Growing awareness of the mental health epidemic in academic settings has spilled over to demand for safeguard supports that benefit clear and front-of-mind support systems across all levels of Higher Education. This is essentially requiring institutions to recognise the omnipresent nature of mental health and acknowledge supporters in teaching as diligently as they do students [5]. It is in this context that ART THINKING offers a game changing approach for the accelerated development of AI in mental health support (Seo et al., 2021).

Tying together mental health outcomes with AI chatbots, ERs and VR therapies through visualization. Figure 1. visualizing AI technologies Chatbots, Early Warning systems and VR therapies in relation to one another and the meta goal — achieve better health outcomes on the subject of mental health.

Figure 1. Flowchart of AI-Powered Mental Health Solutions

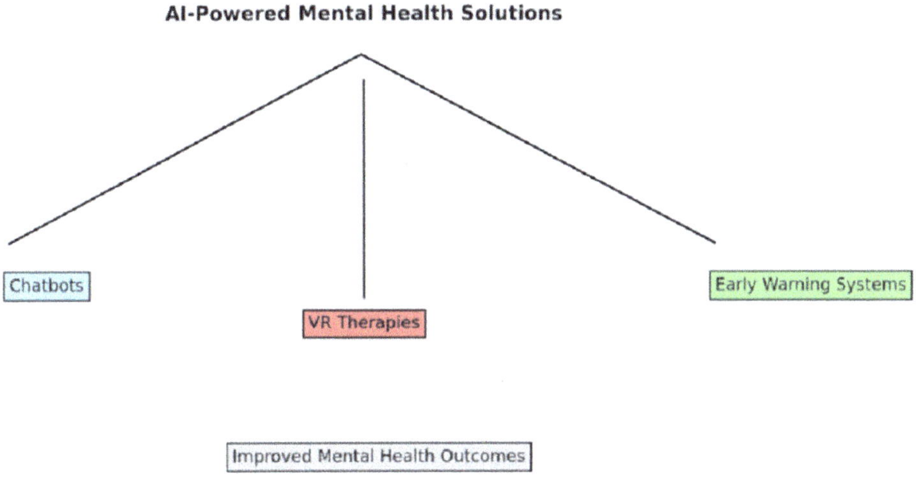

Role of AI in Mental Health Support

AI is changing mental health to be more ready, efficient and personalised for the future. AI, or advanced technologies as the case may be brings attention to some of the many weaknesses in traditional mental healthcare delivery systems. Scaling and timely interventions with offer of bespoke support is one way in which this could help tackle the mental health impacts of being a student.

Highlighting main points such as availability, cost effectiveness and ability to detect early on as in with kind of importance. Bar graph Figure 2 detailing the top 11 AI benefits such as accessibility, economic efficiency and early warning systems.

Figure 2. Bar Chart for Benefits of AI in Mental Health Support

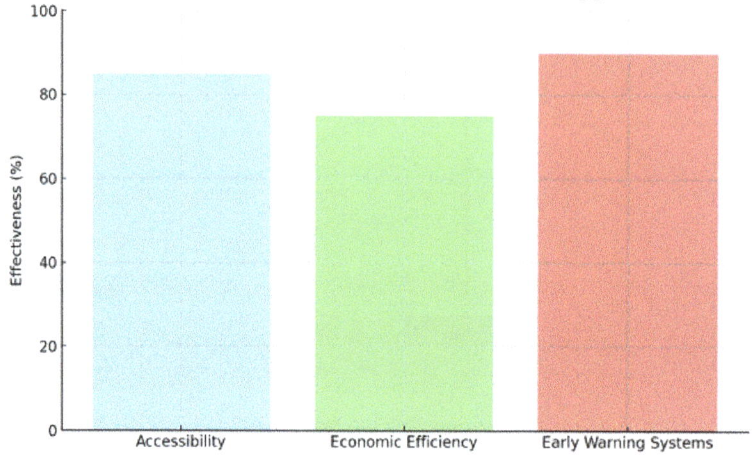

Scalability

In mental health, I would argue that the most important benefit of AI is its ability to scale. Mental health services are constrained by both resource limitations and a global dearth of mental health professionals (Rodway & Schepman, 2023). AI-based solutions including chatbots and digital platform provide scalable solutions for supporting different population segments. These systems are not limited to geography or inability from the professionals, and institutions can use that to stretch care to constituents (Nakshine et al., 2022).

For example, AI chatbots are set to oblige natural human interactions by providing on-the-spot help. This can tackle some of the most common mental health issues they will encounter like stress management or teaching users coping strategies and how to reach out for their first support. This accessibility allows people who are seeking help to immediately link with an existing resource and be freed of access barriers (Malik et al., 2024).

On digital platforms, a multitude of stuff can be uploaded like self-help modules, guided meditation, training materials related to psychoeducation (Luckin et al., 2022). These already equip people to do their own would be treatment, and relieve the overwhelming pressures of overburdened professional care-givers (Makhambetova et al., 2021).

Timely Interventions

AI has the knack for in-time monitoring and managing, essential in early identification of mental health cases. This behavioral data can be analyzed regarding things like sleep changes, physical activity and social interactions that are tracked by wearables, mobile apps and online platforms feeding AI. Some of these insights will help to identify mental health issues, well before they become crises (Labadze et al., 2023).

E.g., AI algorithms in which behavioral signals suggestive of depression or anxiety can generate warnings for both users and mental health professionals (Kamalov et al., 2023). This by standing approach helps to catch it early, and not let problems spiral out of control. In the fast-paced environment of higher education where mental health issues can be accelerated to crisis status quickly (González-López et al., 2021), early intervention can have a meaningful impact on outcomes.

Add to that, AI tools can streamline crisis intervention through quick access to crisis helplines, critical resources, or a campus support services in advance (Erebak & Turgut, 2021). These features keep it so that the incapacitated recipient get the best help right away, thereby decreasing the chance of bad results (Dwivedi et al., 2023).

Personalization

AI in mental health support from another perspective is providing of personalized care. AI platforms evaluate users data (preferences, previous engagement, psychological profile…) to provide tailored therapeutic approach and resources (Crawford et al., 2024). This tailoring enables mental health interventions to be more effective; they are more finely tuned to the unique needs of each patient.

For instance, suggestions on mindfulness and CBT activities that an AI system recommends or lifestyle changes relevant to a certain person's situation. The specific support enables higher mental health strategy adherence and engagement (Chan & Hu, 2023), resulting in a better outcome Additionally personalization creates a feeling of being seen and heard, which can foster commitment to have care needed (Cambra-Fierro et al., 2024).

AI platforms are the remote support another core functionality of AI-driven. AI ensures that the mental health care is available at home and remote therapy sessions, self-help programmes and tools to interact are being made available to people. Stigma Reduction: Increased accessibility in seeking help can reduce a burden on specific resources (Budhwar et al., 2022).

Bridging Gaps in Mental Health Services

The incorporation of AI technologies into mental health care systems can help to fill significant service gaps. Wait Times Since the oldest of mental health services often suffer from short supply, scarcity of workforce and geographical unevenness. By minimizing these constraints with on-demand assistance, AI enhances the scalability and availability to the cohorts of the underserved (Bhutoria, 2022).

AI solutions can be an invaluable support to the existing mental health resources in higher education, where services often overwhelmed by demand. Take platform recommendations with AI-driven screening and triage that will rush some cases depending on severity; directing patients that need immediate attention to the front of the queue. This increased efficiency leads to better use of resources and an improved mental services output (Akgun & Greenhow, 2021).

Ethical Considerations and Challenges

AI for mental health support shows much promise, but it is critical to engage with the ethical issues, and challenges involved in this domain. Security of user privacy & data is at great importance as confidential mental information must be fortified against breaches someone else misuse it in reality. Build trust and adoption of AI based solutions: Institutions must establish extensive safeguards involving transparent policies (Al-Zahrani, 2024).

Furthermore, AI systems should be designed in a way that augments, not substitutes for human mental health practitioners. AI although helpful can't replace good old human touch when dealing with complex and fine-grained mental health problems (Fagherazzi et al., 2021). Our integration of AI tools in parallel with mental health professionals looks to ground care in the physical and psychological.

Algorithmic Bias another concern can occur, creating an uneven access or treatment recommendations. Reducing this risk requires a more inclusive approach and balanced training of AI systems through diverse datasets that match the goals of different population groups (Uban et al., 2021).

Future Implications

AI integration in the mental health support systems for higher education has large transformative potential. Through the mitigation of service gaps, increase accessibility and patient-centredness AI can help to restore emotional homeostasis among university communities (Khurana et al., 2022). The evolution of AI research will almost certainly be spurred by the uptake of new disruptive strategies around mental health, thus offering fresh avenues of investigation for treatment and prevention (Zhang et al., 2022).

More sophisticated capabilities are developed through continued advancements in AI technologies such as predictive modeling for mental health trends, real-time feedback on intervention effectiveness. They can furnish data-driven interventions and pave the way for never-ending quality improvement in mental health care delivery (Davenport & Kalakota, 2019).

AI-Powered Mental Health Solutions

Using AI-based platforms, institutions can fill the service gaps, intervene early and deliver calibrated support that accommodates the needs of the varied segments (Graham et al., 2019) of the societies they are part of. The challenges we need to tackle are of course ethics and algorithmic bias, but the help in mental health support that AI can offer is far-reaching (Molnar, 2024).

Moving forward in the evolution of higher education, leveraging AI for mental care is a crucial time to build resiliency and student/faculty well-being for students & faculty. Preaching these advancements pave the way for academic institutions to be in heads when dealing with the mental health crisis confronting their communities, fostering environments in which people can flourish personally and professionally.

Chatbots for Mental Health

AI chatbots (Woebot and Wysa are at the forefront) are a new frontier in mental health resources. A NLP-powered solution in conversational support systems that can be easily accessed, emotionally compliant and performative for the people who are suffering from Mental health issues. From a functionality perspective, they address many the main aspects in mental health care:

Empathetic Conversations No Judgement

AI chatbots are probably one of the biggest advantage in the fact that they create a safe and judgement-free zone. These tools put the users in a space where they were able to discuss their feelings openly and empathetically. This initial comfort is crucial in mental health care, as it allows individuals to come forward and get the help they need without fear of judgment or ridicule (Peake et al., 2018).

Evidence-Based Methods & Techniques

AI chatbots have been integrated with empirically tested strategies, e.g., cognitive-behavioral therapy, to provide assistance for mental health problems. They are supplying them with useful strategies for managing stress, anxiety and depressive thoughts. These software empower individuals to take control of their mental health, leading people through therapeutic techniques (Balcombe, 2023).

Mood and Emotional Check-Ins

Most often, chatbots contain elements better known as Participant Mood/Emo-checks (regular) —part of the even consistency of a positive mood & emotional wellness monitoring.

Check-ins help users see what they have been progressing in their mental health, learn from patterns and triggers. This feature not only helps self awareness but also can be used as a precious data for long-term mental health monitoring (Rodrigues, n.d.).

Key Advantages of Chatbots in Mental Health

Benefits of using chatbots: AI-powered chatbots are a critical asset in the world of mental health care that should not be take for granted.

1. **Availability 24/7:** One of the major breakthroughs with chatbots is that they are literally available all through day and night. As the AI chatbots give instant support whether it is working hours everyone can avail immediate support unlike human counselors. It is to allow the most timely help to people who need it, decreasing the risk of a crisis stemming from timeliness in seeking solution due to delays at factor (Strickland, 2019).
2. **Anonymous: De-Stigmatization:** Traditional counseling is often shunned by many who fear being judged or shamed. To solve this, chatbots can come in and provide anonymity (which is why `mental health' support becomes easily within reach. This anonymity makes people come out and play, where it normalizes; increases help seeking behaviors [30].
3. **Diligence in Relief of Resource Shortages** — The overutilization of Mental Health services in most institutions and communities results from lack of resources because of understaffed services, meaning long wait times or limited access. Chatbots are a second-line solution for less severe (and preliminary/supportive) problems Chatbots take small part in the workload of mental health

professionals, so they can process those cases where machine-learning approaches are not quite enough (Strickland, 2019) for.

4. **Scalable Solutions:** AI chatbots can reach across massive volumes of users without adding the need for more employees or other material bulk. Their scalability is especially appealing within educational setting, where demand for mental health services outpaces available resources ("PTSD Help - a Randomized Controlled Trial of a PTSD Mobile Health App," 2019)

Applications in Higher Education

Among students and faculty, we see a lot of mental health problems and stress in higher education that AI chatbots in this environment deliver multiple well-targeted benefits:

- **For Students:** Immediate academic, social and financial stress Students will undoubtedly face increasing stress because of everything that happens in the academic life? Chatbots can direct them to mindfulness exercises, breathing methods and tips for stress management in those moments where it is needed.
- **Add- on Support to Faculty:** Faculty are also overloaded with the additional responsibilities of teaching our research our inescapable administrative stuff and enjoy chatbot support too. They provide tools to be instantly available, relieving the burden of coping work-related stress and managing mental health.
- **Crisis Management resource:** Chatbots may be used to guide the user to emergency numbers, campus mental services or other crisis resources depending on when asynchronous helps is required. Agent ship means that they can act as enabler to ensure people in distress getting timely support.

Ethical Considerations and Future Directions

Although AI chatbots are absolutely revolutionary perspective in the future if we consider long term point of view, the ethical issue has to be solved to be able get effectively utilized and accepted.

1. **Data Privacy and Security** — User-sensitive data should be protected very well. Developers need to put in the best security that can secure data and assure user's confidence.
2. **Adding Along Side Human Counselors:** Chatbots view it that way, as added resources for counselors. They exist to be the first layer of support and on less challenging issues, leaving more complex, serious cases to human professionals.

3. **Algorithmic Bias:** Chatbots need diversity datasets for training so as not to have any kind of bias towards which could adversely affect the quality of care being provided to different demographic groups of people.

AI chatbots (ex: Woebot & Wysa) are some of the amazing tool we will need to change the face of mental health support nearly universally in our communities. Designed to provide compassionate, empirically validated and accessible care they are aimed at filling some of the largest holes in traditional mental health services. In higher ed, their breadth and reach makes them an irreplaceable tool for academic communities to build emotional resiliency.

Early Warning Systems

AI-fuelled early warning systems are transforming mental health care through predictive analytics in helping individual in risk to mental health conditions. These systems scan large volumes of data in search of very slight distress markers, creating a time-sensitive intervention. Especially with the ubiquitous nature of mental health problems in higher education, these systems offer incredibly important perspectives to allow prevention from turning into a full-blown crisis. Further, in this Read-Along let us understand the fundamental aspects and advantages of the AI-based WEBS in mental health support ("Talkspace Receives NIH Grants to Conduct Telepsychiatry Research," 2021a). Showing trends in academic performance versus timeline of interventions. Figure 3 outlines how academic performance is improving and intervention cases are interacting with time.

Figure 3. AI-Driven Early Warning Outcomes

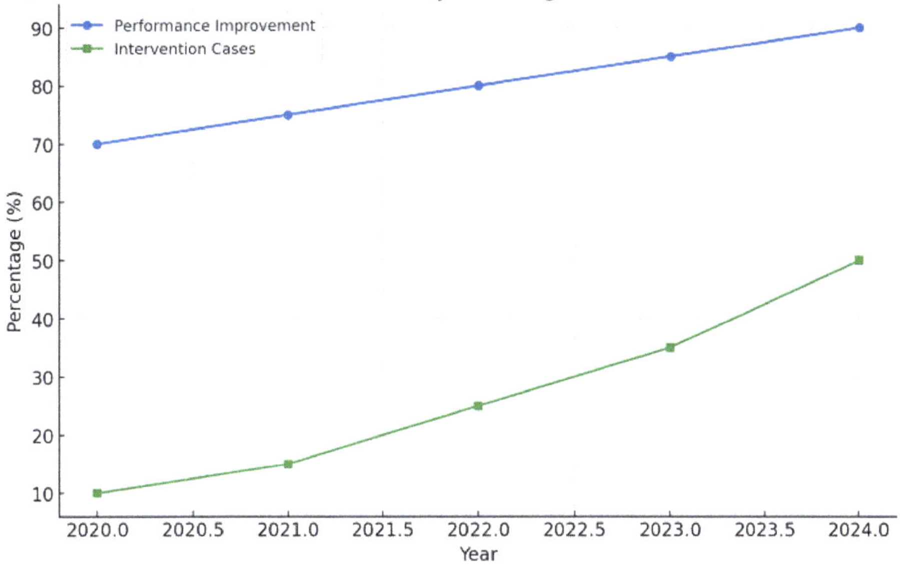

Key Indicators Analyzed by Early Warning Systems

AI systems explore a variety of data points in order to look for patterns and signals of possible emotional/psycholgocial distress. Some of the top indicators are:

1. **Academic trends in performance:** A sudden loss, or a significant drop and let's say more than a threshold amount in terms of the student performance usually indicates stress burnouts or mental health/end emotional problems. for instance, a student who is normally a high performer but starts to have difficulty keeping their grades should they be dealing with emotional or psychological issues. Academic performance markers — AI algorithms can register trends in student performance that signal educators or mental health counselors to intervene with follow up. This allows those who require it, support can be delivered before the situation deteriorates further ("Talkspace Receives NIH Grants to Conduct Telepsychiatry Research," 2021b).
2. **Grades**: Disturbing charts of attendance generally point towards other mental issues such as anxiety, depression or burnout. Increased absence from both classes and/or lab, as well as work-related activities is an emergence sign. AI can also observe attendance data to identify the individuals how seem to be faltering and the chance of catching a timely intervention in these cases. Through the

identification of attendance patterns, AI brings to attention underlying issues and is helping ensure no one gets left behind (Wan, 2021).

3. **Digital Health Metrics:** shifts in digital life patterns like language use for communication, social media activity or type of conversations that take place online can give us an indication of what might be happening with mental health. For example, less online involvement, changes in written communication style, especially over time or an abrupt quit of social media can be signs of distress emotions. These behavioral changes are evaluated by an AI algorithm that determines if the individual is falling into early warning signs for mental health deterioration. By analyzing digital footprints, AI systems provide a proactive means of detecting emotional malaise and enabling prompt support (Wan, 2021).

The Role of AI in Early Warning Systems

The AI-driven early warning system uses complex algorithms to bring together data from multiple sources. Combining academic performance patterns, attendance data and digital health signals across time, Such systems produce in aggregate all big picture of mental well-being on individual. This method of working helps in the accurate prediction and timely intervention [33]. How does it work

1. **CSR:** AI systems get data from different sources like academic details, turn-in statistics and digital interactive sessions. By integrating different datasets to identify patterns that signal mental health struggles. For instance, grades that are falling apart with inconsistency in attendance and decrease in social media presence might be a sign the student is stressed/depressed.
2. **Pattern Detection and Forecasting–** A machine learning can be used by AI to identify trends and patterns which people fail to pick automatically. These algorithms use historical data to create baselines for what normal behavior looks like, and trip-wires departures from those norms that could indicate trouble. A student who regularly misses deadlines but suddenly starts delivering assignments on time might be the first to flag that they are having a problem.
3. **Risk Screening and Alerts:** And when risks are being indicated the system sends alerts to pertinent stakeholders (mental health care provider, educators or administrators). Enable stakeholders with these alerts to read the patterns and apply appropriate action. The Type of Alerts: An alert can be the process of calling a student who looks to be in distress for a conversation or referring the student to counseling.

Benefits of Early Warning Systems

AI- Powered Early Warning Systems in Higher Ed has several critical NEW Improvements over traditional methods

1. **Quick Reactions:** With the brain disorders being detected at initial stage, helps in addressing mental health issues before they transform into a crisis. Timely Intervention: Inhibit the deterioration of mental health conditions, mitigates future problems and enhances long term outcomes. For example, early identification of a student at risk of burnout gives valid support that the student can use effectively to rebalance and avoid academic withdrawal [34].
2. **Individualized Interventions –** Over broad, one-size-fits-all one will not be able to address the individual mental health needs. Early warning systems allow the delivery of better support by determining the concrete problems each person experiences. A student with anxiety might be able to try mindfulness but an anxiety of depression that could be helped by therapy or medication Even when definitions across studies are somewhat disparate- AI Tailored interventions increase relevance and adequacy of support [35].
3. **Efficient Resource Allocation-** Limited mental health resource availability in higher education so it is necessary to allocate the available resource. SRS (silent reading systems) help focus resources on priority individuals, directing where it is most needed at times. For example, based on imminent risk this high-risk student will be scheduled for an urgent counseling session; less critical concerns might help using a variety of self-help materials or peer support programmes [34].
4. **Pre emptive Mental Health Management:** Early warning systems leave traditional mental health care behind from reactive to preventive. Instead of merely reacting when individuals come seeking help, these systems intervene with at-risk individuals prior to them reaching crisis levels. This preventative approach enables the preventive culture, lowering academic communities whole mental health problem [34].

Challenges and Ethical Considerations

Ethical and technical issues of early warning systems, though premier (Blackwell & Heidenreich, 2021), are implemented with great care;

1. **Anonymity and Data Security:** Use of sensitive data of an individual including academic records and digital footprints brings in questions about privacy and security. Single sign-on (SSOs), and more comprehensive security systems

for user data along with enforcement of laws (GDPR or HIPAA) will need to implemented in order to offer safeguards by design when it comes to protecting user privacy Finally transparency around how your user data is collected and used is pivotal to better establish trust with users.

2. **Preventing False Positive and Negatives:** AI are no Gods to be followed 100% of time; they may specify false positives[flag innocent people] or simply fail when it comes to identifying at-risk individuals (false negative). Algorithm continuous improvement and validation against real-world data must be done to reduce these errors, thereby making the system more accurate.
3. **Stigma and Widening the User Base:** Some may not want to use systems that observe their behaviour or flagging for intervention Some institutions must focus more on the supportive qualities of early warning systems and need to ensure that interventions are delivered with care and regard for individual autonomy.
4. **Automation vs human judgement:** While AI learn from the ground and give rich insights, human professionals are indispensable to make sense in data delivery care. Each early warning system should buttress, not substitute for, the praxis of mental health practitioners.

Future Directions

As early warning systems continue to refine, we may soon see the capabilities of these get bigger. Upcoming advancements could be:

- **Improved Predictive Analytics:** by using higher order algorithms to increase quality and reliability (Flanagan et al., 2021).
- **Wearable Devices:** Gathering fitness trackers data, health monitors for a more complete analysis of one's physical and mental state (Tutun et al., 2022).
- **Immediate Response:** Feedback to users of their mental stability real time so people can take the step to proactive (Uban et al., 2021).

Integration of EWS in mental health care for higher education is a paradigm shift that will help to build high quality and resilient academic communities. AI can help institutions to promote a proactive mental health approach, so the students and faculty have everything they need for their well being, personally as well professionally (Graham et al., 2019).

Virtual Reality and AI-Enhanced Therapies in Mental Health Care

Artificial Intelligence (AI) and its VR: boosts therapeutic interventions for mental health that are easily, engagingly and personalized. The technologies harness the power of immersive experiences in combination with AI-enabled personalization for an efficacious and ground-breaking way to tackle lots of mental health issues.

This combination of the technologies delivers rich experiences along with an AI-powered customisation, making it an effective and a creative way to solve many mental health problems. Lastly, I will delve into the important utilities of AI enabled VR therapies with its advantages and how can change the landscape in mental health care.

Applications of AI-Enhanced VR Therapies

AI-VR Solutions converge to generate different mental health therapeutic tools meeting multiple needs. The most pioneering implementations are:

Virtualised Relaxation, Mindfulness Hacks with VR Contexts

These include integrating users into VR environments to experience relaxing/ peaceful places like beaches, forests, or even a plain white background. Virtual spaces targeting stress reduction and mindfulness.

How it works: AI tunes these environments to the user's likes and physiological signs such as heart rate or stress in order for achieving personalized relaxation. For instance, if there is high anxiety one might gain an ease to move into few soothing environments that are calm and accompanied with satisfying sound visualizations.

- Beneficiaries:
    - Reduces stress and anxiety through an interactive platform for meditation [18].
    - Makes it easier to relax in a safe place, this is really helpful when you cannot picture calm by yourself.
    - Provides a stronger experience of mindfulness by exposing users to rich, interactive virtual environments.

Exposure Therapy for Anxiety and Phobias

A safe controlled exposure therapy to treat anxiety disorders, phobias.... [10] These systems are designed on real-life scenarios inducing feelings of fear or anxiety that permit patients to "expose" themselves, and habituate from these triggers .

o Examples:-

For someone that have a specific phobia let's say we're dealing with acrophobia or fear of heights — they can use VR to incrementally get exposed to varying heights from low platforms to taller structures. To practice public speaking or simulate social interactions in a faux social environment, with individuals with social anxiety.

o Advantages:
- Exposure in control: The users are taken through their fears gradually, subsequent fearful exposure help reduce anxiety over time.
- Personalization: The exposure treatments are customized on the progress or non-progress and tolerance of an individual.
- Safety: The virtual setting makes users comfortable during therapy, and hence makes them more willing to confront their fears.

Gamified Simmulated Counseling Sessions: With VR traditional counseling sessions get better with creating face-to-face (you can say virtual) simulations of the therapist or AI therapist avatars.

Sitting in these sessions makes therapy feel more interactive and less isolated for people who have logistical or emotional barriers to in-person therapy.

o Key Features:
- •Gamified: Process of counselling sessions to keep it an engaging one which removes the layers of intimidate mostly seen in traditional counselling.
- Accessibility: Co-location can be applied to dwellers of rural areas or disabled people who could not attend therapy otherwise.

Human Avatars: Human Like Interactions: AI avatars respond natural language support in human like style to actually provide empathetic, human interactive support.

o Use Cases:
- Lite/break the ice-treatment for first time clients who might be anxious about traditional therapy.

- People who have agoraphobia or are so anxious on social situations that they cant get out of the house.

Benefits of AI-Enhanced VR Therapies

The best of all worlds in terms of immersion, personalization and accessibility, AI + VR are a powerhouse combination that can re-write mental health care and make treatment feel less like everything it's currently marketed as. Some of the key highlights include:

1. **High level engagement:** VR provides environments that evoke high levels of engagement, and engage their full focus to increase the effectiveness of therapeutic interventions. In contrast to regular methods that resort to verbal or written instruction, VR sends user into multisensory world and does therapy impact much more than it should. Our simulations are realistic and users can try coping mechanisms in an UNFAKEABLE scenario. Impatient environments enhance interaction and help more likely setup will happen in terms for evidence-based therapy to work.
2. **Individualized Therapy: AI** provides added value to VR therapies by reviewing user-specific parameters (behavioural pattern, emotion response, physiological metrics) and designs individualised treatment plans. This personalization makes each session specifically catered to what they are going through at the moment and or need. For example in a AI system could scale up how far or how long virtual exposure therapy session should be based on the users heart rate, or self-reported anxiety levels.
3. **Real time feedback:** The user can see where they stand and modify their goals. 3. Relaxed & Available: No more logisitical hurdles from traditional mental health care in VR therapy freed by eradicating travel time, conflicts scheduling, & geographic bottlenecks. Users can access therapy sessions at the convenience of their home, this way mental health care become more available and not a big deal. This is especially the part that is benefit to people in underserved areas, for example rural residents or away areas [40].
4. **Decrease Stigma:** AI + VR therapies provide an anonymous and confidential treatment setting that helps reduce the stigma of mental health care seeking. Individuals who feel uncomfortable with the thought of attending traditional in-office sessions can be eased through private and discreet therapeutic experiences.
5. **Cost-Effectiveness:** With scale, VR therapy can be cheaper than traditional in-person treatment as healthcare costs rise over time.

Challenges and Ethical Considerations

AI-Driven VR Therapies: Opportunities & Potential but also Challenges, Ethical Issues for the Future

1. Technological Barriers

High cost of VR hardware and software may put some users or institutions out of reach. As a large portion of users are unaware and new to VR or AI systems, Tech-literacy is a bottleneck for users [24].

2. Privacy and Security Issues

Requiring all the sensitive mental health data obtained from VR sessions is to be properly constrained in a secure manner and avoided from getting hacked. Privacy by default policies are critical to keep users from cheating and complying with privacy laws.

3. Over-Reliance on Technology

AI and VR are incredibly powerful tools, they do not replace the need for us as human therapists. If it is not human supervision, user data could be misinterpreted and complex mental health issues not adequately catered for.

4. Ethical Use of Immersion

The creation of VR experiences has to be done very carefully to not be distressing or harmful. For example, puny exposure scenarios in VR can compound a users perceived fear instead of reducing it .

Future Prospects of AI-Enhanced VR Therapies

We are witnessing some exciting developments in the early stages of AI-fused VR therapeutics. Potential future advancements are:

1. **Sensor Data from Wearable Devices:** One attendance where VR systems are able provide instantaneous data are into physiological and emotional states by using wearable sensors (fitness trackers/EEG headsets).

2. **Expanded Applications:** Besides usages of anxiety and stress reduction, VR therapies could be applied for other psychological problems such as PTSD, autism spectrum disorders as well chronic pain management.
3. **Collaborative Virtual Environments:** Multi-player VR environments can be implemented to conduct group therapy sessions or peer-support networks for a shared understanding [38].
4. **Predictive Analytics powered by AI-based:** With powerful AI algorithms, we may be able to mine user data to predict future mental state trends and provide preventive data for more effective applications of VR therapis.

AI VR Therapies are a significant innovation within the domain of mental health care, providing intervention solutions via immersive (VR) and personalized (AI) pathways for different complexities. Using AI to synthesize the analytical capacity of AI with VR immersive experiences empowers users and lifts them to a personal position within their mental wellness.

What these technologies will do as they evolve is provide the mental health sector with an increased hook that can increase engagement, effectiveness and inclusiveness. Overcoming the present bottlenecks and welcoming future opportunities AI-based VR therapies will be key in making mental healthcare support more targeted, individualized and accessible.

II. AI-POWERED CRISIS HOTLINES: TRANSFORMING MENTAL HEALTH SUPPORT SYSTEMS

Crisis hotlines are extremely important in the face of a mental health crisis and provide immediate help to those who need it. AI is transforming these hotlines, making them user friendly, accessible and responsive through the integration of Artificial Intelligence (AI) [38]. Crisis hotlines automated with AI enrich a traditional toolkit of crude emotional assessments, to-tell interventions and long-term piping to make certain no one feels adrift through even the darkest hours [39].

Further, this includes an explanation of how AI makes crisis hotlines more effective — technologies involved and advantages/disadvantages prospective systems will require [40].

First interaction to solution, with the help of AI as an enhancement to our human support. Figure 4. The pivotal journey of how the process evolves from calligraphy to end with AI and human counselor integration.

Figure 4. AI-Powered Crisis Hotline Process

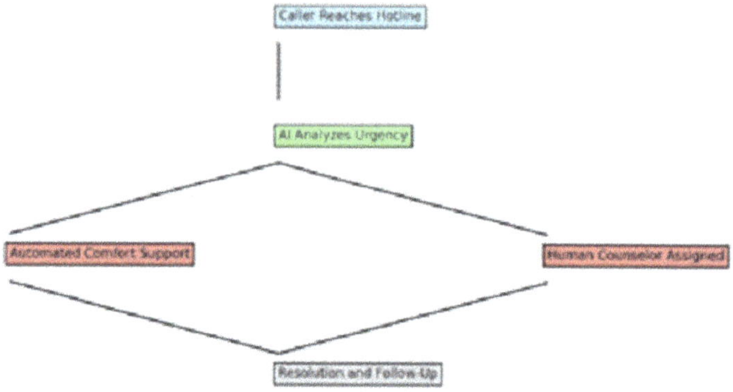

Core Features of AI-Powered Crisis Hotlines

1. **Precise Measurement of Emotional and Trigger Levels:**

Natural Language processing (NLP) and voice sentiment analysis are some of those AI technologies can measure emotional states in very high precision. By extracting text messages, voice tone, diction and conversational cadence AI systems a have the ability to determine the emotional sharpness of a caller and assist in prioritising cases based on perceived time urgency.

How does it work: gain more sophisticated meaning from the linguistic and paralanguage signals (pauses, pitch variation, pace of speech) going into stress, anxiety, fear or hopelessness as AI algorithms (Makhambetova et al., 2021). For example:

- A phrasing might be enough to elevate from LOW priority "I can't go on anymore" text message or "I feel so lonely"
- Trembling or irregular speech patterns detected by voice analysis indicate distress [35].

Impact: By enabling immidiate evaluation, hotlines will be able to identify people most at risk and provide necessary support in real time.

2. **Immediate Action for Serious Cases:**

AI systems are very good at triaging cases — subclassifying them on basis of urgency and severity of problems/patients.

Questioning capability decrease response time to individuals in crisis and eliminates life threatening delays.

Example:

Any person presenting thoughts of suicide with a plan or intent would automatically escalate to next level protocol AI can be used to alert human responders or emergency medical service so they can act in real time with the pertinent context [38].

Benefit:

Stopping the call volume from overwriting critical cases.

And the response to an issue is more appropriate when you can rely upon and adapt for each instance with a better crisis assessment.

3. **Automated Initial Comfort and Support:**

When human counselors are not immediately available, e.g., during peak demands AI chatbots or voice assistants they fill-in as intermediates for customers seeking help.

These systems enable callers temporary emotional support and counselling until they are connected with a live human counsellor.

Functions of AI Assistants

- **Emesis Simulation:** Using programmed responses to communicate empathy and calm the individual. We can immediately offer comfort for example by responding with things like, "I am here for you, and so are your feelings.
- **Coping Resources**: Using AI to direct callers on how to access coping resources like breathing programs or grounding.
- **Inquire:** request of necessary information from the caller so that human counsclors can bcst flow with the conversation.

Advantages:

- Makes sure each caller is not ignored while in peak traffic.
- This ensures that human counselors can concentrate on the emergencies and yet drop general good care for everyone else.

Benefits of AI-Powered Crisis Hotlines

1. Enhanced Capacity and Accessibility:

Shortages of staff and lack of resources are prevalent among traditional crisis hotlines. AI systems come to the rescue for amping up social distancing:

- Free from 24/7 operational cost: with a lean staff.
- By using Language processing for different types of population making sure that non-native speakers get the help to which they are entitled.

2. Scalability and Efficiency

AI hotlines are able to consolidate large call and message traffic, resulting in decreased response time especially when dealing with emergencies. For example,

- AI could for instance rank and prioritise urgent cases at the time of natural disasters or public emergency.

3. Alternate Perspectives for Improving Services

AI examines multiple hotspot interaction datasets allowing for important trends in mental health support to be identified and improved upon in the following AI-assisted decisions:

- Recognizing trends and patterns from crises
- Assessment of Intervention Strategies Value
- They will sharpen the training of counselors, streamline workflows and influence government policy around public mental-health.

4. Enhanced Personal Support and Continual Care

AI Assisted Programs: Custom responses based on previous interactions — hence you get more effective assistance reasoning for the personal aid. Like for example:

- For example, a caller with anxiety might get biofeedback or mantras [14].
- Meanwhile regular callers get follow through as AI remembers information from past conversations.

5. **Less Stigma, more anonymity** (fewer shame-inducing letters on your forehead)

AI hotlines help to keep things anonymous enabling more reaches out without self-censoring. AI crisis hotlines make support services better, safer and faster which finally improves mental health on a larger level.

Technologies Underlying AI-Powered Crisis Hotlines

1. **Natural Language Processing (NLP):** the glue that allow AI systems to understand human languages and respond. This tech is the backbone of text-based hotlines that interpret messages based on the content, tone & context in which they are sent to gauge emotional states.
2. **Sentiment Analysis:** Sentiment analysis helps to determine the emotions that voice or text depicts along with urgency levels and emotional distress.
3. **Voice Stress Analysis:** Utilizing AI for voice recognition, understands vocal patterns that are similar to stress, sadness and anger to give a more comprehensive emotional assessment.
4. **Machine Learning Algorithms:** As AI system learns through machine learning, their capability to judge emotional state and respond appropriately using past interactions with feedback is improved over time.
5. **Integration with Emergency Services:** Some state-of-the-art AI can interface directly with emergency staff, allowing them job logs and other contextual information for rapid response.

Ethical Considerations and Challenges

1. **Confidentiality and Secrecy:** AI phone hotlines have access personal data so deep privacy is a must for these systems. To keep users trust, data security and compliance of privacy laws (e.g., GDPR, HIPAA) have to be ensured.
   - o **Possible threats:** data thieves could steal the most private of personal information and all kinds of bad things could happen.
2. **Bias and Fairness:** AI learned from datasets that have biases (often under-representing whole groups) will replicate what it sees. For example, differences in Linguistic or cultural background should have no effect on the quality of help provided.
3. **Over reliance on AI:** AI augments the hotline but does not automatically mean that human counsellors can be replaced. AI is not capable of the empathy and subtle understanding needed to help with deep emotional challenges.
4. **Accuracy and False Alarm Rates:** AI may classify emotional cues incorrectly from time to time, resulting in inappropriate allocation of cases. High accuracy must be maintained to control second order effects.
5. **Skillful Automation Utilization:** Device initial responses for genuine help not only superficial comfort The intention is that it augment human intervention, not fully automate.

Future Directions and Opportunities

1. **Integration by Wearable Devices:** AI call hotlines could be integrated with wearable devices, like fitness trackers or smartwatches for physiological distress signs (heart rate, sleep patterns) and take a proactive approach in providing support.
2. **Multilingual and Culturally Sensitive:** Improving language options, as well as cultural sensitivity was just non-negotiable to make sure hotlines are fully available the entire palette of populations.
3. **Super AI Advanced Personalization:** Future systems can hyper-personalize the assistance by combining historical interactions, behavioural data & raw data from the moment.
4. **Shared Crisis Communities:** AI would be able to allow hotlines to seamlessly partner with other mental health resources so clients have a full ecosystem of support… For example:
   - Sharing data with therapists or community orgs for continuity of care
   - Transferring callers to your local support groups or resources (per identified needs) (Fagherazzi et al., 2021).
5. **Predictive Training for Counselors:** AI-insights can train human counselors in advance so they have data-driven strategies to efficiently respond to potential crisis situations [34].

AI-enabled crisis hotlines are a major breakthrough for mental health care—they leverage mass, speed and accuracy that was not really possible before. Using the cutting edge technologies called NLP, Sentiment analysis and Machine learning in confluence these systems increase the speed of delivery of crisis response services that will be personalized for every individual (Al-Zahrani, 2024).

There are many complications of course, some being privacy incidents and the notion that we might lean too much on work automation but AI hotlines would also be a game-changer on a number of levels. If further innovated and implemented ethically, these systems could prove invaluable in the quest for more access to mental health support services that increasingly buildlands they save lives and ensure world well-being (Budhwar et al., 2022).

III. ETHICAL AND PRACTICAL ISSUES

Artificial Intelligence (AI) in mental health services is a ground breaking integration which have the ability to augment the balance of access, precision and enhancement of mental health care. Such a hopeful technology however also creates ethical and pragmatic hurdles that have to be dealt with to guarantee reliable, equitable, and useful deployment. Privacy, Bias and AI augment & not replace human professionals in mental health care with AI: below delineate the most important issues.

1. Privacy and Confidentiality: Safeguarding Sensitive Data

AI mental health systems rely on large datasets: including personal information about individuals' mental health, behaviors and backgrounds. This information to be safe [39] protecting

- **Challenges**:
    - o **Data breaches**: AI systems are also at risk from cyberspace and a breach could lead to the inadvertent release of harmful information which may lead to psychological consequences, stigma or discrimination.
    - o **Informed Consent:** As they do not know how their data has been collected/ stored or used thus, raises questions on consent & transparency.
- **Solutions:**
    - o **Encryption and Secure Storage:** Mental health organizations use advanced encryption techniques with controlled data storage to reduce breaches.
    - o **Anonymization:** Sensitive information is anonymized, people do not identify individuals from the data.
    - o **Open and transparent Data Policies:** Data collection, usage and sharing policy must be explained transparently to users.
    - o **Regulations & Standards:** Compliance of well known privacy laws like GDPR, HIPAA or regional regulation are critical to gain trust and stay ethical.

2. Bias and Equity: Ensuring Fairness and Inclusivity

Bias in AI systems is a significant ethical concern, especially in the context of mental health care, where cultural and demographic differences profoundly impact diagnosis and treatment.

- **Causes of Bias**
    - o **Poor Representational Data Sets:** Most AI models are trained on Data Sets that are mainly from small base sets defining various population (western, rich or english-speaking).
    - o This produces biased algorithms that can perform poorly in serving a more diverse population.

- o **Cultural:** AI models are genre blind, the contextual understanding is missing to solve mental health problems aesthetics or cultural contexts.
- **Consequences of Bias:**
  - o Inequity to care for marginalized.
  - o Incorrect diagnosis and individualized advice for underserved populations.
- **Solutions:**
  - o Data sets should include diverse populations in all their varied manifestations: age, gender, ethnicity, SES, background.
  - o Monitoring is ongoing: audits and upgrades of AI systems can root out potential biases.
  - o Human in the loop: AI should perform as an assistant to human professionals who can provide culturally sensitive care and correct the possible miss-interpretation of the algorithm.
  - o Diversity & Inclusivity: Getting diverse stakeholders involved in the development of AI systems ensures that everyone is looked after and the system is fair.

3. The Role of Human Professionals: Balancing Automation with Empathy

AI is great at crunching big data sets, finding trends and automating processes however some parts of mental health care (empathy, human interaction and judgement) remain entirely out of scope for AI.

- **Limitations of AI in Mental Health:**
  - o **Empathy Deficit**: Machines do not have emotional intelligence and empathy, thus it is not able to trust, bond with the individual.
  - o **Trickier Decision Making:** Mental health diagnoses and treatments usually depend on nuance learned from understanding subtle, dependant factors that AI may deem insignificant.
  - o **Ethical Judgments:** Ethical issues run deep in much of the mental health care decision making and require human values and reasoning.
- **Human-AI collaboration**
  - o **Not Add-In but Augumenation**: AI should be viewed as an augmentation of the mental health professionals, not a replacement. Such as:
    - ✓ AI can help recognize patterns or early signs of people in the risk, but human counselors will have to assess and provide care.
    - ✓ AI can help reduce overhead and make the time of professionals available for patient-patient encounter.

- o **Emotional Intelligence and Connection:** The relation and trust are too vital that can only be provided by humans, hence of form algorithm cannot be replace.

4. Ethical Use of Automation

AI in the Psychiatry domain will automate several workflows from screening/ diagnosis to early check-ups and crisis interventions. Automation is an efficiency booster, it surprisingly triggers some ethical debates on how to use it correctly.

- **Ethical Issues**
  - o **Over-Reliance on AI:** Over reliance on automated systems can result in decreased human oversight and errors due.
  - o **Lost Tailoring:** automated pandering lacks individualized care required for complex or unusual needs.
- **Balancing of Automation and Personalization**l
  - o Examples to automate tasks that do not involve human element e.g., data analysis, appointment scheduling or a single screening
  - o Keep complex matters and emotional dealings to the human professionals.

5. Accountability and Transparency

AI systems must operate in a public & accountable manner to protect public trust and integrity of AI

- **Challenges:**
  - o **Black Box:** A lot of algorithms are considered black box as the algorithms are deciding for us without making us understand our decision-making proccss.
  - o **Error Accountability:** Blame for AI errors—whether the developers blundered, or institutions tuned in insensitivity or users inconsistence—is a complicated issue.
- **Solutions:**
  - o **AI Explainable:** The developers need to produce explainable Ailies,because they must be able to explain their solutions.
  - o **Lucid Framework of Accountability:** For any AI interventions outcomes, the AI-powered drug firms or institutions must also mint clear frameworks about who is accountable.
  - o **Action by regulatory bodies:** Governments and professional organizations should have rules for AI practice in mental health care.

6. Accessibility and Affordability

AI can help to scale mental health care and become more accessible, but the flip side risk seems to be that will just deepen current inequalities.

- **Challenges:**
  - o **Digital Divide:** Not everybody have the technology to receive mental services from AI-run mental health service.
  - o **Echnological Barriers:** On the high-cost end of spectrum, advanced AI systems are beyond reach for low-resource settings to develop and deploy.
- **Solutions:**
  - o **Scalable approaches:** The design of AI cost-effective solutions which can be implemented in various settings working from rural or under-served regions.
  - o **Partnerships and Resources Buy-in:** Government — non-profits, and private organizations can help subsidize the costs of AI-based mental health services.
  - o **Education and Training:** Digital integration programming for the youth as well as professionals is very important as more and more people would be able to use and adopt on AI technologies.

Integration of AI in mental healthcare could lead to large potentialities for improved access, efficiency and outcomes. But this innovative technology requires a measured implementation, considering the hurdles of ethical and operational limitations. We ensure that AI works together with human wisdom and provides equitable, high-quality mental health care by tackling all issues including: privacy, bias, and the inability to automate everything

As AI grows in maturity, we will require cooperative efforts from techies, mental health professionals, government bodies as well across a variety of social demographics to navigate over these challenges and leverage the power of AI-based mental health solutions. We can use this to tap the potential of technology in a way that creates a mentally healthier society that is more open, compassionate and capable.

IV. DIGITAL LITERACY

Digital literacy is critical to the adoption of AI based mental health tools in a university environment. As these tools are embedded deeper within the crux of education and mental health services it is imperative that faculty, as well as students have knowledge and skills not only to utilize them righteously but responsibly. The educational sector can work towards a more even and beneficial tone in mental health care by raising awareness about how AI tools operate, the data fed and procured with, all limitations included. We go into more depth on the essentials, the challenges and solutions for digital literacy this way below.

Illustration of relative user engagement rates within chatbots, predictive analytics and VR therapies. Figure 5 presenting rates of usage between chatbots, predictive analytics and VR therapies.

Figure 5. Pie Chart for AI-Driven Mental Health Usage

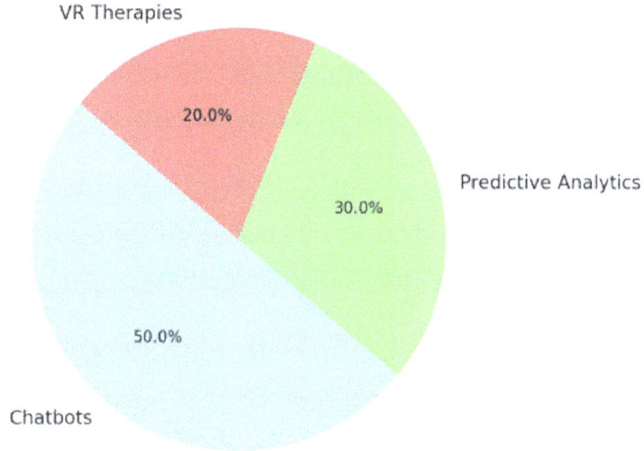

1. **Understanding AI-Powered Tools:** Chatbots, predictive algorithms and VR platforms are just a few of the AI technologies gaining prominence in mental health care. Everybody needs to understand what those functionalities do and why in order for them to fully serve students, faculty, mental health practitioners.
    - **Components of Digital Literacy in AI**:
        - o **How AI Works:** Basic concept of how AI handles data, sees patterns and come out with outputs (Shahzad et al., 2024).
        - o **Types of data and their Utilization:** Help users understand the data which AI is collecting — student performance trends, absences or social media posts and showing that data for example
        - o **Ethical Discourses:** Calling for transparency, informed consent and privacy breaches and exploited — along with the associated dangers of over-reliance on AI-driven systems.
    - **Practical Application:**
        - o Students and faculty should understand that AI chat bots or early warning systems can help uncovered and manage mental health

problems, but they are not to replace human empathy as well professional counselling. That a chatbot could provide instantaneous responses but cannot be substitue for individualized therapy.

2. **Training Faculty and Mental Health Professionals:** Both Faculty and mental health professionals would be key in how to use AI driven mental health tools efficiently. With their high level of digital literacy these technologies are used as intended and not at expense of the mental health and school climate of students.
   - **Training Programs for Faculty:**
     - o **Awareness Workshops**: Short sessions to train faculty regularly about new AI tools, its capabilities & mental healthcare.
     - o **Practical Demonstrations** Hands-on trainings to faculty with respect to AI systems (for example: reading early warning alerts, operating AI operating systems).
     - o **Ethical Education**: Educating teachers on how to handle issues of bias, privacy and heavy reliance on AI solutions.
   - **Training Of Counselors in the Profession:**
     - o **AI Integration:** Psychologists demand the tools of AI and how to plug them into their practice for recognizing high-risk patients by means, like predictive analytics.
     - o **Interdisciplinary team building:** Call for joint work of AI experts and counselors in the development of tools that are both cutting-edge, and clinically efficient.
     - o **Lifelong Learning:** Allowing professionals to learn the new advancements in AI and mental health care.
3. **Educating Students on AI and Mental Health** Main end users of AI-based mental health tools in academic/campus environments, are students. They must be carefully educated on digital literacy to grow a more trustful audience and prevent irresponsible usage.
   - **Key Areas of Focus**:
     - o **How AI capabilities and limitations:** Students should be aware of what AI tools can or cannot accomplish. AI, for example; can detect early symptoms of mental ill-health but cannot perform a professional evaluation or therapy.
     - o **Privacy Awareness:** Informing Students about how their data is gathered, stored and safeguarded in AI systems and underpin their rights as well the importance of consent.
     - o **Responsible Usage**: Encouraging responsible AI applications like not depending only upon chatbots for emotional support and follow up when necessary.
   - **Examples of Educational Initiatives:**

- o **Workshops and Seminars**: arranging the general events where AI tools are demonstrated to students and what their role is in mental health care.
  - O **Digital Literacy Modules:** Instituting AI and mental health topics in the class curriculum to give the students an introductory base.
- o **Peer Good Programs:** Some example of this is training student volunteers as digital literacy ambassadors, who provide help to their fellowmen in using AI tools wisely.

4. **Addressing Challenges in Digital Literacy:** Importance of digital literacy is widely recognized, but there are many difficulties to where we have actually gotten with making it a reality. This recognition and handling of these issues are essential for the general use of AI technologies in mental health care
   - **Challenges:**
     - o **Inequality of Technology:** Not every student and/or faculty member was granted the devices with internet connectivity required to employ AI tools.
     - o **Change Resistance:** People are not going to embrace AI in mental health because the general public is unclear on its applications.
     - o **Complexity of AI Systems**: Users may struggle to understand how AI tool works, which makes them confused or does not use it properly.
     - o **Ethical Considerations:** The concern of privacy and dread of misuse data push individuals to not use AI-driven answers.
   - **Solutions:**
     - o **Bridging Digital Divide** – Offering access to tech, as in the institutional initiatives lend device or offer low-cost or no charge internet access.
     - o **Reinforce Trust:** Out right communication of both the benefits and limitations along with safeguards AI tools presents will help alleviate very skeptical minds
     - o **Reduce complexity of interfaces:** Make the user-friendly AI tools with easy to use interfaces will hence lower the complexity barrier.
     - o **Enforcing Best Practices:** Developing superior data protection policies and advocating ethical use in training.
5. **Long-Term Benefits of Digital Literacy:** From an academic point of view, investing in the digital literacy of students as well as faculties from AI-led mental health solutions has diverse long term benefits.
   - **Digital literacy:** AI tools are used correctly, resulting in timely interventions and improved mental health support.

- **Empowered users:** students and faculty using digital literacy know how to think critically about their mental health care, which can help reduce dependency or mis-using any AI tools [20].
- **Increased Institutional Brand:** When institutions focus on digital literacy, it sends a message of innovating in patient care and student welfare that pull in students and faculty valuing these aspects.
- **Future Tech Adaptability:** Digital literacy means that individuals can get involved in new technology to create a culture of continuous learning and change for the future.

6. **Future Directions:** To continue and enhance the benefits of digital literacy in AI-driven AI mental health, academic institutions should take a future perspective with policymaking.
   - **Research & Development:** Investing in research on the role of digital literacy in AI adoption and mental health outcomes, to further guide future initiatives.
   - **Policy Frameworks:** Establishing policy that drive digital literacy, takes ethics in AI and bridging the decedence causes of technology access.
   - **Global Collaboration:** Working with intercountry organizations and institutions for best practices and available resources ensuring quality digital literacy in mental health care.

Successful Integration of AI-Mental Health in Academic Settings: Foundational to Digital Literacy For ensuring all humans accept AI-driven solutions for mental health integration, education must begin by training faculty, students and mental health faculty on capabilities and limitations of AI tools as well as informing on ethics of their uses. If we tackle extra-strength challenges such as technology imbalances and impeding the transition, these systems should be ready for widespread adoption and trust.

The real-world use of AI tools also means not only amplify what digital literacy does but also to navigate our relationship with mental healthcare for ourselves. As AI receives the embracement of educational institutions, however, a robust digital literacy component will be key in insuring an equitable approach that is both inclusive and technically sound to the practice of mental health support. By continued work and collaboration, we can create a world where AI and the human mind work together to enhance mental health outcomes for everyone.

CONCLUSION

AI-powered tools have the potential to transform mental health care in academia by offering scalable, accessible, and personalized support to both students and faculty at an affordable cos. Emerging technologies, including chatbots, early-warning systems, and VR therapies, enable students to navigate mental roadblocks that impact academic performance and overall wellness. Yet, what will allow their real success is addressing ethics in terms of privacy, bias, and equity regarding the application of such technologies. Responsible deployment of AI solutions must be demanded by institutions to ensure that their use is not only effective but also equitable and fair. By fostering a responsible AI framework, higher education institutions can build healthier communities that promote well-being, resilience, and academic success. In the end, AI will revolutionize the way mental health care is delivered for the good of the community by providing more effective and trusted modes of care in a more efficient manner to those who are potentially going through a crisis. Through innovation and ethics-driven deployments, we can properly engineer AI to play a gigantic role in sculpting a vibrant, thriving academic ecosystem.

REFERENCES

Akgun, S., & Greenhow, C. (2021). Artificial intelligence in education: Addressing ethical challenges in K-12 settings. *AI and Ethics*, *2*(3), 431–440. DOI: 10.1007/s43681-021-00096-7 PMID: 34790956

Al-Zahrani, A. M. (2024). Unveiling the shadows: Beyond the hype of AI in education. *Heliyon*, *10*(9), e30696. DOI: 10.1016/j.heliyon.2024.e30696 PMID: 38737255

Balcombe, L. (2023). AI Chatbots in Digital Mental Health. *Informatics (MDPI)*, *10*(4), 82. DOI: 10.3390/informatics10040082

Bhutoria, A. (2022). Personalized education and Artificial Intelligence in the United States, China, and India: A systematic review using a Human-In-The-Loop model. *Computers and Education: Artificial Intelligence*, *3*, 100068. DOI: 10.1016/j.caeai.2022.100068

Blackwell, S. E., & Heidenreich, T. (2021). Cognitive Behavior Therapy at the Crossroads. *International Journal of Cognitive Therapy*, *14*(1), 1–22. DOI: 10.1007/s41811-021-00104-y PMID: 33584950

Budhwar, P., Malik, A., De Silva, M. T. T., & Thevisuthan, P. (2022). Artificial intelligence – challenges and opportunities for international HRM: A review and research agenda. *International Journal of Human Resource Management*, *33*(6), 1065–1097. DOI: 10.1080/09585192.2022.2035161

Cambra-Fierro, J. J., Blasco, M. F., López-Pérez, M.-E. E., & Trifu, A. (2024). ChatGPT adoption and its influence on faculty well-being: An empirical research in higher education. *Education and Information Technologies*, *30*(2), 1517–1538. DOI: 10.1007/s10639-024-12871-0

Chan, C. K. Y., & Hu, W. (2023). Students' voices on generative AI: Perceptions, benefits, and challenges in higher education. *International Journal of Educational Technology in Higher Education*, *20*(1). Advance online publication. DOI: 10.1186/s41239-023-00411-8

Crawford, J., Allen, K.-A., Pani, B., & Cowling, M. (2024). When artificial intelligence substitutes humans in higher education: The cost of loneliness, student success, and retention. *Studies in Higher Education*, *49*(5), 883–897. DOI: 10.1080/03075079.2024.2326956

Davenport, T., & Kalakota, R. (2019). The potential for artificial intelligence in healthcare. *Future Healthcare Journal*, *6*(2), 94–98. DOI: 10.7861/futurehosp.6-2-94 PMID: 31363513

Dwivedi, Y. K., Kshetri, N., Hughes, L., Slade, E. L., Jeyaraj, A., Kar, A. K., Baabdullah, A. M., Koohang, A., Raghavan, V., Ahuja, M., Albanna, H., Albashrawi, M. A., Al-Busaidi, A. S., Balakrishnan, J., Barlette, Y., Basu, S., Bose, I., Brooks, L., Buhalis, D., & Wright, R. (2023). Opinion Paper: "So what if ChatGPT wrote it?" Multidisciplinary perspectives on opportunities, challenges and implications of generative conversational AI for research, practice and policy. *International Journal of Information Management*, *71*, 102642. DOI: 10.1016/j.ijinfomgt.2023.102642

Erebak, S., & Turgut, T. (2021). Anxiety about the speed of technological development: Effects on job insecurity, time estimation, and automation level preference. *The Journal of High Technology Management Research*, *32*(2), 100419. DOI: 10.1016/j.hitech.2021.100419

Fagherazzi, G., Fischer, A., Ismael, M., & Despotovic, V. (2021). Voice for Health: The Use of Vocal Biomarkers from Research to Clinical Practice. *Digital Biomarkers*, *5*(1), 78–88. DOI: 10.1159/000515346 PMID: 34056518

Flanagan, O., Chan, A., Roop, P., & Sundram, F. (2021). Using Acoustic Speech Patterns From Smartphones to Investigate Mood Disorders: Scoping Review. *JMIR mHealth and uHealth*, *9*(9), e24352. DOI: 10.2196/24352 PMID: 34533465

González-López, Óscar. R., Buenadicha-Mateos, M., & Sánchez-Hernández, M. I. (2021). Overwhelmed by Technostress? Sensitive Archetypes and Effects in Times of Forced Digitalization. *International Journal of Environmental Research and Public Health*, *18*(8), 4216. DOI: 10.3390/ijerph18084216 PMID: 33923407

Graham, S., Depp, C., Lee, E. E., Nebeker, C., Tu, X., Kim, H.-C., & Jeste, D. V. (2019). Artificial Intelligence for Mental Health and Mental Illnesses: An Overview. *Current Psychiatry Reports*, *21*(11). Advance online publication. DOI: 10.1007/s11920-019-1094-0 PMID: 31701320

Kamalov, F., Santandreu Calonge, D., & Gurrib, I. (2023). New Era of Artificial Intelligence in Education: Towards a Sustainable Multifaceted Revolution. *Sustainability*, *15*(16), 12451. DOI: 10.3390/su151612451

Khurana, D., Koli, A., Khatter, K., & Singh, S. (2022). Natural language processing: State of the art, current trends and challenges. *Multimedia Tools and Applications*, *82*(3), 3713–3744. DOI: 10.1007/s11042-022-13428-4 PMID: 35855771

Labadze, L., Grigolia, M., & Machaidze, L. (2023). Role of AI chatbots in education: Systematic literature review. *International Journal of Educational Technology in Higher Education*, *20*(1). Advance online publication. DOI: 10.1186/s41239-023-00426-1

Luckin, R., Cukurova, M., Kent, C., & du Boulay, B. (2022). Empowering educators to be AI-ready. *Computers and Education: Artificial Intelligence*, *3*, 100076. DOI: 10.1016/j.caeai.2022.100076

Makhambetova, A., Zhiyenbayeva, N., & Ergesheva, E. (2021). Personalized Learning Strategy as a Tool to Improve Academic Performance and Motivation of Students. *International Journal of Web-Based Learning and Teaching Technologies*, *16*(6), 1–17. DOI: 10.4018/ijwltt.286743

Malik, A. S., Acharya, S., & Humane, S. (2024). Exploring the Impact of Security Technologies on Mental Health: A Comprehensive Review. *Cureus*. Advance online publication. DOI: 10.7759/cureus.53664 PMID: 38455776

Molnar, A. (2024). Prescription Digital Therapeutics: Assertions. *Health Affairs*, *43*(6), 897–897. DOI: 10.1377/hlthaff.2024.00152 PMID: 38830162

Nakshine, V. S., Thute, P., Khatib, M. N., & Sarkar, B. (2022). Increased Screen Time as a Cause of Declining Physical, Psychological Health, and Sleep Patterns: A Literary Review. *Cureus*. Advance online publication. DOI: 10.7759/cureus.30051 PMID: 36381869

Peake, J. M., Kerr, G., & Sullivan, J. P. (2018). A Critical Review of Consumer Wearables, Mobile Applications, and Equipment for Providing Biofeedback, Monitoring Stress, and Sleep in Physically Active Populations. *Frontiers in Physiology*, *9*. Advance online publication. DOI: 10.3389/fphys.2018.00743 PMID: 30002629

PTSD Help - a Randomized Controlled Trial of a PTSD Mobile Health App. (2019). *Case Medical Research*. https://doi.org/DOI: 10.31525/ct1-nct03862703

Rodrigues, R. S. (n.d.). *Sarcopenia e atrofia cerebral como preditores de prognóstico funcional em pacientes com aneurisma cerebral*. https://doi.org/DOI: 10.11606/t.5.2024.tde-18062025-095403

Rodway, P., & Schepman, A. (2023). The impact of adopting AI educational technologies on projected course satisfaction in university students. *Computers and Education: Artificial Intelligence*, *5*, 100150. DOI: 10.1016/j.caeai.2023.100150

Seo, K., Tang, J., Roll, I., Fels, S., & Yoon, D. (2021). The impact of artificial intelligence on learner–instructor interaction in online learning. *International Journal of Educational Technology in Higher Education*, *18*(1). Advance online publication. DOI: 10.1186/s41239-021-00292-9 PMID: 34778540

Shahzad, M. F., Xu, S., Lim, W. M., Yang, X., & Khan, Q. R. (2024). Artificial intelligence and social media on academic performance and mental well-being: Student perceptions of positive impact in the age of smart learning. *Heliyon, 10*(8), e29523. DOI: 10.1016/j.heliyon.2024.e29523 PMID: 38665566

Strickland, E. (2019). IBM Watson, heal thyself: How IBM overpromised and underdelivered on AI health care. *IEEE Spectrum, 56*(4), 24–31. DOI: 10.1109/mspec.2019.8678513

Talkspace receives NIH grants to conduct telepsychiatry research. (2021a). *Mental Health Weekly, 31*(3), 8–8. https://doi.org/DOI: 10.1002/mhw.32648

Talkspace receives NIH grants to conduct telepsychiatry research. (2021b). *Mental Health Weekly, 31*(3), 8–8. https://doi.org/DOI: 10.1002/mhw.32648

Tutun, S., Johnson, M. E., Ahmed, A., Albizri, A., Irgil, S., Yesilkaya, I., Ucar, E. N., Sengun, T., & Harfouche, A. (2022). An AI-based Decision Support System for Predicting Mental Health Disorders. *Information Systems Frontiers, 25*(3), 1261–1276. DOI: 10.1007/s10796-022-10282-5 PMID: 35669335

Uban, A.-S., Chulvi, B., & Rosso, P. (2021). An emotion and cognitive based analysis of mental health disorders from social media data. *Future Generation Computer Systems, 124*, 480–494. DOI: 10.1016/j.future.2021.05.032

Wan, E. (2021). "I'm like a wise little person": Notes on the Metal Performance of Woebot the Mental Health Chatbot. *Theatre Journal, 73*(3), E-21–E-30. DOI: 10.1353/tj.2021.0068

Xie, T., Pentina, I., & Hancock, T. (2023). Friend, mentor, lover: Does chatbot engagement lead to psychological dependence? *Journal of Service Management, 34*(4), 806–828. DOI: 10.1108/josm-02-2022-0072

Zawacki-Richter, O., Marín, V. I., Bond, M., & Gouverneur, F. (2019). Systematic review of research on artificial intelligence applications in higher education – where are the educators? *International Journal of Educational Technology in Higher Education, 16*(1). Advance online publication. DOI: 10.1186/s41239-019-0171-0

Zhai, C., Wibowo, S., & Li, L. D. (2024). The effects of over-reliance on AI dialogue systems on students' cognitive abilities: A systematic review. *Smart Learning Environments, 11*(1). Advance online publication. DOI: 10.1186/s40561-024-00316-7

Zhang, T., Schoene, A. M., Ji, S., & Ananiadou, S. (2022). Natural language processing applied to mental illness detection: A narrative review. *NPJ Digital Medicine, 5*(1). Advance online publication. DOI: 10.1038/s41746-022-00589-7 PMID: 35396451

Chapter 2
Foundations of AI Literacy

Jatin C. Modh
https://orcid.org/0000-0002-4221-3480
GLS University, Ahmedabad, India

Tejaskumar P. Bhatt
https://orcid.org/0000-0002-1092-4624
GLS University, Ahmedabad, India

Darshita Kalyani
https://orcid.org/0000-0001-6976-9553
GLS University, Ahmedabad, India

Aakanksha Jain
https://orcid.org/0009-0006-2527-1773
GLS University, Ahmedabad, India

ABSTRACT

This chapter introduces the notion of AI literacy and covers its definition, importance, and various facets, such as its technological, ethical, sociological, and creative aspects. It offers a historical view on the development of AI, emphasizing crucial turning points. Additionally, the chapter explores fundamental AI ideas such as robotics, computer vision, natural language processing, machine learning, and deep learning. It also describes the steps involved in developing AI, including gathering data, training models, evaluating them, and deploying them. Lastly, it explores at various types of AI, including rule-based systems, expert systems, and evolutionary algorithms, with a focus on how they might be used in a variety of fields.

DOI: 10.4018/979-8-3373-2297-1.ch002

1. INTRODUCTION

1.1 What AI Literacy means

Artificial Intelligence (AI) is one of the most transformative technologies of the 21st century, influencing how we work, communicate, and make decisions. It plays a critical role in domains such as healthcare, finance, education, and entertainment, enhancing efficiency and enabling intelligent decision-making (Brynjolfsson & McAfee, 2017).

As AI becomes increasingly embedded in everyday life, individuals must develop **AI literacy**—the capacity to understand, critically evaluate, and responsibly interact with AI technologies. This includes knowing how AI systems function, such as through machine learning or data-driven algorithms, and understanding their ethical, social, and legal implications (Ng, 2021; Long & Magerko, 2020).

AI literacy differs from general digital literacy by emphasizing comprehension of how intelligent systems make decisions, influence human behavior, and impact society. It includes recognizing the role of algorithms in curating social media feeds, the biases in AI-driven decisions, and the implications of AI in privacy and surveillance (West & Allen, 2018; Crawford, 2021).

Importantly, AI literacy promotes a realistic view of AI's capabilities and limitations. It dispels common myths, such as the belief that AI will replace all human jobs or that it can function with infallible accuracy. Instead, AI literacy helps individuals navigate these technologies thoughtfully and ethically, advocating for fair and transparent systems (Eubanks, 2018; Floridi et al., 2018).

In professional settings, AI literacy enables workers to adapt to shifting job requirements, collaborate with intelligent systems, and remain competitive in AI-influenced industries. It also supports lifelong learning and innovation in education and business (Bughin et al., 2018).

In sum, AI literacy is no longer optional. It is a crucial skill for individuals to engage with the digital world responsibly, safeguard their rights, and shape AI technologies to align with societal values (UNESCO, 2021).

1.2 Why AI Literacy is Crucial

Being AI-literate allows individuals to understand and question the systems influencing their lives, especially as AI technologies increasingly shape critical societal functions. This literacy enables recognition of ethical challenges like bias, accountability, and privacy, particularly in high-stakes domains such as criminal justice, hiring, and financial decision-making (Ng, 2021; Long & Magerko, 2020).

Transparency in AI decision-making is vital, especially when systems operate as opaque "black boxes." AI literacy empowers people to demand explainability and fairness in systems that affect them (UNESCO, 2021; Eubanks, 2018).

Moreover, AI is reshaping labor markets. Individuals equipped with AI literacy are better positioned to adapt to evolving job roles and contribute to innovation, while governments and institutions that prioritize AI education help ensure inclusive participation in the AI-driven economy (Bughin et al., 2018; West & Allen, 2018).

In sectors such as healthcare, finance, and education, AI introduces both opportunities and risks. While AI tools can improve diagnostics, financial forecasting, and personalized learning, errors or biases may cause harm if users lack awareness of AI's limitations (Topol, 2019; Crawford, 2021; Luckin, 2018).

Furthermore, AI systems impact privacy, democracy, and public discourse. Social media algorithms influence beliefs, and surveillance tools raise ethical concerns. With AI literacy, individuals can better detect manipulation, advocate for responsible practices, and participate in shaping technology policy (Floridi et al., 2018; European Commission, 2021).

In conclusion, fostering AI literacy is essential for building an informed, empowered society capable of engaging constructively with AI technologies and ensuring their development aligns with ethical and equitable goals.

1.3 Different Dimensions of AI Literacy

Artificial Intelligence (AI) is transforming industries, economies, and daily life, making AI literacy an essential skill for individuals across all sectors (Bughin et al., 2018). AI literacy refers to the ability to understand, evaluate, and interact with AI technologies effectively (Long & Magerko, 2020). It encompasses technical knowledge, ethical awareness, and critical thinking about AI's societal impact (Ng, 2021).

This chapter explores the different dimensions of AI literacy, including technical understanding, critical thinking, ethical awareness, socio-cultural context, and practical application. These dimensions collectively provide a framework for preparing individuals to interact responsibly and intelligently with AI technologies.

1.3.1. Technical Understanding of AI

The foundation of AI literacy lies in understanding how AI systems function (West & Allen, 2018). This includes:

- **Basic Concepts**: Knowledge of machine learning, neural networks, and data-driven decision-making (Brynjolfsson & McAfee, 2017).
- **How AI Learns**: Recognizing that AI relies on training data, which can introduce biases if not properly managed (Crawford, 2021).
- **Limitations of AI**: Understanding that AI lacks human-like reasoning and can make errors when faced with unfamiliar data (Tegmark, 2017).

Without technical literacy, individuals may overestimate AI's capabilities or fear it irrationally (Floridi et al., 2018). Educational initiatives must simplify these concepts for non-experts to foster informed discussions (UNESCO, 2021).

1.3.2. Ethical Considerations in AI

AI raises significant ethical concerns that require public awareness (Eubanks, 2018). Key issues include:

- **Bias and Fairness**: AI systems can perpetuate discrimination if trained on biased data (Crawford, 2021).
- **Privacy Risks**: AI-driven surveillance and data collection threaten personal privacy (Zuboff, 2019).
- **Accountability**: Determining responsibility when AI makes harmful decisions (Floridi et al., 2018).

Ethical AI literacy empowers individuals to demand transparency and fairness in automated systems (West & Allen, 2018). Policymakers and corporations must prioritize ethical guidelines to prevent misuse (UNESCO, 2021).

1.3.3. Practical Applications of AI

AI literacy involves recognizing how AI is used in everyday life (Brynjolfsson & McAfee, 2017). Examples include:

- **Healthcare**: AI assists in diagnostics but requires human oversight to avoid errors (Topol, 2019).
- **Finance**: Algorithmic trading and fraud detection improve efficiency but pose systemic risks (Tegmark, 2017).
- **Education**: Adaptive learning tools personalize education but may reinforce inequalities (Eubanks, 2018).

Understanding these applications helps individuals use AI tools effectively while remaining cautious of their limitations (Long & Magerko, 2020).

1.3.4. Societal and Economic Impact of AI

AI is reshaping labor markets and social structures (Bughin et al., 2018). Key societal dimensions include:

- **Job Displacement vs. Creation**: AI automates routine tasks but also generates new roles (Brynjolfsson & McAfee, 2017).
- **Digital Divide**: Unequal access to AI education exacerbates socioeconomic disparities (Eubanks, 2018).
- **Democracy and Misinformation**: AI-powered social media algorithms influence public opinion (Zuboff, 2019).

AI literacy enables citizens to advocate for policies that ensure equitable benefits (Floridi et al., 2018). Governments must invest in reskilling programs to mitigate job losses (UNESCO, 2021).

1.3.5. Critical Thinking and AI Skepticism

Blind trust in AI can be dangerous (Crawford, 2021). AI literacy encourages:

- **Questioning AI Decisions**: Not all AI outputs are accurate or fair (Eubanks, 2018).
- **Recognizing MHistory of AI:** Evolution and Key Milestone

1.4 AI Policies and Global Governance

As Artificial Intelligence (AI) technologies increasingly permeate society, industry, and governance, the development of comprehensive global AI policies has become essential. AI policies aim to address issues related to ethics, accountability, data protection, inclusivity, transparency, and the mitigation of potential harms. Governance, in this context, refers to the frameworks, laws, and institutions that guide the responsible development and deployment of AI. Several national and international bodies have taken major steps to regulate and shape AI development, reflecting a global consensus on the importance of responsible innovation.

1.4.1 European Union AI Act

One of the most prominent efforts in AI regulation is the European Union's AI Act, proposed in April 2021. This legislation is the first major attempt to establish a legal framework to govern AI across a large jurisdiction. The Act categorizes AI applications into four risk categories: unacceptable, high-risk, limited risk, and minimal risk. Applications deemed "unacceptable" (e.g., social scoring or manipulative systems) are banned, while high-risk systems (e.g., biometric identification, credit scoring) must meet strict regulatory requirements (European Commission, 2021). The AI Act aims to ensure safety and fundamental rights while fostering innovation through regulatory sandboxes and support for startups.

1.4.2 OECD AI Principles

The Organisation for Economic Co-operation and Development (OECD) has also played a key role in global AI governance. In 2019, it released the *OECD Principles on Artificial Intelligence*, which emphasize inclusive growth, sustainable development, and well-being; human-centered values and fairness; transparency and explainability; robustness and security; and accountability. These principles were adopted not only by OECD member countries but also by several non-member states, reflecting their broad applicability and global influence (OECD, 2019).

1.4.3 UNESCO's Global AI Framework

UNESCO has taken a culturally inclusive approach to AI governance. In 2021, UNESCO's General Conference adopted the *Recommendation on the Ethics of Artificial Intelligence*, a globally binding normative framework signed by 193 member states (UNESCO, 2021a). It emphasizes human rights, environmental sustainability, and data governance. Notably, UNESCO's AI Competency Framework for Students outlines key skills and values young learners should acquire, including understanding AI applications, data literacy, critical thinking, and ethical awareness (UNESCO, 2021b). This initiative aims to promote global AI literacy and prepare future generations to engage responsibly with AI technologies.

1.4.4 United States Executive Order on AI

In October 2023, the United States issued a significant Executive Order on the Safe, Secure, and Trustworthy Development and Use of Artificial Intelligence. This order mandates AI developers to share safety test results with the federal government and sets standards for AI use in public sectors like healthcare, education, and defense. It also emphasizes civil rights, consumer protection, and AI workforce development (The White House, 2023). The U.S. approach focuses on innovation leadership while introducing safeguards to prevent misuse.

1.4.5 Global South and Non-Western Approaches

Efforts to shape AI governance are not limited to the West. Several non-Western nations have also initiated policy frameworks tailored to their socio-economic and cultural contexts. For instance:

- **India's National Strategy for Artificial Intelligence (NSAI)** outlines an "AI for All" vision, emphasizing inclusive growth and the use of AI in agriculture, healthcare, education, and smart mobility (NITI Aayog, 2018).
- **China's AI development plan**, released in 2017, aims to become the world leader in AI by 2030, with a focus on integration in military, economic, and social systems. The Chinese government has also begun drafting AI ethical guidelines and standards for responsible use (State Council of China, 2017).
- **Rwanda** and other African nations, in collaboration with UNESCO and ITU, have started national AI strategies that prioritize education, infrastructure, and ethical use, especially in healthcare and agriculture (UNESCO, 2021a).

These efforts highlight the need to balance innovation with ethical safeguards while adapting AI governance to diverse social, economic, and cultural realities.

1.4.6 Toward a Unified Global Framework

While national policies are crucial, the transboundary nature of AI systems—such as generative models, surveillance technologies, and algorithmic decision-making—demands international cooperation. Multilateral efforts are underway to harmonize AI standards, promote transparency, and prevent a fragmented global AI landscape. Institutions like the **Global Partnership on AI (GPAI)**, initiated by the G7, seek to bridge research and policy by fostering collaboration across borders and sectors.

However, challenges remain. Differing legal traditions, data protection regimes (e.g., GDPR in Europe vs. sectoral approaches in the U.S.), and geopolitical interests can hinder the formation of a truly unified governance model. Still, initiatives like the UN AI Advisory Body and cross-regional collaborations continue to build momentum toward cohesive, ethical, and sustainable AI governance.

2. HISTORY OF AI: EVOLUTION AND KEY MILESTONE

Artificial Intelligence (AI) has evolved from a speculative concept in computer science to a transformative force reshaping industries, economies, and daily human experiences. Its journey has been marked by groundbreaking innovations, periods of intense optimism (often called "AI summers"), and phases of skepticism and reduced funding (known as "AI winters"). These cycles reflect the dynamic interplay between technological potential and real-world challenges. This explores AI's historical development, highlighting key milestones that have defined its growth. Understanding AI's origins provides context for its current capabilities and future potential (Russell & Norvig, 2021).

2.1 Primal Foundations of AI (1940s–1950s)

- The roots of Artificial Intelligence (AI) date back to the mid-1900s, when researchers first started investigating how machines could be designed to replicate human-like cognitive abilities. One of the earliest milestones was the development of the first electronic computers, such as the ENIAC (Electronic Numerical Integrator and Computer) in 1945, which demonstrated that machines could perform complex calculations (McCulloch & Pitts, 1943).
- Alan Turing's Contributions (1950): British mathematician Alan Turing proposed the Turing Test, a foundational test for machine intelligence proposes that if a machine can replicate human responses in a way that is indistinguishable from a real person, it can be considered intelligent. it could be considered "intelligent" (Turing, 1950).
- The formal inception of Artificial Intelligence as an academic discipline can be traced to the Dartmouth Conference of 1956, where pioneers John McCarthy, Marvin Minsky, Nathaniel Rochester, and Claude Shannon introduced the term "Artificial Intelligence" during a landmark workshop that laid the groundwork for future research in the field. Early AI research focused on problem-solving and symbolic reasoning, leading to programs like the Logic Theorist (1956), developed by Allen Newell and Herbert A. Simon, which could mimic human problem-solving skills.(McCarthy et al., 1956)

2.2 The Golden Age of AI (1960s–1970s)

- Early optimism led to significant breakthroughs, though progress was slower than anticipated.The 1960s and 1970s saw significant advancements in AI, driven by optimism and increased funding. Researchers developed expert systems, which were designed to replicate human decision-making in specialized fields. One notable example was DENDRAL (1965), an AI system that could analyze chemical compounds, demonstrating practical applications of AI in science (Buchanan & Feigenbaum, 1978).

- ELIZA (1966): Joseph Weizenbaum developed ELIZA, an early natural language processing program that simulated conversation, demonstrating AI's potential in human-computer interaction (Weizenbaum, 1966).
- Shakey the Robot (1969): The first general-purpose mobile robot, Shakey, used logic-based reasoning to navigate and solve problems, laying the foundation for robotics and automated planning (Nilsson, 1984).
- Despite early progress, the development of AI was hindered by limited computing capabilities and overly ambitious expectations. As a result, by the late 1970s, enthusiasm waned and financial support diminished, ushering in the first "AI winter"—a phase marked by declining interest and investment in artificial intelligence research.

2.3 AI Winter and Challenges (1970s–1990s)

- Overpromising and under delivering led to funding cuts, known as the AI Winter. However, research continued in niche areas.
- Expert Systems (1980s): AI applications shifted toward expert systems, rule-based programs that emulated human expertise in fields like medicine (e.g., MYCIN for diagnosing infections) (Shortliffe, 1976).
- Backpropagation Algorithm (1986): Geoffrey Hinton and others refined neural network training techniques, reviving interest in machine learning (Rumelhart et al., 1986).

2.4 The Ascent of Machine Learning and Neural Networks (1980s–1990s)

- The 1980s witnessed a revitalization in the field of artificial intelligence, primarily driven by the emergence of machine learning techniques and the development of neural networks. During this period, there was a notable transition from traditional rule-based approaches to data-driven learning algorithms. A pivotal advancement came with the refinement of the backpropagation algorithm, which significantly enhanced the ability to train multi-layer neural networks efficiently (Rumelhart et al., 1986).
- During this period, expert systems gained commercial success, particularly in industries like healthcare and finance. For example, MYCIN (1976), an AI system for diagnosing bacterial infections, demonstrated the practical benefits of AI in medicine (Shortliffe, 1976).

- However, by the late 1980s, the limitations of expert systems became apparent—they were expensive to maintain and lacked adaptability.

2.5 The Ascent of Modern AI (1990s–2010s)

- Computational power and data availability fueled AI's resurgence.
- Deep Blue vs. Kasparov (1997): IBM's Deep Blue defeated chess champion Garry Kasparov, showcasing AI's strategic decision-making abilities (Campbell et al., 2002).
- Machine Learning Boom (2000s): Advances in algorithms (e.g., Support Vector Machines, Random Forests) and big data enabled practical AI applications in finance, healthcare, and more (Hastie et al., 2009).

2.6 The Deep Learning Revolution (2010–Present)

- The 21st century has witnessed unprecedented advancements in AI, driven by big data, improved algorithms, and powerful computing hardware.
- Neural networks, powered by GPUs and massive datasets, transformed AI capabilities.
- Machine Learning and Deep Learning: The rapid growth in data availability, coupled with advancements in computational capabilities—particularly the use of Graphics Processing Units (GPUs)—has driven significant progress in deep learning techniques. A landmark achievement occurred in 2012 when AlexNet, a deep convolutional neural network, triumphed in the ImageNet Large Scale Visual Recognition Challenge. This breakthrough model markedly enhanced the accuracy of image classification tasks, highlighting the transformative potential of deep learning (Krizhevsky et al., 2012).
- Natural Language Processing (NLP) Breakthroughs (Generative AI (2020s)): AI models like GPT (Generative Pre-trained Transformer) by OpenAI (2018) and BERT (Bidirectional Encoder Representations from Transformers) by Google (2018) revolutionized NLP, enabling machines to understand and generate human-like text (Vaswani et al., 2017).
- Developing skepticism prevents over-reliance on AI and promotes human oversight (Tegmark, 2017).
- AI in Everyday Applications:

AI is now integrated into daily life through:

Virtual assistants (Siri, Alexa, Google Assistant), Autonomous vehicles (Tesla, Waymo), Healthcare diagnostics (IBM Watson, AI-powered radiology)

- Ethical and Societal Challenges: As AI becomes more pervasive, concerns about bias, privacy, and job displacement have emerged. Governments and organizations are now focusing on AI ethics and regulation (Bostrom, 2014).

The evolution of artificial intelligence reflects a dynamic narrative marked by groundbreaking innovations, periods of stagnation, and remarkable revivals. Originating from abstract theoretical foundations, AI has progressed to sophisticated deep learning systems that are reshaping both industries and everyday experiences. Despite ongoing hurdles, the horizon of AI promises transformative developments across domains such as automation, medical technology, and the interface between humans and machines.

2.7 AI Literacy for K–12 and Higher Education

Artificial Intelligence (AI) is increasingly permeating every sector of society, making it vital for both K–12 and higher education systems to integrate AI literacy into curricula. AI literacy empowers students and educators to understand how AI functions, engage critically with its applications, and contribute responsibly to its development (Long & Magerko, 2020). For educational institutions, developing AI literacy is no longer a futuristic luxury—it is a present-day imperative.

2.7.1 Importance of AI Literacy in Education

In the digital age, AI literacy extends beyond understanding technical mechanisms to include ethical reasoning, critical thinking, and informed decision-making (Ng, 2021). It enables students to discern the workings and implications of AI tools embedded in platforms they interact with daily, such as search engines, recommendation systems, or virtual assistants (Floridi et al., 2018). For educators, it provides the foundational knowledge needed to foster interdisciplinary learning and to prepare students for AI-augmented work environments.

Integrating AI literacy in schools equips young learners with essential skills in data analysis, algorithmic thinking, and ethical awareness. This early exposure ensures that students grow up not only as digital consumers but as informed citizens and potential creators of AI technologies. In higher education, AI literacy supports the development of domain-specific AI applications across disciplines like healthcare, finance, education, and social sciences (Luckin, 2018).

2.7.2 Case Study: Finland's "Elements of AI"

One of the most influential global efforts to promote AI literacy is Finland's Elements of AI initiative. Launched in 2018 by the University of Helsinki and technology firm Reaktor, this free online course aims to demystify AI by teaching foundational concepts to people of all backgrounds—students, professionals, and policymakers alike (University of Helsinki, 2018). The program emphasizes accessibility and inclusivity, avoiding heavy technical jargon and instead focusing on how AI affects society and individual decision-making.

By 2021, over 750,000 people across more than 170 countries had enrolled in the course, and it has been translated into multiple languages. Finland even offered the course to all EU citizens as a diplomatic gesture to promote AI literacy across Europe (Reaktor & University of Helsinki, 2019). The program exemplifies how governments can collaborate with academia and industry to implement scalable AI literacy strategies.

2.7.3 Case Study: IBM's AI Education for K–12

IBM's AI Education initiative targets K–12 educators and students in the United States with comprehensive resources designed to introduce AI concepts in an age-appropriate manner. Developed in collaboration with ISTE (International Society for Technology in Education), the curriculum includes instructional modules, interactive tools, and real-world case studies tailored to young learners (IBM, 2020).

This program not only builds students' understanding of machine learning and natural language processing but also emphasizes the ethical and societal implications of AI. Teachers receive training to incorporate AI into subjects like science, mathematics, and social studies, making AI a cross-curricular topic. Moreover, students engage in projects that simulate real-world AI applications—such as developing chatbots or analyzing bias in algorithms—fostering both creativity and critical thinking (ISTE & IBM, 2020).

2.7.4 Integrating AI Literacy into Curriculum Design

Effective AI literacy education must be scaffolded across different age groups. For example, elementary-level curricula may focus on understanding the concept of algorithms and recognizing AI in everyday life. Middle school programs can introduce data ethics, algorithmic bias, and AI's role in media consumption. In high school and college, students can delve into machine learning, robotics, natural language processing, and ethical frameworks.

Project-based learning, case-based analysis, and gamified learning platforms are effective pedagogical strategies to promote engagement and comprehension (West & Allen, 2018). Additionally, collaboration with tech companies and open-access platforms can enrich curriculum resources and provide real-world relevance.

2.7.5 Challenges and Future Directions

Despite its importance, AI literacy faces several barriers in education. These include limited teacher training, lack of standardized curricula, and unequal access to technological resources (UNESCO, 2021). Addressing these challenges requires systemic investment in teacher professional development, inclusive educational policy, and public-private partnerships.

To ensure inclusive AI literacy, efforts must also prioritize underrepresented groups, including women, rural populations, and economically disadvantaged students. Equitable access to AI education can bridge the digital divide and promote societal resilience against automation-related job displacement (Bughin et al., 2018).

AI literacy is foundational for navigating the challenges and opportunities of the 21st century. By embedding AI education across K–12 and higher education systems, we can cultivate a generation that not only understands the mechanics of AI but also engages critically with its ethical, social, and economic dimensions. Initiatives like Finland's Elements of AI and IBM's K–12 AI Education program offer replicable models for inclusive, scalable, and impactful AI literacy education. Moving forward, fostering cross-sector collaboration and policy alignment will be key to making AI literacy universal.

3. CORE AI CONCEPTS

Bird's-eye view on Core AI Concepts

Artificial Intelligence (AI) has appeared as a revolutionary development in the digital era. Artificial Intelligence represents a paradigm-shifting technology and groundbreaking advancement in technology, enhancing the competence of artificial systems to emulate human intelligence in accomplishing activities that traditionally required cognitive functions such as learning, reasoning, perception, and choosing between alternatives. AI is gradually evolving into a core element of daily life, powering everything to carry out day-to-day tasks. Its ability to solve complex problems, improve efficiencies, and create new possibilities has made it a key catalyst for technological advancement in the present era.

Artificial Intelligence (AI) is a transformative branch of computer science aimed at creating and constructing systems equipped to accomplish activities traditionally requiring human intelligence. The scope of these tasks covers logical reasoning, learning from experience, addressing complex problems, perceiving the environment, and understanding human language. These functions include the ability to reason, adapt through learning, solve challenges, recognize patterns, and interpret language. AI has become integral to numerous industries, such as healthcare, finance, education, and transportation, transforming how people interact with technology and data (Russell & Norvig, 2021).

AI today plays a central role in fields ranging from medicine and finance/banking, agriculture to transportation and autonomous vehicles, education, the manufacturing industry, retail and e-commerce, and cybersecurity. Often, the concepts of AI are also applied in the fields of entertainment and media, defense and security, environment and climate science, and smart cities and urban planning. The concept of AI uses self-directed algorithms that do not require human intervention. These algorithms are coded/trained to independently determine their course of action and make decisions.

At its core, AI integrates algorithms, data, and computational resources to develop systems capable of solving problems, addressing challenges, perceiving patterns, and adapting to changing environments. It is not a solidified concept or cohesive theory, but rather a broad field encompassing multiple interconnected areas, including machine learning, deep learning, natural language processing, computer vision, and robotics. AI concepts and algorithms are applicable across various disciplines in this digital era.

The following Figure 1 conveys the idea of core concepts of AI, which are essential for grasping how AI works and how it continues to shape the future.

Figure 1. Core Concepts of AI

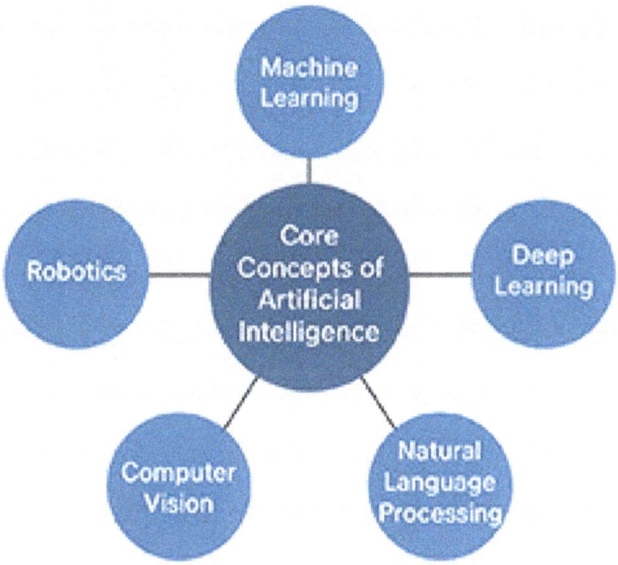

This chapter delves into these core concepts in depth. By understanding each concept thoroughly, readers will gain insight into how AI systems function and how they are driving the evolution of innovation and human interaction. The following sections provide a detailed and comprehensive exploration of core AI concepts.

3.1 Machine Learning

Machine Learning (ML) forms a vital part of AI, enabling machines to acquire skills through learning.that enables systems to learn and improve from experience without being explicitly programmed.Machine Learning (ML) is a fundamental branch of AI that allows systems to acquire knowledge through experience. It involves the development of algorithms that can identify patterns in data and make decisions or predictions based on it. ML is broadly categorized into supervised learning, unsupervised learning, and reinforcement learning. Supervised learning uses labeled data to train models, while unsupervised learning deals with unlabeled data to uncover hidden structures. Reinforcement learning, on the other hand, is based on reward systems to guide learning through interactions with the environment (Goodfellow, Bengio, & Courville, 2016).

In supervised learning, algorithms such as linear regression, logistic regression, support vector machines, and decision trees are commonly used. These models learn a mapping from inputs to outputs and are evaluated based on their predictive accuracy. Unsupervised learning techniques like k-means clustering and principal component analysis (PCA) help in discovering intrinsic patterns within data without any labels. Reinforcement learning has gained popularity due to its success in games like AlphaGo by DeepMind, where agents learn optimal strategies through trial-and-error interactions.

ML applications span numerous fields, including fraud detection (e.g., PayPal using ML to monitor transactions), recommendation systems (such as Netflix's personalized movie suggestions), personalized marketing (targeted ads on platforms like Facebook), and predictive maintenance in manufacturing industries. With the emergence of automated machine learning (AutoML), even users with limited technical expertise can build and deploy ML models effectively.

3.2 Deep Learning

Deep Learning (DL) is a specialized field within machine learning that uses neural networks with many layers (hence "deep") to model complex patterns in large datasets. DL excels in areas such as image and speech recognition, natural language processing, and game playing. Deep learning models like Convolutional Neural Networks (CNNs) and Recurrent Neural Networks (RNNs) have enabled significant advancements in AI capabilities. DL requires vast amounts of data and computational power but often achieves state-of-the-art performance in various tasks (LeCun, Bengio, & Hinton, 2015).Deep learning models automatically learn representations of data through multiple layers of computation, hence the term "deep" in deep learning. This approach has led to significant breakthroughs in AI, enabling the development of self-driving cars, facial recognition systems, and virtual assistants.

Deep learning models are composed of multiple layers of neurons (artificial neurons or nodes) that process information in a hierarchical manner. These layers can automatically extract high-level features from raw data, making deep learning particularly effective for tasks like image classification or speech recognition.

CNNs are particularly effective in computer vision tasks due to their ability to automatically learn spatial hierarchies of features from images. For example, Google Photos uses CNNs for automatic image classification and face recognition. RNNs and their variants, such as Long Short-Term Memory (LSTM) networks, are well-suited for sequence data like text and time series. More recently, the introduction of attention mechanisms and transformer architectures (e.g., BERT, GPT) has revolutionized how deep learning handles sequential and language data. An example is OpenAI's ChatGPT, which can generate human-like text responses and summaries.

Deep learning encompasses various specialized architectures designed for different types of tasks. These architectures are the backbone of modern AI systems, enabling breakthroughs in areas such as computer vision, natural language processing, and reinforcement learning. It focuses on different architectures like Convolutional Neural Networks (CNNs), Recurrent Neural Networks (RNNs),Generative Adversarial Networks (GANs),Transformer Networks etc.

Despite its capabilities, deep learning has limitations. These include high training times, the need for large labeled datasets, and the "black box" nature of deep models that make them difficult to interpret. Researchers are actively exploring techniques to improve model explainability, robustness, and fairness. One example of ongoing research is IBM's AI Explainability 360 toolkit, which aims to make deep learning decisions more transparent.

3.3 Natural Language Processing

Natural Language Processing (NLP) is centered on how computers interact with human languages.Natural Language Processing (NLP) is concerned with enabling computers to understand and process human languages.The goal is to enable machines to understand, interpret, and generate human language in a way that is both meaningful and useful. Applications of NLP include machine translation, sentiment analysis, speech recognition, and chatbots. Advances in NLP have been driven by deep learning techniques, especially transformer-based models like BERT and GPT (Jurafsky & Martin, 2020).

NLP tasks can be broadly divided into syntax-related and semantics-related activities. Syntax tasks include part-of-speech tagging, parsing, and word segmentation. Semantic tasks involve named entity recognition (NER), sentiment analysis, and question answering. The evolution from rule-based methods to statistical models and, more recently, to neural networks has significantly improved the accuracy and versatility of NLP systems.

Natural Language Processing (NLP) plays a key role in the realm of Artificial Intelligence (AI) that enables machines to understand, interpret, and generate human language. NLP is a blend of computational linguistics, machine learning, and linguistics, designed to help computers communicate with humans in their natural language. It focuses on developing algorithms that allow machines to process and analyze large amounts of natural language data to perform tasks like speech recognition, language translation, sentiment analysis, and question answering.

Large language models (LLMs), such as OpenAI's GPT series and Google's BERT, have shown remarkable capabilities in generating coherent text, answering questions, and performing summarization. These models are trained on vast corpora of text and fine-tuned for specific tasks using transfer learning techniques. For example, Google's Gmail uses NLP for Smart Compose, which suggests sentence completions. As NLP continues to evolve, challenges such as bias, misinformation, and data privacy remain important areas of research.

In today's world, where communication through text and voice is a primary form of interaction, NLP is essential for improving human-computer interaction. NLP's ability to understand and generate human language makes it foundational for virtual assistants like Siri, Alexa, and Google Assistant, as well as chatbots, language translators, and other AI-driven communication systems.

Natural Language Processing is a pivotal part of AI. As essential aspect of AI, Natural Language Processing empowers machines to analyze, understand, and generate human language. As technology advances, NLP continues to evolve, addressing challenges such as language ambiguity and multilingualism, bringing us closer to a future where human-computer interaction through natural language is seamless, intuitive, and efficient.

The concept of NLP can be applied to language translation, chatbots and virtual assistants, text summarization, information retrieval and search engines, speech recognition, text classification, and document categorization, among others.

3.4 Computer Vision

In the field of AI, Computer Vision trains machines to process and interpret visual information to make decisions. It includes image classification, object detection, facial recognition, and video analysis. Computer vision combines methodologies from ML, DL, and signal processing to understand visual content. With the help of CNNs, computer vision systems have achieved human-level performance in several image recognition tasks (Szeliski, 2022).

Key techniques in computer vision include edge detection, feature extraction, and image segmentation. These methods enable the identification and classification of objects within images and videos. Object detection frameworks like YOLO (You Only Look Once) and Faster R-CNN have enabled real-time applications such as autonomous driving (e.g., Tesla's Autopilot system) and surveillance.

Facial recognition technology is another prominent application, widely used in security systems and personal devices. Apple's Face ID and airport security systems are examples. However, it raises ethical concerns regarding surveillance, consent, and data protection. Similarly, image generation techniques like Generative Adversarial Networks (GANs) are powerful tools used by companies like NVIDIA to generate synthetic human faces but also contribute to the spread of deepfakes and misinformation.

The future of computer vision lies in multi-modal learning, where visual data is combined with other types of data (e.g., audio, text) to build more comprehensive

AI systems. Research in this area aims to develop machines that can perceive and reason about the world in a human-like manner.

As AI has advanced, computer vision has expanded beyond traditional image processing to include real-time visual interpretation, making it a crucial part of intelligent systems. These systems are designed to analyze and make sense of visual inputs, enabling machines to perform tasks ranging from simple recognition to more complex tasks like interpreting scenes and understanding visual relationships.

The early days of computer vision focused on basic image processing tasks, such as edge detection, filtering, and simple object identification. Over time, as computational power and datasets grew, computer vision expanded to more complex tasks. The development of machine learning techniques and deep learning methods, particularly Convolutional Neural Networks (CNNs), allowed for substantial progress in image classification and object detection. Today, computer vision is not just about recognizing images but about interpreting the world in a way that was once thought to be exclusive to humans.

The concept of computer vision can be applied to Autonomous Vehicles, Healthcare and Medical Imaging, Retail and E-commerce, Security and Surveillance, Augmented and Virtual Reality (AR/VR) etc.

3.5 Robotics

Robotics is a cross-disciplinary field that merges AI and mechanical engineering with mechanical engineering and electronics to create machines capable of performing a wide range of tasks. AI in robotics enhances autonomy, adaptability, and decision-making in robots, enabling them to operate in dynamic environments. Applications include industrial automation, autonomous vehicles, medical surgery, and space exploration. AI allows robots to learn from their environment, plan actions, and collaborate with humans (Siciliano & Khatib, 2016).

Modern robotics integrates sensors, actuators, and control systems with AI to develop intelligent agents capable of perception, planning, and manipulation. For example, self-driving cars use AI for path planning, obstacle detection, and decision-making under uncertainty. In manufacturing, robotic arms equipped with computer vision and ML algorithms perform tasks with high precision and adaptability. Amazon Robotics, for instance, uses mobile robots in warehouses to streamline logistics.

Humanoid robots and service robots are also gaining traction in healthcare, hospitality, and education. For instance, SoftBank's Pepper robot is widely used in retail and customer service environments; it can recognize faces, interpret emotions, and engage in basic conversations. In healthcare, robots like TUG, developed by Aethon, navigate hospital corridors autonomously to deliver medications and supplies. Meanwhile, in the field of education, the NAO robot is used as a teaching assistant to help children learn programming and social skills through interactive lessons. These examples demonstrate how humanoid and service robots are not only technologically advanced but also provide tangible value in real-world settings. in healthcare, hospitality, and education. For example, SoftBank's Pepper robot can recognize faces and emotions and is used in retail and customer service. In hospitals, robots like TUG autonomously deliver supplies and medications. In classrooms, robots such as NAO assist in teaching programming and social interaction skills.

These robots rely on speech recognition, gesture detection, and emotion analysis to interact naturally with humans. Challenges in robotics include real-time learning, safety, energy efficiency, and ethical implications related to job displacement and privacy.

3.6 Conclusion

Understanding the core concepts of AI—machine learning, deep learning, natural language processing, computer vision, and robotics—is essential for grasping how AI technologies are revolutionizing modern life. These domains interconnect to form intelligent systems capable of performing complex tasks with increasing autonomy and efficiency.

As AI continues to evolve, interdisciplinary collaboration and responsible development practices will be critical in ensuring that AI technologies benefit society. This includes addressing ethical issues, fostering transparency, and ensuring equitable access to AI innovations. By deepening our understanding of AI's core concepts, we can better prepare for a future where intelligent systems are an integral part of human life.

The core concepts of AI—Machine Learning, Deep Learning, Natural Language Processing, Computer Vision, and Robotics—are the building blocks of intelligent systems that are rapidly transforming industries and societies. Understanding these concepts is essential for individuals and organizations seeking to stay competitive in an increasingly AI-driven world. As AI continues to evolve, it will unlock new opportunities and challenges, making it more important than ever to grasp the foundational principles that drive innovation. Whether it's enhancing customer experiences, improving healthcare outcomes, or driving automation, AI's core concepts are fundamental to shaping a future where intelligent systems play an integral role in solving complex problems and improving quality of life.

4. AI DEVELOPMENT PROCESS

AI has emerged as a transformational technology, influencing nearly every facet of modern society. From recommendation engines and voice assistants to autonomous vehicles and predictive analytics, Applications of AI are changing how people use information and technology. But the power and utility of Artificial Intelligence systems stem from rigorous development processes rooted in scientific methodology, data analytics, and computational principles. Understanding the AI development process is therefore crucial for developing AI literacy, particularly for students, educators, professionals, and policymakers who interact with or design AI systems.

This section unpacks the AI development lifecycle, presenting it not merely as a technical pipeline but as a structured and iterative methodology. The lifecycle encompasses five essential stages: Problem Definition, Data Collection and Preparation, Model Selection and Training, Model Evaluation, and Deployment and Maintenance. Each stage is examined in detail to provide foundational understanding as well as practical insight into how AI systems are conceptualized, built, and sustained.

4.1 Problem Definition

The identification and formal characterization of the problem is the first, and possibly most important, stage in the development of AI. Not all real-world challenges are suitable for AI solutions. Rule-based systems or human decision-making may be more effective in solving some issues, particularly when data is sparse, ambiguity is high, or ethical considerations prevail.

To frame a problem appropriately for AI, it is necessary to analyze its structure, data dependencies, and expected outcomes. AI-suited issues, for instance, frequently entail pattern recognition, large-scale data analysis, or ambiguous decision-making. Common domains include disease prediction in healthcare, customer segmentation in marketing, and fraud detection in financial services (Russell & Norvig, 2021).

A clear articulation of objectives and success criteria is essential. These objectives define what the AI system is intended to accomplish—whether it is classification, regression, clustering, or optimization. Correspondingly, Key Performance Indicators (KPIs) must be defined to assess system effectiveness. Metrics like accuracy, latency, precision, recall, and user satisfaction often guide the development and refinement of models. Furthermore, contextual KPIs such as cost reduction or increased engagement can be established depending on organizational goals.

4.2 Data Collection and Preparation

Data is often referred to as the "fuel" of AI. AI systems cannot work consistently without data, particularly data of high quality, representativeness, and relevance. Data collection and preparation are both essential and labor-intensive phases of AI development. It includes acquiring raw data, cleaning it, transforming it into usable formats, and sometimes augmenting it to improve coverage and variability.

4.2.1 Data Acquisition

AI systems rely on data that mirrors the complexity of the real world. Sources of data may include:

- Internal databases from existing organizational systems.
- Public datasets from government and research bodies.
- IoT devices and sensors for real-time data.
- APIs or web scraping for large-scale external data.
- Manual labeling through crowdsourcing platforms like Amazon Mechanical Turk.

Labeled data is necessary in supervised learning tasks, where each input is associated with the proper result. In unsupervised learning, unlabeled data is sufficient, allowing algorithms to identify patterns or groupings without human guidance (Goodfellow, Bengio, & Courville, 2016).

4.2.2 Data Cleaning and Preprocessing

Raw data is typically messy. It may contain missing values, inconsistencies, duplicate records, and noise. Cleaning the data ensures it reflects accurate and consistent values, which is crucial for training robust models. Preprocessing steps may include:

- **Normalization and Standardization**: Numeric features are being adjusted to fit a common scale.
- **Encoding**: Converting categorical variables into numerical values.
- **Imputation**: Filling in missing values using statistical methods or algorithms such as mean substitution, K-nearest neighbors, or predictive modeling.
- **Balancing**: Addressing class imbalances using techniques like oversampling and undersampling.
- **Outlier detection** to eliminate data points that may skew model behavior (Zhang et al., 2021).

4.2.3 Feature Engineering and Data Augmentation

Once cleaned, data may still need enhancement.

Feature engineering is the practice of developing new input features to improve model learning. Domain knowledge often plays a vital role here. For example, extracting sentiment scores from text data or computing body mass index (BMI) from weight and height can provide better predictors than raw data alone.

Feature engineering involves selecting, transforming, and creating relevant input variables—called **features**—using raw data to enhance the model's performance. Features are essentially the pieces of information that the model uses to learn and make predictions. For example, when building a model to predict housing prices, features might include the size of the property, the number of rooms, the location, and the year built. In some cases, raw data might not be immediately useful, and engineers need to derive meaningful features—such as calculating the age of a house from its construction year or creating an interaction between variables like location and size. Feature engineering also involves techniques like normalization, encoding categorical data, handling missing values, and reducing dimensionality. Well-crafted features help the model uncover patterns more effectively, whereas poor features can lead to weak performance. Since the quality of input features often has a greater impact on the outcome than the choice of algorithm itself, feature engineering is considered both an art and a science, playing an important role in developing accurate and reliable AI systems.

Data augmentation is particularly relevant in image or audio tasks, where transformations like rotation, cropping, or noise injection help simulate new data, improving generalization and mitigating overfitting (Chollet, 2018).

Data augmentation is the technique of artificially extending a dataset by making updated versions of existing data that retain the underlying meaning. This technique is widely used in computer vision and natural language processing. For example, in image-based tasks, augmentation might involve rotating, flipping, scaling, or adding noise to images to simulate different viewing conditions. In text-based models, it could include techniques like synonym replacement, sentence rephrasing, or back translation. The primary goal of data augmentation is to help AI models generalize better and avoid overfitting by exposing them to varied examples during training. This leads to more robust performance when the model encounters new, unseen data. Data augmentation is a cost-effective way to improve the reliability and accuracy of AI systems by adding training data diversity and volume without manual labeling.

4.3 Model Selection and Training

The crux of AI development lies in selecting a model architecture that fits the type of problem and the nature of the data. With numerous algorithms and architectures available, the decision depends on factors such as interpretability, scalability, accuracy, and computation cost.

4.3.1 Choosing the Right Algorithm

Different problems require different AI paradigms:

- **Classification tasks** benefit from models like decision trees, support vector machines (SVM), or neural networks.

In a classification task, the goal is to teach the AI system how to assign data items into predefined categories or classes. For example, an AI model may be trained to distinguish whether an email is spam or not or to identify whether an image contains a bird, a cat, or a dog. This process starts by feeding the model with labeled data—datasets where the correct category for each item is already known. The AI then learns to recognize patterns or features that help it differentiate between classes. Classification can be **binary**, where there are only two possible outcomes, such as "yes" or "no," or **multi-class**, where there are several distinct categories. There is also **multi-label classification**, where an item may belong to more than one class at the same time. Metrics like accuracy, precision, recall, and F1-score are used to assess effective classification models and make sure they produce accurate predictions. Classification plays an important role in many real-world applications, including medical diagnosis, sentiment analysis, fraud detection, image recognition, and more, making it a foundational concept in the AI development process.

- **Regression tasks** may use linear regression or ensemble methods like random forests.

In a regression task, the goal is to focus on predicting continuous numerical values rather than classifying data into distinct categories. Unlike classification, where the output is a label or category, regression tasks involve estimating quantities such as price, temperature, age, or sales figures. For instance, a regression model can be trained to predict the price of a property based on features like location, number of bed-rooms, and square footage. The AI system analyzes patterns in training data to determine the relationship between input variables and target numeric output. One of the simplest forms of regression is **linear regression**, which tries to fit a straight line through the data to make predictions. More advanced techniques like **polynomial regression** or **support vector regression** are used when the data relationships are more complex. Metrics like Mean Squared Error (MSE), Root Mean Squared Error (RMSE), or Mean Absolute Error (MAE), which quantify the difference between the expected and actual values, are typically used to assess a regression model's performance. Regression plays an important role in domains like finance, weather forecasting, healthcare, and marketing, where accurate numeric predictions can drive strategic decisions and automation.

- **Clustering tasks** typically employ K-means, DBSCAN, or hierarchical clustering.

Clustering is a key task within the AI development process, particularly under **unsupervised learning**. Unlike classification, where data is labeled, clustering involves discovering patterns or groupings within a dataset without any predefined labels. The goal of clustering is to organize data into meaningful groups, or "clusters," so that data points within the same group are more similar to each other than to those in other groups. Customer segmentation in marketing, where an AI model divides clients according to their demographics, preferences, or purchase patterns, is a typical example of clustering. K-Means, Hierarchical Clustering, and DBSCAN are well-known clustering methods that can be used for various dataset types and clustering requirements. Since there are no predefined categories, evaluating clustering results can be challenging, but metrics like **Silhouette Score**, **Davies-Bouldin Index**, and **intra-cluster vs inter-cluster distance** are often used to assess the quality of the grouping. Applications for clustering are numerous and include anomaly detection, image processing, social network analysis, and recommendation systems. By revealing hidden structures within data, clustering plays a critical role in exploratory data analysis and supports deeper insights that drive AI-based decision-making.

- **Sequential or time-series problems** are best tackled with Recurrent Neural Networks (RNNs) or Long Short-Term Memory (LSTM) networks.

The trade-off between model complexity and interpretability is also a major consideration. Logistic regression and decision trees are transparent but may underperform on complex tasks. Deep learning models offer high performance but function as "black boxes" with limited interpretability (Goodfellow et al., 2016).

4.3.2 Model Training and Hyperparameter Tuning

Training a model involves optimizing it to minimize prediction errors. This is achieved by feeding the model training data and adjusting internal parameters using optimization algorithms like stochastic gradient descent (SGD), Adam, or RMSprop.

Model performance heavily depends on hyperparameters, which are parameters set before training begins (e.g., learning rate, batch size, number of layers). Hyperparameter tuning methods include:

- Grid search
- Random search
- Bayesian optimization

Cross-validation, a method that separates data into several subgroups to guarantee consistent performance across various data samples, is frequently used for training and tuning.

4.4 Model Evaluation

No model should be deployed without rigorous testing. Evaluation helps in determining whether the model works effectively on unseen data as well as the training set. This is critical for ensuring the system's generalizability—its ability to work reliably in real-world conditions.

4.4.1 Common Evaluation Metrics

Key evaluation metrics include:

- **Accuracy**: Proportion of correct predictions to total predictions.
- **Precision**: Correctly predicted positives divided by total predicted positives.
- **Recall (Sensitivity)**: Correctly predicted positives divided by total actual positives.
- **F1 Score**: Harmonic mean of precision and recall.
- **AUC-ROC**: Area under the curve for receiver operating characteristics, useful in binary classification (Sammut & Webb, 2017).

4.4.2 Avoiding Overfitting and Underfitting

Artificial intelligence algorithms can **overfit** by memorizing training data, resulting in poor performance on new data. . On the other hand, **underfitting** happens when the model is too basic to identify patterns in the data. Strategies to combat these issues include

- Regularization techniques (L1, L2)
- Dropout layers in deep learning models
- Early stopping during training
- Model ensembling (e.g., bagging, boosting)

4.4.3 Ethical and Fair Evaluation

Modern AI systems are increasingly used in high-impact decisions, making fairness and bias critical evaluation dimensions. Discriminatory results can arise from biased training data, particularly in applications related to law enforcement, healthcare, and employment. Techniques such as fairness-aware learning and model auditing help ensure ethical AI development (Barocas, Hardt, & Narayanan, 2019).

4.5 Deployment and Maintenance

Once an AI model passes evaluation, it must be integrated into operational environments where it can offer real-world value. Deployment transforms a theoretical model into a live service or application component.

4.5.1 Deployment Practices

Deployment typically involves

- Packaging the model using containers (e.g., Docker).
- Hosting it on cloud platforms such as AWS, GCP, or Azure.
- Providing API endpoints for application integration.
- Ensuring security, scalability, and latency optimization.

Tools such as TensorFlow Serving, ONNX, and MLflow streamline these workflows.

4.5.2 Monitoring and Performance Tracking

Post-deployment, continuous monitoring of key metrics such as latency, throughput, and error rates is crucial. AI models often face data drift—a situation where the input data distribution changes over time. This necessitates mechanisms for alerting, diagnosis, and possibly model retraining (Sculley et al., 2015).

4.5.3 Model Versioning

To maintain relevance, models must be periodically retrained with fresh data. Maintaining version control helps track changes in models, configurations, and data pipelines. Tools like DVC (Data Version Control) and Git for ML projects are widely used for this purpose.

4.6 Challenges in AI Development

Data Privacy and Ethics

Handling sensitive data raises privacy concerns, particularly under regulations like GDPR and HIPAA. Developers must adopt privacy-preserving techniques such as differential privacy and federated learning to address these challenges (Dwork, 2008).

Interpretability and Explainability

AI models, especially deep learning ones, are often seen as "black boxes." Tools like LIME and SHAP allow developers to interpret predictions, increasing user trust and transparency.

Scalability and Resource Constraints

Training large models requires significant computational power. Although they offer scalable resources, cloud systems like AWS, Google Cloud, and Microsoft Azure can raise issues with pricing and security.

4.7 Future Directions in AI Development

Automated Machine Learning (AutoML)

The entire machine learning process, including feature selection, model selection, and hyperparameter tuning, is automated by autoML. This makes it possible for non-experts to create reliable AI systems with little coding.

MLOps and AI Lifecycle Management

MLOps is a set of practices that combines machine learning with DevOps. It ensures model reproducibility, scalability, and governance throughout the lifecycle (Allam et al., 2021).

Human-Centered AI

Future AI systems will increasingly focus on augmenting human capabilities rather than replacing them. Human-in-the-loop (HITL) techniques guarantee that crucial decision-making procedures incorporate human judgment.

5. TYPES OF AI

Based on its methodology and capabilities, artificial intelligence can be divided into a number of categories. The main categories of AI systems will be examined in this section.

5.1 Rule-Oriented Systems

The first examples of artificial intelligence are Rule-Oriented Systems. These systems leverage an ordered set of "if-then" statements and logical inference techniques to execute tasks or make conclusions. The mechanism is accessible and transparent as the information is openly expressed in the form of rules that domain experts offer (Giarratano & Riley, 2005).

In Fraud detection, these systems have been frequently employed, where questionable transactions may be flagged by established criteria (Bolton & Hand, 2002). It has been included into automated customer service platforms, including chatbots, which provide consistent, rule-based answers to user questions.

Figure 2. Methodology for Rule Oriented Systems

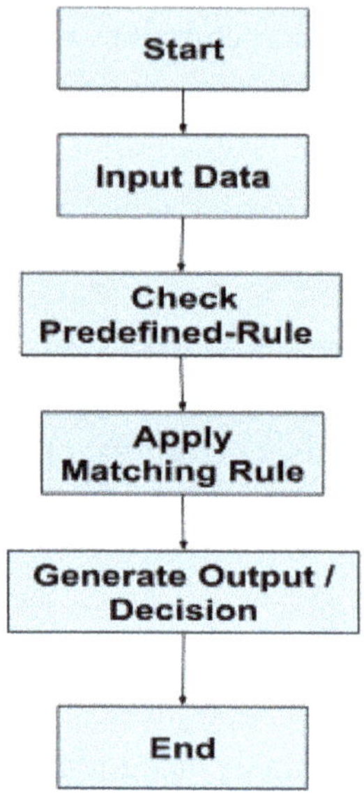

The procedure commences when the rule-based system warms up and helps prepare for receiving input. Data is submitted into and acquired by the system from user interactions as well as external sources. It then assesses if any requirements are satisfied by examining established rules that are kept in its knowledge base. The system implements the appropriate regulation to the input data in the event that a matching situation arises. The system accomplishes the procedure and brings a stop to the process by producing an output or decision based on the applicable rule.

A system which employs previously determined "if-then" procedures to interpret incoming quantities data and deliver alternatives or outputs is depicted in this flowchart.

Example: Rules like "If a transaction exceeds $10,000 and occurs outside the country of residence, then flag it for review" might get employed by a fraudulent activity detection system.

The Inference Engine Algorithm, also known as Forward Chaining or Backward Chaining, is the fundamental algorithm utilized in rule-based systems. By using rules of the type "IF condition THEN action," the system iteratively infers additional facts until a goal is achieved. This process is known as forward chaining.

Rule-based systems come in a variety of forms, each having special traits and uses. Forward Chaining Systems start with the facts that are presently accessible and use inference rules for gathering further data until an objective is achieved.

Their organizations are frequently employed in diagnostic systems that must analyze symptoms with the goal to determine a cause since they are data-driven. Systems that use backward chaining begin with an objective and work backward to identify the facts that support it. They work well in applications like legal reasoning and theorem proving because they are goal-driven. Deterministic Rule-Based Systems, rules provide unambiguous, predictable results. They work well in areas that are clearly defined and have inputs and outputs.

Fuzzy logic is utilized by fuzzy rule-based systems for dealing with imprecise or uncertain data. Algorithms are frequently used in systems like environmental monitoring or control systems when the input data is not strictly binary. In order to improve performance and flexibility, particularly in complex or changing contexts, hybrid rule-based systems integrate rule-based logic with additional strategies like machine learning or probabilistic models.

Advantages: High comprehension and reasoning for decision control.

Limitations: Rigidity and inadequate capacity to adjust to changing or unpredictable circumstances.

5.2 Expert Systems

The concept of systems based on rules is strengthened by systems with expertise, whose approximate human expert thinking by integrating a larger knowledge base with an inference engine. By mirroring human experts' processes for making decisions, researchers attempt to facilitate deciding in exacerbated contexts (Jackson, 1999).

One prevalent application for systems of experts is in medical diagnostics. As an instance, the MYCIN system, which was created in the 1970s, used a set of questions and knowledge criteria to diagnose bacterial illnesses and suggest treatments (Shortliffe, 1976). In a comparable way, expert systems in the legal realm assess legal precedents and legislation to offer advisory help.

Figure 3. Workflow of Expert Systems

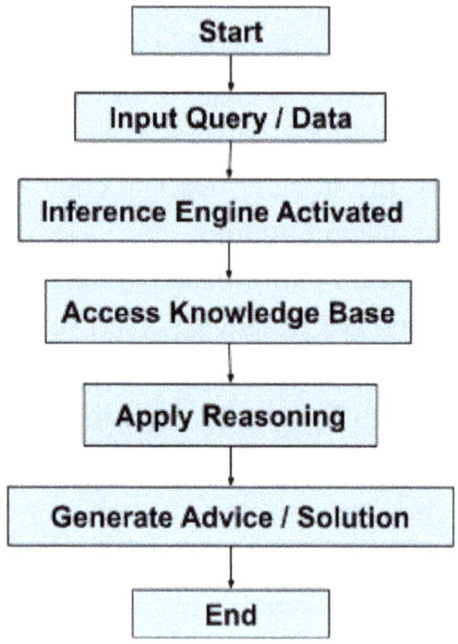

Depending on the input of users, the process diagram demonstrates the ways an expert system yields expert-level inferences or suggested actions by executing a machine learning engine alongside a knowledge base.

Example: Strategies for treatment may be proposed by an oncologist expert system based on tumor characteristics and patient history.

Expert systems work on designated knowledge and rules and are domain-dependent. Expert systems emerge across various forms, including fuzzy, rule-based, frame-based, model-based, and hybrid systems. Each is suitable for various distributed forms and levels of complexity. Fuzzy expert systems, for illustration, are helpful for making conclusions based on ambiguous or unpredictable input, such in weather forecasting.

Benefits include dependable expert logic imitation and structured decision-making. Limitations comprise limited learning capacity and challenges in growing and upgrading knowledge bases.

5.3. Machine Learning-Based AI

Algorithms that learn from data as opposed to relying on explicit programming constitute a component of machine learning (ML), an evolution in AI technique. In broad terms, supervised learning, unsupervised learning, semi-supervised learning, and reinforcement learning are the categories into which machine learning models fall (Jordan & Mitchell, 2015).

Though unsupervised learning detects patterns in unlabeled information, supervised learning uses data with labels to train the model to derive predictions. These kinds of models have significance effective recommendation systems, image recognition, spam detection, and predictive analytics (LeCun, Bengio, & Hinton, 2015).

Figure 4. Methodology for Machine Learning based AI Systems

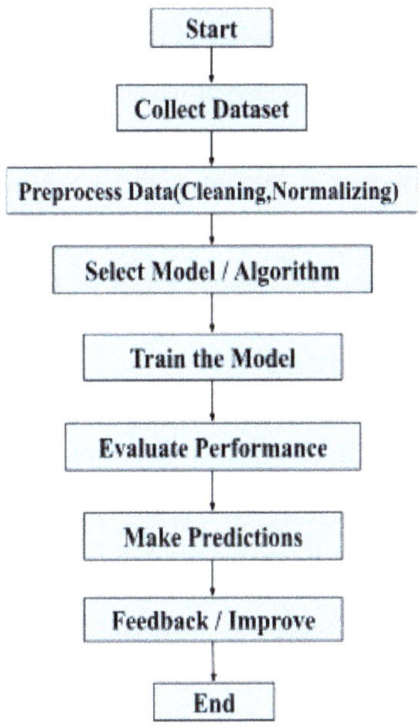

The ML pipeline is portrayed in the above graphic, starting with collection of data and and ending with trained models, assessment, and prediction together with feedback for continual improvement.

Example: Netflix's recommendation engine analyzes user activity to generate content recommendations employing machine learning.

In terms of mathematics, machine learning primarily relies on optimization, calculus, linear algebra, and probability theory. The Support Vector Machine (SVM) is another important method that increases the margin between data classes to choose the best hyperplane for categorizing them. Naive Bayes classifiers are computationally advantageous for text classification and spam detection because they use Bayes' theorem under a foundation of feature independence. Training, validation, and testing steps are necessary for machine learning models in application. The algorithm uses training data for altering its internal parameters throughout training. Testing assesses how well the finished model generalizes to new data, whereas validation aids in hyperparameter adjustment.

PyTorch, TensorFlow, Scikit-learn, and Keras are some prominent instances of libraries and frameworks used in modern machine learning development which provide pre-built functions and patterns for quicker deployment. Both complex deep learning networks and conventional machine learning models could probably be developed with the use of such technologies.

The fields of healthcare (disease diagnosis), finance (fraud detection), manufacturing (predictive maintenance), and entertainment (recommendation systems) have collectively seen major changes thanks to machine learning. Interpretability issues, data bias, overfitting, and the requirement for huge, high-quality datasets are some of the drawbacks of machine learning, despite its achievements.

Benefits incorporate perpetual learning and scalability and flexibility to new data. Limitations include the need for substantial datasets; interpretability of the model may be restricted.

5.4. Evolutionary Algorithms

Biological evolution, notably Evolutionary natural selection, serves as the inspiration for evolutionary algorithms, or EAs. Over several generations, develop solutions to optimization issues through mechanisms including crossover, mutation, and selection (Back, Fogel, & Michalewicz, 1997).

These algorithms work especially well in fields like financial modeling, engineering design, and robotic route planning that call for optimization under intricate restrictions (Eiben & Smith, 2003). A frequently utilized subset of EAs, genetic algorithms have been adopted to control system optimization and neural network evolution.

Figure 5. Methodology for Evolutionary Systems

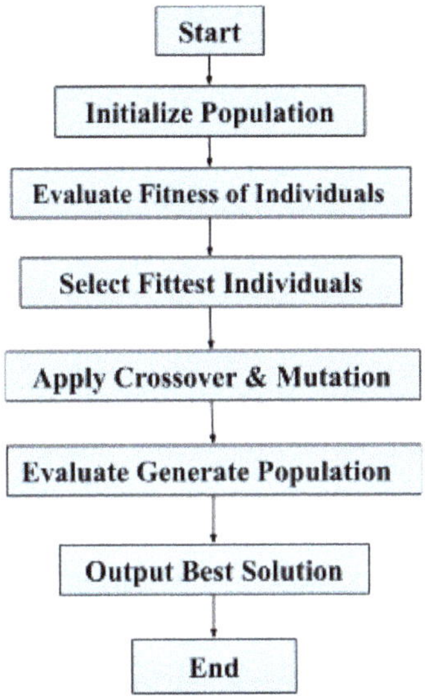

The steps of a simple evolutionary algorithm are as follows:

Initialization: Randomly create a starting population of solutions.

Selection: Select the most fit people to have children.

Recombination, or crossover, is the process of combining the genetic material of two parents to produce a child.

Mutation: To preserve genetic variety, introduce arbitrary alterations into progeny.

Replacement: Create a new generation by choosing from both existing and newly formed people.

Termination: Continue doing the aforementioned actions until a stopping condition is satisfied, such as convergence or the number of generations.

The evolutionary process is demonstrated by the flowchart, through which solutions become established through generations using crossing, mutation, and selection until the best outcome emerges.

The population-based search paradigm is the foundation of EAs. In order to determine an ideal or nearly ideal response, a population of possible solutions—often described as chromosomes or individuals—is established across several generations as opposed to emphasizing a single solution. A measure of fitness that evaluates the quality of the answer in relation to the problem is used to assess each member of the population.

Example: Evolutionary algorithms in robotics can imitate and determine the most beneficial motions to optimize a robot's mobility.

Genetic algorithms belong to the most prominent evolutionary algorithm types (GA). Ordinarily, vectors with real values or binary strings are used to represent candidate solutions in GAs. Each individual x's competence can be evaluated utilizing a fitness function f(x)f. For selecting individuals for reproduction, methods of selection which comprise methods like tournament selection, roulette wheel selection, or rank selection are employed. While crossover may employ uniform, two-point, or one-point crossover processes, mutation frequently entails bit flipping or marginally altering values.

Genetic Programming (GP) represents another class whereby the individuals are expression trees or computer programs. GP may automatically produce algorithms or mathematical expressions by evolving not just parameter values but also the structure of solutions.

Benefits encompass flexibility in troubleshooting and a willingness to innovate out of local optima. Constraints: costly to compute; delayed convergence.

5.5 Generative AI and Large Language Models (LLMs)

The term "generative AI" emphasizes artificial intelligence systems that have a capacity not only adept at monitoring or operating upon preexisting data, yet additionally of producing new material, encompassing text, photos, music, videos, and even code. These algorithms create new instances that have similar properties after learning the underlying patterns of the data during training.

Employing a generator and discriminator, GANs (Generative Adversarial Networks) generate photorealistic pictures that are employed in fashion and art. To create new samples for anomaly detection and picture editing, VAEs (Variational Autoencoders) model data distributions. Autoregressive models, such as GPT, provide material gradually for chatbots and narratives. Stable Diffusion and DALL·E 2 constitute two examples of technologies that utilize diffusion models, effectively inverting noise to produce high-quality photos. Transformer-Based Models assist in code creation, translation, and natural language processing through the utilization of self-attention for lengthy, coherent sequences.\

Tasks like blog writing, AI art, and auto-coding have been rendered possible by the application of generative AI in text, picture, music, and code production. It maintains privacy in healthcare by simulating patient data for model training.

Prominent forms of generative AI comprise:

- **GANs (Generative Adversarial Networks)**: Apply a discriminator and generator to produce photorealistic pictures, which are frequently utilized in art, entertainment, and fashion.

- **VAEs (Variational Autoencoders)**: Investigate data distributions for offering fresh samples for style transfer, picture restoration, and anomaly detection.
- **Autoregressive Models:** Chatbots, text creation, and dialog systems are driven by GPT (Generative Pretrained Transformer), and it produces content token by token.
- **Diffusion Models:** Examples including DALL·E 2 and Stable Diffusion create realistic, high-quality pictures by inverting random noise.
- **Transformer-Based Models:** These algorithms are excellent at tasks like code creation, machine translation, and long-form text synthesis because of their attention-based structures.

Numerous Applications are Enabled by Generative AI:

Synthetic patient information produced using LLMs aids in model training in the healthcare industry while maintaining patient privacy. In low-resource industries it facilitates data augmentation, game design, and instructional simulations easier.

LLMs' Potential, Dangers, and Implications for Critical Thinking

The way humans interact with machines has been fundamentally altered by large language models (LLMs) such as ChatGPT, Claude, and Gemini. Multi-modal reasoning, machine writing, natural conversation, and semantic search may all be employed to achieve this.

Key competencies of LLMs consist of:

- Sentiment analysis, translation, and summarization are automated.
- Coding assistance
- Multi-modal integration

Generative AI and LLMs models have some critical risks, like misinformation propagation, over-reliance that can reduce the ability for thoughtful reflection and problem-solving, bias amplification, and plagiarism.

AI Literacy Must Evolve to Navigate Challenges

- Obtain the capacity to critically examine AI results.
- Acknowledge the ethical and model limits.
- cross-check material, especially during high-stakes and academic settings.

LLMs and generative AI utilized are formidable equipment; however, correct application depends on critical awareness, ethical frameworks and open practices in industry and education.

5.6 Explainable AI (XAI)

The concept of "explainable AI" (XAI) highlights artificial intelligence methods and approaches that enhance the transparency and human-understandability of AI systems' strategic selection processes. The goal of XAI is to make sure that users can understand and grasp the explanations provided for the predictions or actions made by AI models.

XAI types include:

Model-specific techniques: These, such as rule-based systems or decision trees, are directly included into the machine learning model to enable interpretation.

Post-hoc explanation techniques: These techniques illustrate how sophisticated models, such deep neural networks, make decisions after they have been trained. SHAP (Shapley Additive Explanations) and LIME (Local Interpretable Model-Agnostic Explanations) are two methods.

XAI improves openness and trust across industries. It enhances confidence in healthcare by discussing AI-driven diagnosis. It addresses fraud detection and credit scoring in the financial industry. It guarantees decision-making transparency for autonomous cars, enhancing safety. Fairness and accountability are supported by ethical and legal AI, particularly in delicate fields like criminal justice.

A variety of disciplines, notably scheduling, game design, robotics, data mining, neural architecture search, and engineering design, benefit from the adaptability and utility of evolutionary algorithms. Algorithms can deal with noisy, discrete, or multi-modal fitness landscapes and don't need gradient information.

5.7. Edge AI

Edge AI is the technique of employing AI models and algorithms directly on edge devices like embedded systems, smartphones, and Internet of Things devices—instead of depending on cloud-based processing. The procedure uses less bandwidth, improves privacy, and lowers latency.

The Edge AI methodology encompasses many techniques. Edge computing uses AI models directly on local devices, such smartphones or industrial machinery, to check data and make decisions without relying on the cloud. Federated Learning minimizes the requirement for centralized data by enabling devices to train models locally on their own data and exchange changes. Through the use of methods like quantization and pruning, compression techniques shrink the size of AI models, making them appropriate for edge devices with constrained resources. By allowing AI models to make inferences in real time on edge devices, on-device inference reduces latency and dependency on the cloud.

Different algorithms that are tailored for local devices are used by Edge AI. Images and videos are processed using CNNs, whilst sequential data tasks are handled by RNNs. Random Forests and Decision Trees are lightweight models that work well in edge applications. For classification with minimal computing demands, SVMs are utilized. Working together to train models without exchanging raw data is made possible by federated learning techniques such as Federated Averaging. In order to ensure quicker processing on edge devices, model compression techniques such as pruning and quantization lower the size of the model. Tasks like anomaly detection and data compression also employ K-means clustering. Effective, real-time AI processing on devices with limited resources is made possible by these methods.

Edge AI has several uses in different industries. Real-time monitoring and diagnoses in healthcare are made possible by wearable technology that locally analyzes health data. It facilitates local data processing for smart grids, environmental sensing, and traffic monitoring in smart cities. Instead of depending on cloud servers, it enables autonomous cars to make decisions in real time. By providing predictive maintenance and anomaly detection in production, edge AI helps industrial IoT by decreasing downtime. It improves inventory control and customer experiences in retail by analyzing consumer activity on-device.

6. HANDS-ON OR PRACTICAL LITERACY TOOLS: PRACTICAL GUIDANCE AND RESOURCES TO BUILD AI LITERACY

Artificial Intelligence (AI) is no longer a distant concept reserved for researchers and tech giants. Today, AI is increasingly interwoven into our daily lives—from voice assistants and smart home devices to recommendation systems and autonomous vehicles. As AI becomes more pervasive, there is a growing need for AI literacy—a foundational understanding of what AI is, how it works, and how to interact with it responsibly and creatively. (Halili, 2019)

AI literacy is essential not only for those aspiring to become data scientists or machine learning engineers but also for everyday citizens. Teachers, students, professionals, and even children should have the tools to understand and engage with AI in a practical, meaningful way. This chapter explores hands-on tools and practical strategies that can be used by individuals and educators to build AI literacy. A curated toolkit of platforms and resources is also provided to support self-learning and classroom integration.

6.1 The Importance of Practical AI Literacy

AI literacy is more than just understanding technical terms. It involves the ability to:

- Understand what AI is and how it functions.
- Use AI tools and platforms in real-world contexts.
- Recognize ethical implications and biases in AI.
- Create or modify simple AI applications.
- Communicate and collaborate effectively with AI systems.

Practical engagement with AI through **interactive tools and project-based learning** significantly enhances the understanding of these concepts. It helps demystify AI and empowers learners to become not just passive consumers but active contributors to an AI-driven world.

6.2 Key Components of Practical AI Literacy

To effectively teach and learn AI, we need hands-on tools that support the following components:

1. **Interactive Learning:** Visual and interactive platforms help learners grasp abstract AI concepts.
2. **Real-world Applications:** Tools that simulate or build AI applications in real contexts (like voice recognition or image classification). (Dougherty, et al., 2020)
3. **No-Code or Low-Code Platforms:** These lower the entry barrier for beginners who may not have a programming background.
4. **Project-Based Learning:** Practical assignments and experiments foster deeper understanding.
5. **Ethical Considerations:** Platforms that encourage discussions around fairness, bias, and privacy in AI.

6.3 Popular Hands-on Tools to Build AI Literacy

Below is a list of platforms and tools specifically designed to make AI learning **accessible**, **interactive**, and **creative**:

6.3.1. Teachable Machine by Google

- **Description:** Teachable Machine allows users to create AI models using their webcam, images, audio, or poses without any coding.
- **Educational Use:** Ideal for schools and beginners to understand image, sound, and pose recognition.
- **Features:**
  - Train models in real-time.
  - Export models to TensorFlow.js or for web/mobile integration.
- **Impact:** Encourages experimentation and builds a foundational understanding of how machine learning models work.

6.3.2. MIT App Inventor with AI Extensions

- **Description:** A visual programming environment that lets users build mobile apps, now integrated with AI-powered features such as image classification and speech recognition.Code.org. (n.d.).
- **Educational Use:** Helps students create real-world mobile apps with AI functions.
- **Features:**
  - Drag-and-drop programming blocks.
  - AI extensions to incorporate vision and NLP (Natural Language Processing).
- **Impact:** Bridges the gap between AI theory and practical app development.

6.3.3. AI for Oceans (Code.org)

- **Description:** An engaging activity that introduces machine learning through a game-like interface.
- **Educational Use:** Great for young learners (Grades 3–8) to learn how AI can be trained to make decisions.
- **Features:**
  - Teaches supervised learning using friendly visuals.
  - Includes lessons on bias and ethics in AI.
- **Impact:** Encourages critical thinking and ethics awareness from an early age.

6.3.4. Cognimates

- **Description:** An AI training platform where children can teach machines to recognize text, images, and voice. (Code.org. (n.d.)).

- **Educational Use:** Designed especially for K-12 classrooms and informal learning.
- **Features:**
- Integrates with Scratch.
- Supports model training and ethical decision-making.
- **Impact:** Empowers students to train and customize AI while learning its limitations and potential.

6.3.5. Machine Learning for Kids

- **Description:** A simple platform that introduces machine learning by connecting it with Scratch and App Inventor. (Dougherty, et al., 2020)
- **Educational Use:** Suitable for ages 8+, great for coding clubs and STEM programs.
- **Features:**
- Offers structured lessons.
- Supports text, image, number, and sound classification.
- **Impact:** Helps learners build confidence by building real AI models and projects.

6.3.6. Microsoft MakeCode with AI Extensions

- **Description:** A beginner-friendly environment for coding hardware like the BBC micro:bit, with AI capabilities.
- **Educational Use:** Allows real-world experimentation with sensors and AI.
- **Features:**
- Simple JavaScript/blocks interface.
- Projects involving speech, motion, and sensors.
- **Impact:** Brings AI into physical computing, making it tangible and exciting.

6.4 Practical Strategies for Educators

While tools are essential, the approach to using them matters just as much. Here are some practical strategies for integrating AI literacy into classrooms or self-learning:

1. **Start with Everyday Examples:** Use tools like voice assistants, Netflix recommendations, or Google Translate to initiate discussions about AI.
2. **Encourage Inquiry-Based Learning:** Pose questions like "Can a machine be fair?" or "How does a camera recognize your face?"

3. **Use the Tools in Projects:** Integrate platforms like Teachable Machine into project work—e.g., build a gesture-controlled game or a speech-based quiz app.
4. **Discuss AI Ethics:** Encourage students to think about bias, privacy, and responsibility in AI systems.
5. **Cross-disciplinary Projects:** Blend AI learning with other subjects—create AI-based art, music, or storytelling projects.
6. **Empower Student Creation:** Let students present their own AI-powered apps or models to develop presentation and critical thinking skills.

6.5 A Toolkit for Building AI Literacy

Table 1. Here's a summary of platforms and resources educators and learners can explore

Tool	Purpose	Ideal For
Teachable Machine	Create ML models without code	Beginners, Class demos
MIT App Inventor + AI	Build AI mobile apps	High school, college
AI for Oceans (Code.org)	Teach ethics + ML basics	Elementary, middle school
Cognimates	Train AI with games + Scratch	Young learners
Machine Learning for Kids	AI + Scratch/App Inventor	Ages 8+, STEM educators
MakeCode + micro:bit	Physical computing + AI	Robotics, practical labs

7. SUMMARY

AI literacy is the ability to understand, use, and critically evaluate AI technologies in various contexts.

It is important for everyone—students, professionals, and the general public—to be AI-literate due to AI's increasing influence in everyday life.

AI literacy includes four key dimensions: technical (how AI works), ethical (responsible use), societal (impact on jobs and life), and creative (AI in art and design).

The evolution of AI began with early theories by Turing and von Neumann, progressed through symbolic AI in the 1950s, and later advanced through machine learning and deep learning to reach today's modern AI systems.

Key AI concepts include machine learning, deep learning, natural language processing, computer vision, and robotics, each with real-world applications.

The AI development process involves defining problems, collecting and preparing data, selecting and training models, evaluating performance, and deploying and maintaining systems.

Different types of AI include rule-based systems, expert systems, machine learning-based models, and evolutionary algorithms, each serving unique purposes.

Gaining AI literacy helps in making informed decisions, engaging in meaningful discussions, and understanding both the potential and limitations of AI in society.

REFERENCES

Aayog, N. I. T. I. (2018). National Strategy for Artificial Intelligence: #AIForAll. https://niti.gov.in/sites/default/files/2021-07/NationalStrategy-for-AI-Discussion -Paper.pdf

Back, T., Fogel, D. B., & Michalewicz, Z. (1997). *Handbook of Evolutionary Computation*. Oxford University Press.

Barocas, S., Hardt, M., & Narayanan, A. (2019). Fairness and machine learning. http://fairmlbook.org

Bolton, R. J., & Hand, D. J. (2002). Statistical fraud detection: A review. *Statistical Science*, *17*(3), 235–255.

Bostrom, N. (2014). *Superintelligence: Paths, dangers, strategies*. Oxford University Press.

Brynjolfsson, E., & McAfee, A. (2017). *Machine, Platform, Crowd: Harnessing Our Digital Future*. W.W. Norton & Company.

Buchanan, B. G., & Feigenbaum, E. A. (1978). DENDRAL and Meta-DENDRAL: Their applications dimension. *Artificial Intelligence*, *11*(1-2), 5–24.

Bughin, J., Hazan, E., Ramaswamy, S., Chui, M., Allas, T., Dahlström, P., & Trench, M. (2018). *Artificial Intelligence: The Next Digital Frontier?* McKinsey Global Institute.

Campbell, M., Hoane, A. J., & Hsu, F. H. (2002). Deep Blue. *Artificial Intelligence*, *134*(1-2), 57–83.

Chollet, F. (2018). *Deep learning with Python*. Manning Publications.

Code.org. (n.d.). AI for Oceans. https://code.org/oceans

Cognimates. (n.d.). Cognimates: AI Education for Kids. https://cognimates.me

Crawford, K. (2021). *Atlas of AI: Power, Politics, and the Planetary Costs of Artificial Intelligence*. Yale University Press.

Dougherty, D., & Eisenberg, M. (2020). Machine learning for kids. https://machinelearningforkids.co.uk

Dwork, C. (2008). Differential privacy: A survey of results. In *Theory and Applications of Models of Computation* (pp. 1–19). Springer.

Eiben, A. E., & Smith, J. E. (2003). *Introduction to Evolutionary Computing*. Springer.

Eubanks, V. (2018). *Automating Inequality: How High-Tech Tools Profile, Police, and Punish the Poor*. St. Martin's Press.

European Commission. (2021). Proposal for a Regulation laying down harmonised rules on artificial intelligence (Artificial Intelligence Act). https://eur-lex.europa.eu/legal-content/EN/TXT/?uri=CELEX%3A52021PC0206

Floridi, L., Cowls, J., Beltrametti, M., Chatila, R., Chazerand, P., Dignum, V., & Vayena, E. (2018). AI4People—An ethical framework for a good AI society: Opportunities, risks, principles, and recommendations. *Minds and Machines*, *28*(4), 689–707. DOI: 10.1007/s11023-018-9482-5 PMID: 30930541

Giarratano, J., & Riley, G. (2005). *Expert Systems: Principles and Programming*. Cengage Learning.

Goodfellow, I., Bengio, Y., & Courville, A. (2016). *Deep learning*. MIT Press.

Google. (2018). Teachable Machine. https://teachablemachine.withgoogle.com

Halili, S. H. (2019). Technological advancements in education and their implications. *International Journal of Emerging Technologies in Learning*, *14*(5), 36–46. DOI: 10.3991/ijet.v14i05.9357

Hastie, T., Tibshirani, R., & Friedman, J. (2009). *The elements of statistical learning*. Springer.

IBM. (2020). AI Education. https://www.ibm.com/skills/ai-education

ISTE & IBM. (2020). AI + Ethics Curriculum Guide. https://cdn.iste.org/www-root/Libraries/Documents%20%26%20Files/AI_Ethics_Curriculum_Guide.pdf

Jackson, P. (1999). *Introduction to Expert Systems* (3rd ed.). Addison Wesley.

Jordan, M. I., & Mitchell, T. M. (2015). Machine learning: Trends, perspectives, and prospects. *Science*, *349*(6245), 255–260. PMID: 26185243

Jurafsky, D., & Martin, J. H. (2020). *Speech and language processing* (3rd ed.). Draft., https://web.stanford.edu/~jurafsky/slp3/

Krizhevsky, A., Sutskever, I., & Hinton, G. E. (2012). ImageNet classification with deep convolutional neural networks. *Advances in Neural Information Processing Systems*, *25*, 1097–1105.

LeCun, Y., Bengio, Y., & Hinton, G. (2015). Deep learning. *Nature*, *521*(7553), 436–444. PMID: 26017442

Long, D., & Magerko, B. (2020). What is AI Literacy? Competencies and Design Considerations. *Proceedings of the ACM CHI Conference*.

Luckin, R. (2018). *Machine learning and human intelligence: The future of education for the 21st century*. UCL Institute of Education Press.

McCarthy, J., Minsky, M., Rochester, N., & Shannon, C. E. (1956). A proposal for the Dartmouth Summer Research Project on Artificial Intelligence. *AI Magazine*, *27*(4), 12–14.

McCulloch, W. S., & Pitts, W. (1943). A logical calculus of the ideas immanent in nervous activity. *The Bulletin of Mathematical Biophysics*, *5*(4), 115–133.

Microsoft. (n.d.). MakeCode for micro:bit. https://makecode.microbit.org

Ng, A. (2021). *AI for Everyone: Demystifying Artificial Intelligence*. Coursera.

Nilsson, N. J. (1984). *Shakey the robot*. SRI International.

OECD. (2019). OECD principles on artificial intelligence. https://www.oecd.org/going-digital/ai/principles/

Reaktor & University of Helsinki. (2019). Elements of AI. https://www.elementsofai.com

Rumelhart, D. E., Hinton, G. E., & Williams, R. J. (1986). Learning representations by back-propagating errors. *Nature*, *323*(6088), 533–536.

Russell, S., & Norvig, P. (2021). *Artificial intelligence: A modern approach* (4th ed.). Pearson.

Sammut, C., & Webb, G. I. (Eds.). (2017). *Encyclopedia of machine learning and data mining*. Springer.

Sculley, D., Holt, G., Golovin, D., Davydov, E., Phillips, T., Ebner, D., . . . Dennison, D. (2015). Hidden technical debt in machine learning systems. In Advances in Neural Information Processing Systems, 28.

Shortliffe, E. H. (1976). *Computer-based medical consultations: MYCIN*. Elsevier.

Siciliano, B., & Khatib, O. (Eds.). (2016). *Springer Handbook of Robotics* (2nd ed.). Springer.

State Council of China. (2017). A Next Generation Artificial Intelligence Development Plan. https://www.gov.cn/zhengce/content/2017-07/20/content_5211996.htm

Szeliski, R. (2022). *Computer vision: Algorithms and applications* (2nd ed.). Springer.

Tegmark, M. (2017). *Life 3.0: Being Human in the Age of Artificial Intelligence.* Knopf.

The White House. (2023). Executive Order on the Safe, Secure, and Trustworthy Development and Use of Artificial Intelligence. https://www.whitehouse.gov/briefing-room/presidential-actions/2023/10/30/executive-order-on-the-safe-secure-and-trustworthy-development-and-use-of-artificial-intelligence/

Topol, E. (2019). *Deep Medicine: How Artificial Intelligence Can Make Healthcare Human Again*. Basic Books.

Turing, A. M. (1950). Computing machinery and intelligence. *Mind*, *59*(236), 433–460.

UNESCO. (2021). AI and Education: Guidance for Policy-Makers. United Nations. https://unesdoc.unesco.org/ark:/48223/pf0000376709

UNESCO. (2021). Recommendation on the ethics of artificial intelligence. https://unesdoc.unesco.org/ark:/48223/pf0000379922

UNESCO. (2021a). Recommendation on the ethics of artificial intelligence. https://unesdoc.unesco.org/ark:/48223/pf0000381137

UNESCO. (2021b). AI Competency Framework for Students. https://unesdoc.unesco.org/ark:/48223/pf0000379868

Vaswani, A., Shazeer, N., Parmar, N., Uszkoreit, J., Jones, L., Gomez, A. N., & Polosukhin, I. (2017). Attention is all you need. *Advances in Neural Information Processing Systems*, *30*, 5998–6008.

Weizenbaum, J. (1966). ELIZA—A computer program for the study of natural language communication between man and machine. *Communications of the ACM*, *9*(1), 36–45.

West, D. M., & Allen, J. R. (2018). *How Artificial Intelligence is Transforming the World*. Brookings Institution.

Zhang, Y., Sheng, Q. Z., Alhazmi, A., & Li, C. (2021). Clean and reliable: Data cleaning and preprocessing in machine learning. *IEEE Access : Practical Innovations, Open Solutions*, *9*, 140008–140021. DOI: 10.1109/ACCESS.2021.3118676

Zuboff, S. (2019). *The Age of Surveillance Capitalism: The Fight for a Human Future at the New Frontier of Power*. PublicAffairs.

Chapter 3
History of AI:
Key Milestones and Figures, Highlighting the Evolution of AI From Its Early Beginnings to Its Current State

A. Elavarasi
https://orcid.org/0009-0004-0463-7372
Velammal College of Engineering and Technology, India

A. Periyanayaki
https://orcid.org/0009-0003-6735-628X
Velammal College of Engineering, India

ABSTRACT

The history of Artificial Intelligence (AI) shows a journey from early ideas about machines and logic to today's powerful technologies. Alan Turing's work in the 20th century laid the foundation for AI, which became a formal field in 1956. After early progress and setbacks during the "AI Winter," AI advanced with machine learning and neural networks. Milestones like IBM's Deep Blue and Google's AlphaGo showed AI's growing strength. Today, AI impacts healthcare, finance, and daily life but also raises ethical concerns about privacy and fairness. The future goal is creating responsible AI that benefits society.

1. INTRODUCTION

A collection of computational methods referred to as artificial intelligence (AI) enables machines to sense, comprehend, act, and learn in a highly human-like manner.

DOI: 10.4018/979-8-3373-2297-1.ch003

AI is not a technology. Scholars and practitioners have varying definitions of artificial intelligence because of its wide and evolving nature. AI consists of a number of subfields, such as computer vision, natural language processing, and machine learning, as opposed to being a single, monolithic system. These methods provide organizations with efficient means of enhancing customer interaction, decision-making, and productivity when integrated with automation tools and data-driven analytics. (Russell, S., & Norvig, P., 2021)

Narrow (or "weak") AI

The majority of the AI applications found in the ordinary worlds belong to the category of narrow AI, or weak AI. They are systems meant to carry out specialized functions within a well-defined range. Some of them include mobile apps that give forecast weather conditions, voice-commanded digital assistants, and business intelligence programs that analyze datasets for the purpose of supporting operational effectiveness. While these systems exist within limited domains, their effects are substantial when used at scale. Narrow AI is still revolutionizing industries through enhanced accuracy, lowered expenses, and the enhancement of human decision-making. (Nilsson, N. J.,2014).

General (or "strong") AI

On the other hand, strong AI, or general AI, refers to theoretical computer innovation of machines that can reason, learn, and evolve in a broad range of activities similar to human cognition. Popular culture tends to portray this type of AI as self-sustaining, conscious entities with the ability for abstract thinking and imagination. Although today's AI can surpass human capabilities in specific tasks like data processing or pattern recognition, the dream of general AI is still to be realized. Therefore, AI today can be described more as a collection of tools augmenting human capabilities and not substituting them, and hence human–machine collaboration remains the focus of technological advancement (Bostrom, N., 2017).

2. EARLY FOUNDATIONS OF AI

2.1 Philosophical and Mathematical Influences

2.1.1 Gottfried Wilhelm Leibniz – Logical Reasoning

(Avance Science Ed) Lee Anderson

I know they're worth my time. Lee Anderson is pictured flying the drones over the Chalk Hill Estate. He is a drone operator based at the grapevines in the Chalk Hill Estate. The drones are an essential tool in helping Lee inspect the grapevine and determine the quality of the grapes. An 85.5 percent share of the total crop is expected to lead to its enhancement in the wine production process at the Chalk Hill Estate and a sustainable performance that makes it the market leader in the region that is mainly concerned with wine production. Lee Anderson is optimistic about the graveyard's success if the new technology is introduced.

Figure 1. Gottfried Wilhelm Leibniz

2.1.2 Drones Over the Vineyard

During those times, advancements in computers regarding artificial intelligence that will allow a machine to think and, incidentally, do things faster will have been made. This will not only save me time but also leave me to care for plants and therefore make the work lighter and more fun. He could likewise explain freely the Platonic laws like the Convention of the Same as the One and the Other. Principle of The Same: Everything that exists is all there is at all.

2.1.3 George Boole – Boolean Algebra and Symbolic Logic

English mathematician, logician, and philosopher George Boole (1815–1864) is best famous for inventing Boolean algebra, the basis for modern symbolic logic and computer science.

Figure 2. George Boole

Boolean Algebra

Boole promoted an algebraic approach to logic with numerical representation of truth values (1 for true, 0 for false) and calculation based on logical operations. Boole's system is mathematics based reasoning and the foundation of computer science and electronic circuits nowadays.

Key Boolean Algebra Concepts:

Binary values:

True (1) and False (0)

Logical Operators:

- AND (•) – True if and only if both inputs are true (A • B)
- OR (+) – True if any of the values being checked are true (A + B)
- NOT (¬) – The inverse of the value (¬A is true when A is false)

Boolean Functions:

- Formulas involving identities and operations (like $F = A \bullet (B + \neg C)$)
- Applied to computer science, set theory, and logic gates

Basic Laws:

- Identity Laws: $A + 0 = A, A * 1 = A$
- Domination Laws: $A + 1 = 1, A \bullet 0 = 0$
- Idempotent Laws: $A + A = A, A \bullet A = A$
- Distributive, Associative, and Commutative Laws.

Symbolic Logic and "The Laws of Thought"

In his book an Investigation of the Laws of Thought (1854), Boole revolutionized logic to the point where logical sentences were utilized as algebraic expressions, making Aristotelian logic formal and replacing it with a mathematical process.

Impact on Computing and Modern Logic

- Boolean algebra is the basis for designing digital circuitry (microprocessors, logic gates, flip-flops).
- Search algorithms utilize Boolean operators (Google searches employ AND, OR, NOT operators).
- It forms the foundation for databases, artificial intelligence, and programming languages.

Boole's contribution turned logic into a rigorous mathematical science, giving rise to the modern computer, electronic circuits, and artificial intelligence.

2.2 Theoretical and Computational Foundations

2.2.1 Charles Babbage (1791–1871) – The Visionary

Babbage was a British inventor. It had primitive features of a modern computer, including:

- An "store" (memory) to hold numbers and intermediate results.
- A "mill" (processor) to execute calculations.
- Input and programming punched cards (based on Jacquard looms).

Conditional branching and loops, in theory making it general-purpose computable. Although Babbage never built a fully functional model due to technological and financial limitations, his design spawned modern computing.

Figure 3. Ada Lovelace (1815-1852) | Charles Babbage (1791-1871)

2.2.2 Ada Lovelace

Some of her main achievements are:

Thinking broadly about computers and imagining what they can do that goes way beyond just basic math – that they can work with things not just numbers but also letters and logical rules. Entering history with the designation as the first computer programmer with the creation of the very first program that was designed for machine execution. Making concepts before present computing usage that date back such as machines' capability to produce graphics and music. Even though the Analytical Engine was never constructed, Lovelace's pioneering concepts formed the foundation for modern computing.

2.3 Alan Turing - Turing Machine and Turing Test

Turing Machine:

The art and science of computation were truly revolutionized in 1936 when British mathematician and logician Alan Turing published a landmark paper "On Computable Numbers, with an Application to the Entscheidungs problem": therein he introduced the Turing Machine, which is a theoretical mathematical model for a simple yet powerful computing device capable of carrying out any conceivable algorithmic computation.

The Turing Machine consists of:

- An infinite tape (or length) consisting of cells which hold symbols.
- A tape head capable of reading and writing and of moving left and right along the tape.

Rules (state transitions) that instruct the machine in accepting the input according to its current state. It is the essence of the Turing Machine to distinguish those things that are computable from those not computable, thereby setting the groundwork for modern computer science. It has also provided insight into problems that cannot be solved by any algorithm, a profound assertion about undesirability.

Figure 4. Alan Turing

Turing's concept of the "Turing Test" (1950)

Thus, Turing proposed the test called the Turing Test in his major paper, "Computing Machinery and Intelligence," 1950 as a criterion by which to assess the extent of intelligent behaviour in machines.

The following is the Turing Test in Turing's words:

An interrogator puts questions to both a human and a machine through a text-only channel. If the interrogator is unable to differentiate, with reasonable confidence, between the human and the machine in terms of answers given, then the machine has passed the test, having demonstrated behaviour indistinguishable from that of a human being.

The Turing Test remains a cornerstone for AI and for much continuing relevance in the debate around machine consciousness, machine intelligence, and chatbot design. It is true that the latest trend in AI, like ChatGPT, would produce an answer that sounds quite intelligent, but the criticism would be that it does not claim to be a seeker of true understanding or real reasoning.

3. THE BIRTH OF AI AS A FIELD

3.1 The Dartmouth Conference (1956)

Many consider the conference at Dartmouth, held in the summer of 1956, to be the beginning of the whole new academic program, artificial intelligence. The conference was organized by four great personalities, because Graham Moore and Marvin Minsky are very often credited among the founders of artificial intelligence. Hampton L.L. was the location of the conference in Hanover, New Hampshire, US.A.

To explore this idea, "any aspect or trait of learning or other aspect of intelligence is, in principle, so precisely described that a machine could be built to simulate it." According to this hypothesis, one could teach any feature of intelligence in computers, and those machines would then work on tasks that we assume require human intelligence. (McCarthy, J., Minsky, M. L., Rochester, N., & Shannon, C. E., 1956).

In this respect, AI became an independent field of academic research. Although the idea of artificial beings or machines with intelligence had been around before, this was the moment when it made an identity for itself as a scientific field. John McCarthy is often credited with coining the term at this conference, and this was the first time it came to represent, in fact, this field. Brilliant aspirations were set in the conference to fabricate machines that would execute human-like intelligent operations, such as proper chess play, solving problems, or learning from experience. The Dartmouth Conference also gathered numerous wishful investors who would influence an unknown future for AI, such as John McCarthy, Marvin Minsky, Allen Newell, and Herbert A. Simon. Although the conference did not suddenly lead to a flurry of developments in AI, it is nevertheless regarded as the moment in AI history when pompousness directed innovation into this field.

3.2. Key Contributors

3.2.1 John McCarthy

John McCarthy is considered a pivotal figure in the field of artificial intelligence and coined this term in 1956. As he and other pioneers of the art—Marvin Minsky, Nathaniel Rochester, and Claude Shannon— organized the Dartmouth Conference at Dartmouth College in Hanover, New Hampshire, it was here that he first propounded the notion that all learning or intelligence can, in principle, be so adequately described that a machine can emulate it. (McCarthy, J., Minsky, M. L., Rochester, N., & Shannon, C. E.,1956). This statement laid the groundwork for AI as a formal academic discipline. The use of the phrase "artificial intelligence" by McCarthy basically denotes the genesis of the new field as a scientific activity or engineering activity intent upon building machines able to perform tasks that normally would require the intelligence of human beings. McCarthy's contributions to AI could also be that he developed the LISP programming language, one dedicated to AI research, some of the work on common-sense reasoning, and also that on machine learning. It was not so much to build machines that would simulate human behaviour, according to McCarthy, as much as it was to have machines which could actually think and reason. All in all, the coining of the phrase "artificial intelligence" at Dartmouth permitted McCarthy to provide a name and a structure for a burgeoning field that would, in years to come, impact modern-day computing and many other technologies.

Figure 5. John McCarthy

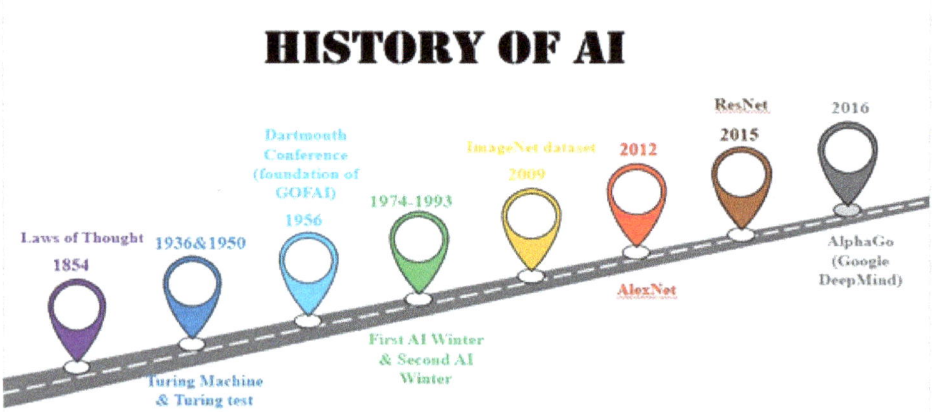

3.2.2 Marvin Minsky

Marvin Minsky can be described as one of the founding fathers of artificial intelligence (AI), contributing in many ways into the early AI research. He is better known for his involvement with machine intelligence theory, neural networks, and the possible capability of machines to mimic human-like cognition. Minsky used his theories and ideas as a way of exploring the suboptimal ways in which such symbolic AI should be implemented. This has been done through the construction of 'maintenance think tanks', simple conceptions of how AI might use its various cognitive functions related to the tasks assigned within AI. At times they were thought mainly as complementary to the fully established rational agent. This perspective was somewhat the one with which his grandfather worked.

Figure 6. Marvin Minsky

Marvin Minsky was, and remains, one of the greatest architects of our understanding of intelligence. Even though he was critical of the early neural networks, contributions in AI, cognitive science, and machine learning shape a philosophy that cannot, for the moment, just be ignored. An ingenious conception of intelligence is interlaced through the interaction of simpler processes, itself just one of the inputs toward accomplishing a breakthrough in equal regard, deep learning, natural language processing, and robotics. The principles that Minsky carried with him into the more extensive AI field forced people, quite rightly, to think carefully about intelligence, the capabilities coding machines have, and what the current technologies cannot do. Minsky will definitely be remembered for a combination of profound theoretical insights and the healthy skepticism with which he approached the goal of an elaborated intelligence and the limitations of early AI systems. In continuous view, Minsky had yet made additional soft contributions in the technical, theoretical, philosophical, and even what you could view as more spiritual senses contributing massively to the road ahead. The mantra should read: Marvin Minsky made more contributions toward propelling AI in diverse equitable stages built actually more than the short-term influence through his critique of neural networks as set by burning the second flame instead through his great wider realization on intelligence as an interacting atmosphere of interplaying parts while deeply imbuing it through and through with insights playing enormously through AI to beholder more quickly, next cognitive science leveraging toward or eventually creating opportunities yet to disposed indirectly through whatever visceral snapshot that goes through an AI build-out complemented through Robotic Consciousness scholarship over there as a capstone.

3.2.3 Herbert Simon and Allen Newell

Simon was well versed in political science, economics, and psychology, whereas Newell was specifically involved in computer science. Together, Simon and Newell worked to model human cognitive processes using artificial systems. Their cooperation formed the basis of what would later become cognitive science. They sought a description of how human thinking proceeds and how one can possibly emulate it with machines. The early group of research involved symbolic AI (commonly termed classical AI or "Good Old-fashioned AI" - GOFAI) working from a perspective of manipulating symbols that represent knowledge and/or particular types of problems. (Simon, H. A., & Newell, A., 1956.) The work of Simon and Newell that proved to be among the most influential was the General Problem Solver. It was widely considered to be an early attempt to simulate human problem-solving through the use of formal algorithms and heuristics. GPS was set to solve problems by searching through possible solutions using a set of rules and operators. The GPS may be seen as a very early example of a rule-based system because it applied a set of production rules to explore the problem space. In fact, GPS was working in principle on a heuristic search, that is, solving problems by means of rules deciding which move or step to take, not by trying to masochistically exhaust all possible solutions. These rules were meant to steer the system in the right direction, not unlike how human problem-solvers use intuition and experience. GPS was to attack the problem first by trying to break it down into smaller sub problems. Often referred to as means-ends analysis, this approach used rules to close the gap between the present state and the goal state.

Production systems: This was the production system model that Simon and Newell also contributed to rule based AI. A production system is a rule-based system in which rules (normally in "if-then" forms) apply to the current state of the system to generate a new state or states. In this view, a rule-based system keeps on firing production rules on its data, changing one state into another according to the conditions defined by these rules, and infers or decides step-by-step according to the rules specified to it.

Figure 7. Herbert Simon and Allen Newell

The cognitive models of Herbert Simon and Allen Newell, from the perspective of rule-based AI, were foundational in shaping the future trajectory of AI research. Their didactic developments of the General Problem Solver and their theories of problem-solving and knowledge representation formed the basis for rule-based systems that still remain important to AI research and applications today. Their interdisciplinary approaches allow them to combine a wide range of fields such as psychology, computer science, and, eventually, artificial intelligence into one big, established, overly important field of research.

3.4 Early AI Systems and Theories

Symbolic AI refers to "good old-fashioned AI" (GOFAI) and appeared in the 1950s and 1960s; it held the notion that knowledge had to be explicitly represented as symbols, which could be manipulated through logical rules for reasoning and problem-solving. The central idea of Symbolic AI consists of encoding and representing knowledge in general through symbols (words, numbers, or some other discrete representation) and, through formal logic on these symbols, deriving conclusions or solutions that would represent an intelligent behaviour. Symbolic AI logic primarily means a logic-based and rule-based means of problem-solving: in which knowledge was represented in symbols and logical statements-propositions or predicates while reasoning was done by means of logical operations-deduction, inference, or resolution-on these symbols (Rosenblatt, F., 1958). The expert systems were rule-based systems made to emulate the decision-making capabilities of a human expert in a particular field of knowledge, such as medicine, engineering, or finance. The elements of Symbolic AI are described as follows: Knowledge representation, which brought into play the formal methods of predicate logic, semantic networks, and frames through which knowledge could be expressed; Inference engines: applying rules to knowledge to infer new facts much like a human would reason logically. Chess had always been from the start one of the very benchmark problems of AI because of its complex decision-making, strategy requirement, and an absolutely well-defined goal. Chess playing programming has always been one of the fields that AI researchers first tried to work within, scientifically validated instead as proving grounds for AI problem-solving methods.

4. AI WINTERS AND REVIVALS (1970S – 1990S)

4.1 First AI Winter(1970s) – Over Promised Expectations Lead to Funding Cuts

The First AI Winter was a period when grand expectations were placed on the development of AI, which proved to be undeliverable at a later stage. In the 1950s and 1960s, several early AI pioneers had the craziest kind of bravado about imminent leaps in machine intelligence. However, that just wasn't the case at the time; first and foremost, there was a lack of computer power, and there existed obstacles like natural language processing or its solving as well as little data; those could count as some methods that also existed and included into more important observations concerning the AI Winter: unrealistic expectations that machines then promised to rival human intelligence were unrealistic by only a couple of decades; the light years between them and actual computers: AI algorithms were too computationally intensive for computers available at that time; the absolute failure of natural language understanding and machine learning fields to create any real-life applications; thus the slashing of funding from governments and agencies since the slow pace of research had led these people to lose faith in AI. The US and the UK finally ceased investment in AI, including the Light hill Report (1973), which had criticized UK AI developments. This stage of AI development was barren until the development of the 1980s revived it.

4.2 Rise of Expert Systems (1980s) – AI Applied in Business and Healthcare

AI Applications in the Business and Healthcare Theories Stemmed in the 1980s. AI researchers got a new lease of life-in the sense that the AI programs were thought to be that of expert systems-a computer program intended to simulate the logic involving a decision-making process performed by a human in a narrow field. (Feigenbaum, 1980.) These systems provided solutions to rather tricky issues using mostly if-then rules and, with the help of knowledge bases, "made" AI operational in real-world situations with a focus on business and healthcare, and later on in manufacturing.

Major Contributions from Expert Systems – Knowledge-Based Systems:

Unlike previous approaches to AI, expert systems relied on extensive rule-based knowledge databases and an inference engine that made deductions over it.

Corporate Transactions:

Clan relations filed expert systems for the purposes of planning, customer support, and decision-making in the finance sector.

Advanced in Medical Assistance:

The diagnostic support systems advanced in interest from the late 1970s into the 1980s, including MYCIN for treating bacterial infections and DXplain for diagnostic support.

Government and Military Ventures:

AI was leveraged towards logistics, planning, and intelligence analysis.
Constraints and Some Declines of the late 1980s saw expert systems stumbling into their frustrations:

Very High Maintenance:

The rule-based system specialists would have to update almost on a daily basis to keep the systems alive.

Scalability Issues:

If the expert system was sound, adding rules only complicated them once again and would, quite possibly, make them less efficient. (McDermott, D., 1987.)

4.3 Second AI Winter (1987-1993) – Limitations of Rule-Based AI models

The Pitfalls of Rule-Based AI Systems the Second AI Winter was largely due to the over-dependency upon expert systems, which rose to importance in the 1980s. Though showing great promise among others, these rule-based AI models eventually failed to scale up, which led to their disillusionment, funding cuts, and slow one to covet and deem AI most worthy as a research function to pursue in the mid-1990s.

Key Reasons for the Second AI Winter

1. High Maintenance Cost:

There is a need for constant updating of the expert systems. In some cases, when new rules are appended, there may be inconsistencies and backward efforts.

2. Scalability issues:

Rule-based systems became arcane and slowly cumbersome as they increased knowledge bases in size. They could not well cope with uncertainty, nor could they adapt to another scenario quickly.

3. The Collapse of the AI Hardware Market:

Some companies included Symbolics, Lisp Machines Inc., and Xerox, for example, which manufactured expensive AI-specific hardware. As a result, these devices were systematically outperformed by now affordable and much more powerful general-purpose computers, conscripting them to obsolescence.

4. High Hopes but Low Returns:

A great hype was almost built up around expert systems functions and processes by research scientists and industry. Therein, belief of the investors and business agents declined, vacuuming up financial activity and halting all progress.

5. Industries and Government Withdraw:

Substantial cuts in AI funding in the U.S. by DARPA. -The Japanese Fifth Generation Computer Systems project to restructure AI did not give any compelling deliverables.

Consequences of the Second AI Winter:

AI moved into niche research, and much of it was stalled. -Most AI start-ups closed their doors, while AI initiation in academia was overwhelmed. -And for the field leapt towards more statistical and data driven approaches that yielded breakthroughs in machine learning in the 1990s and 2000s.

4.4 Machine Learning Revival (1990s) –Shift Toward Data-Driven Approaches

With the closure of the Second AI Winter (1987-1993), the AI field witnessed revival in the 1990s as it gradually swayed from rule-based expert systems toward data-driven machine learning (ML) approaches. (Rumelhart, D. E., Hinton, G. E., & Williams, R. J.,1986.) Rather than relying on manually programmed rules, researchers began to shift their focus onto statistical models, neural networks, and algorithmic learning from data.

Reasons Behind the Revival of Machine Learning

1. Improvements in Computing Power:

Faster microprocessors and GPUs allowed for training complex models. Instead of expensive AIcentric hardware, cheap yet powerful computers gained prominence within the field. (Schapire, R. E. 1990).

2. Data Availability:

The Internet and digital storage opened the gates to allowing huge volumes of both structured and unstructured data to come in (Vapnik, V., 1995). Machine learning flourished in this data-driven paradigm, using real-life scenarios to improve its performance.

3. Neural Networks Brought to Life Again:

By bringing together other deep learning researchers and the back-propagation algorithm, Geoffrey Hinton and a few others were able to train multi-layer neural networks much more efficiently . Although the initial concept of deep learning did appear, the hardware limitations set a cap on their potential (Hinton, G. E., Osindero, S., & Teh, Y. W.,2006.)

4. Change toward Probabilistic Models:

Research began to settle down to studying Bayesian networks, Hidden Markov Models (HMMs), and Support Vector Machines (SVMs). (Pearl, 1988). These models worked on outperforming rule-based AI under the conditions of uncertainty and pattern recognition. (Dempster, A. P., Laird, N. M., & Rubin, D. B., 1977.)

5. Industry Adoption& Practical Application:

Speech recognition, fraud detection, recommendation systems, etc. provided scopes of application for machine learning. First successful applications included spam filters, financial modelling, and medical diagnostics. (Brynjolfsson, E., & McAfee, A.,1997) Impacts of the ML Revival AI research regained its credibility again, earning investments from tech industries and indeed governments as well. It laid ground works for big data analytics, computer vision achievements, and deep learning advancements in the years 2000 and 2010. IBM, Google, and Microsoft started integrating machine learning into their different products.

5. THE RISE OF MACHINE LEARNING AND DEEP LEARNING

5.1 Advancements in Computational Power and Data Availability

The exponential increase of machine learning (ML) and deep learning (DL) in the 2000s and 2010s was driven primarily by progress in computational powers and available data. Innovations or applied innovations developed over these two decades were a result of these two drivers. Let us observe how these drivers pushed ML and DL forward. (Hinton, G. E., Osindero, S., & Teh, Y. W., 2006.)

5.1.1 Progress in Computational Powers

a. Graphics Processing Units (GPUs)

While initially used to produce video game graphics, the parallel processing capabilities of GPUs made them natural choices to train deep learning models. While

CPUs execute instructions sequentially, GPU architecture executes thousands of calculations simultaneously, thereby being well suited to train large neural networks. (Goodfellow et al., 2014). Researchers using deep learning started embracing GPU acceleration for model training in the early part of the late 2000s and early 2010s. This was revolutionary, as it was too slow with traditional CPU-based computation beforehand to do model training of deep learning models and thus was impractical for experimentation and research purposes. By rendering their GPUs deep learning exercise relevant, NVIDIA literally branded itself a pioneer in AI. CUDA's introduction in 2006 expedited additional utilization of general-purpose computing by GPU and garnered substantial interest in machine learning with GPUs.

b. Computing and Distributed Computing:

Massive adoption of cloud computing environments, such as Amazon Web Services (AWS), Google Cloud, and Microsoft Azure, made it possible for researchers, start-ups, and firms to acquire the computing capabilities at a negligible rate compared to making the investment for building supercomputers in-housed. Cloud computing offered scalable infrastructure so that teams could train large models and experiment with humongous datasets without necessarily spending money on expensive hardware. Access to the computation power deep learning needed became democratized as a result. The practice of distributed computing was more common. Researchers were able to train models across multiple machines at the same time, thereby dispersing the computation load and accelerating the training process significantly.

c. TPUs, or special hardware

Google in 2015 presented Tensor Processing Units (TPUs), hardware especially developed for boosting machine learning activities, specifically deep learning. TPUs are better suited for performing matrix operations that are the heart of deepest learning algorithms. TPUs then advanced the frontiers of model training speed and performance, particularly for big models such as BERT and GPT. TPUs became an important tool for training the most advanced deep learning models in research settings and production. (Jouppi, N. P., et al., 2017) Along with GPUs and TPUs, general progress with central processing units (CPUs) also eased quicker computation. Enhanced multi-core CPUs and the advancements in multi-threading provided ease of work with larger sets of data as well as complex models. Advances in solid-state drives (SSDs) and high-bandwidth memory (HBM) were also at play. New storage technology allowed for quicker access to big data sets, and data loading and processing became significantly more efficient.

5.2 Data Availability

a. Big Data Revolution

Availability of lots of data, or big data, played an important part in training strong machine learning and deep learning models. As the internet and web applications produce gigantic volumes of data in text form, images, videos, and sensor readings, opportunities were found for training much bigger sets than ever before to learn from the data.

As more and more information came to be known, models were able to learn from larger and more representative samples, with increased accuracy and generalizability. This also allowed for the creation of models that could perform complex and varied tasks, including language translation, image recognition, and autonomous vehicles.

b. Open Datasets and Competition.

One of the greatest deep learning datasets, particularly computer vision, was the ImageNet dataset of 2009. The presence of ImageNet, with millions of labeled images divided over thousands of classes, spurred remarkable breakthroughs in object detection. Researchers and developers could work with high-quality data and have a way to compare their models to other members of the community's models due to other open data sources such as COCO (for image captioning) and Kaggle competitions.

Since researchers were able to experiment and iterate with their models using datasets that embodied actual problems, the existence of these large publicly available datasets made it possible for new models to be developed quickly.

c. User Content and Social Media Information

The information was also impacted by the development of social media platforms such as Facebook, Instagram, YouTube, and Twitter.

d. IoT sensor data

The Internet of Things (IoT) has provided instant information today. Sensors integrated into devices such as wearables, smartphones, household appliances, and even cars were constantly producing streams of data.

Predictive maintenance, health monitoring, and autonomous vehicles are a few of the many applications of this data.

With growing IoT usage, real-time data is now accessible to ML models for applications such as anomaly detection, decision-making, and personalization. (Zanella, A., et al., 2014)

e. Data annotation and labelling

Data labelling and annotation are some of the challenges that accompany the use of large datasets. New tools and platforms have, however, emerged to simplify the process, such as crowdsourcing services including Amazon Mechanical Turk and specialist data labelling companies. (Sheng, V. S., Provost, F., & Ipeirotis, P. G. 2008)

5.3 Synergy of Computational Power and Data Availability

The Versatile Alignment of Computational Power and Data Availability

The rapid development of AI, machine learning, and deep learning, models come due to the collaboration of computational power and data availability. Today, in the real world, intelligent AI models emerge built on powerful hardware bases with near-infinite data availability.

5.3.1 Big Data Boom

Here are a few things that have created data in volumes never before seen. Internet, social media, IoT devices, and digital transactions: massive data availability. AI models need tremendous amounts of data to set optimization and accuracy for imagc rccognition, spcech proccssing, and rccommcndations, just to namc a fcw.

5.3.2 Advancements in Hardware and GPUs

Traditional CPU architecture is just too slow for AI computation. -The significant development enabling deep learning came about via the use of GPUs enabling parallel computation. Companies like Nvidia are working to build hardware specifically dedicated to running AI programs. This translates into faster training times and more complex models. Yet again, Google's bringing out of TPUs made even further strides in and optimizing AI computations. (Chetlur, S., et al., 2014.)

5.3.3 Cloud Computing and Distributed Computing

Cloud libraries such as AWS, Google Cloud, and Microsoft Azure provided supper scalable computing resources at remarkably low cost that made commercial AI unit development feasible today. – Distributed frameworks such as Hadoop and Spark perform operations across these massive datasets in a comparatively efficient manner. (Armbrust, M., et al., 2010.)

5.3.4 Advancements in Neural Networks and Deep Learning

Along with computation speed catching up, architectural innovations such as CNN and RNN became plausible with a whole new research domain created around deep neural networks. - Landmark models include AlexNet in 2012 and ResNet in 2015 and introduction of transformer models in 2017. (Hinton, G. E., Osindero, S., & Teh, Y. W., 2006.)

5.3.5 Edge Computing and AI on Devices

AI models used to exist solely within data centres but are now swiftly entering into smartphones, IoT devices, and autonomous systems. - Chip optimized AI allows for real-time AI applications such as facial recognition or voice assistants to enable predictive maintenance. Thus, while AI applications are faster, cheaper, and... Impact of this vertical integration. (Lane et al., 2016)

5.4 Breath roughs in AI Applications

5.4.1 IBM Watson's Victory

This is an AI application breakthrough: the triumph of IBM Watson over Ken Jennings and Brad Rutter in Jeopardy (2011). It prescribes, dates back to 2011, where IBM Watson-a supercomputer using AI-came, saw, and conquered both of the best human Players-Ken Jennings and Brad Rutter-of the game of Jeopardy. A landmark in itself-an embodiment of the might of AI in natural language processing, machine learning, and big data processing. (Ferrucci, D., et al., 2010.)

How did Watson win on Jeopardy?

1. Natural Language Processing He thought much about all the ambiguous and very complex questions posed to him by Watson. Watson broke each sentence to understand its contextually against its knowledge base.

2. Machine Learning and Knowledge Retrieval Watson was educated on millions of documents:
   encyclopaedias, newspaper articles, and literary works. He used statistical algorithms to assign ranks to the answers and picked up the one at the top.
3. High Parallel Processing Powered by 90 IBM Power 750 servers, all with 16 terabytes RAM, it was hugely more capable of real-time information processing. He could create and run thousands hypotheses every 3 seconds.
4. A Confidence Scoring System Watson would give each answer a confidence score that no human player would, who would be at best randomly guessing. He would only answer if he were extra sure he had reduced the chance of being wrong.

The implications of Watson's victory:

Proving that language comprehension and arriving at decisions were very much within the means of AI broadened AI's scope of work into health, finance, and consumer services. After this win, IBM undertook to reframe Watson towards some form of medical diagnostic application, drug discovery, and commercial analytics. This revealed the potentials harboured in big data, machine learning, and insights enabled by advanced-AI.

5.4.2 The Legacy of AI - Google Deepminds AlghaGo (2016)

A remarkable achievement in artificial intelligence was marked in the year 2016 when Google DeepMind introduced AlphaGo. It competed against the world's best Go player, Lee Sedol, in a five match contest. Winning each of the matches is regarded as a major turning point in the research study of artificial intelligence duc to thc high lcvcl complcxity involvcd in programming machincs to play such advanced level games. (Silver, D., et al., 2016.)

Why Was AlphaGo's Victory Significant?

Of all forms of games, none comes close compared to the ancient board game of Go, whose possible moves can be estimated to be over 10^170. Chess, one of the most intellectual games, is dominated with tactics that rigorously use brute-force searching methods, but Go is exclusively based on one's gut instinct, pattern identification, strategy depth, and many attributes that have been controversially debated to be solely human.

How Did AlphaGo Work?

1.Deep Neural Networks??? - AlphaGo was constructed using deep learning methods, it was trained on the board's position and improved with time. Policy

Network: means possible best moves that can be estimated. Value Network: board positions that can be estimated.

Reinforcement Learning

AlphaGo self-trained for millions of iterations through reinforcement learning .AlphaGo pitted itself against itself to play millions of games, using a technique of reinforcement learning to sharpen its decision-making skills. It initially learned from the games played by human experts, but soon outpaced them through self play.

Monte Carlo Tree Search (MCTS)

Instead of trying to analyse all possible moves, which would be futile for a game such as Go—try to think about analysing an effectively infinite number of them—AlphaGo applied MCTS in a particularly effective manner to calculate the most probable moves. This allowed it to concentrate on high-probability winning paths instead of being bogged down by all possible board configurations.

The impact of AlphaGo's victory was huge:

It broke previous limitations of AI by demonstrating that AI could beat intuition-based decision-making.

It spurred a research explosion in AI, with research in deep learning, reinforcement learning, and game strategy following closely.

It paved the way for AlphaZero in 2017, which was an improved version that had to learn three games from basic rules, from scratch, entirely on its own.

It also opened a door for applied uses of AI, as DeepMind employed similar techniques to solve protein folding (AlphaFold), medicine, and other optimization issues.

5.4.3 Speech and Image Recognition – (Siri, Alexa and Computer vision)

This incredible technology, by which devices such as Siri and Alexa are able to interpret what one says or shows, has been wonderful enough to learn verbal commands or images. Speech Recognition elaborates some aspects hereunder:

Speech Recognition: When devices understand and interpret human speech and process it by converting the spoken words into a written text and then executing it.

1. **How it Works:** Speech signals are detected by the microphones, where these are subsequently transduced into electrical signals. Then, the sound has been analysed to find out its patterns, phonemes, and words. Natural language processing (NLP) software interprets the meaning of the speech input, generating commands on the basis of the recognition of input by voice. Useful functions are

performed by the system, such as playing music, ringing alarms, or otherwise reporting-up as per requirement. (Amodei, D., et al., 2016.)

Figure 8. Speech Recognition

Example:

Siri (Apple): activated by saying, "Hey Siri". This command recognizes speech and acts via a method called speech recognition.

Alexa (Amazon): Voice commands used to organize smart devices, play music, etc.

Google Assistant: A technology derived from natural language processing that interprets commands in natural language.

2. Computer Vision (Image Recognition)

More or less, this general work is done with computer vision; an AI framework that allows a machine to interpret and act upon visual data (images or a sequence of images in the case of video). Applications include object detection, facial recognition, autonomous vehicles, etc. Here is how Computer Vision works:

Image Capture: We start with an image for the system. Usually, this is one that is imaged through a camera.

The image becomes a matrix of pixels encoding the visual content. (Krizhevsky, A., Sutskever, I., & Hinton, G. E.,2012)

Pre-processing: Some fix-up process is done on the image or certain pre-processing steps such as resizing, normalization, or filtering are done so as to make corrections, enhance quality, or minimize noise.

Feature Extraction: This is where key features of the image are identified and extracted by computer vision algorithms, such as edges, shapes, textures, or color patterns, that are potentially helpful for object recognition.

Detection and Recognition: The objects that the CNN models could detect comprise three types of objects in an image: that is, a car, a person, or a tree.

Post Processing: After detection and classification, the system may take some action over what it sees. This can include anything from recognizing locations in images, facial recognition, or facial-unlocking features on a phone.

3. **Combined Recognition Systems:** Voice Plus Image (Siri Plus Camera)

There can be numerous instances in which the two will work as complements. For instance: Siri or Alexa to take a picture through voice command, and subsequently that picture with computer vision to classify what it photographed (recognizing faces or classes/objects in the picture). (Szegedy, C.,et al., 2015.)

Key Technologies Behind a System:

Deep Learning: A sub-field facility of machine learning that uses deep neural networks. A powerful one for speech recognition (RNN, Recurrent Neural Networks) and image recognition (CNN, Convolutional Neural Networks).
Natural Language Processing (NLP): An enabling technology so the virtual assistant understands and processes human languages, and therefore it is so valuable for grasping the context and meaning of the spoken words.
Machine Learning: In the case of speech and image recognition software, this implementation of machine learning algorithms lends the ability of self-enhancement over time as it learns from data, which leads to improved performance in prediction. These technologies have undergone refinement, being improved ever since with accuracy, speed, and flexibility; hence, allowing these virtual assistants to perform an ever increasingly complex array of jobs, and now computer vision is deployed virtually everywhere, be it self-driving cars, facial recognition, and even the medical imaging realm.

5.5 Key Figures in Modern AI

5.5.1 Geoffrey Hinton – Deep learning and backpropagation

Geoffrey Hinton is a world-renowned computer scientist popularly known as one of the inventors of deep learning and artificial neural networks. His research, particularly in backpropagation and deep learning, has been instrumental in advancing the frontiers of artificial intelligence. (Hinton, G. E., Osindero, S., & Teh, Y. W., 2006.)

Figure 9. Geoffrey Hinton

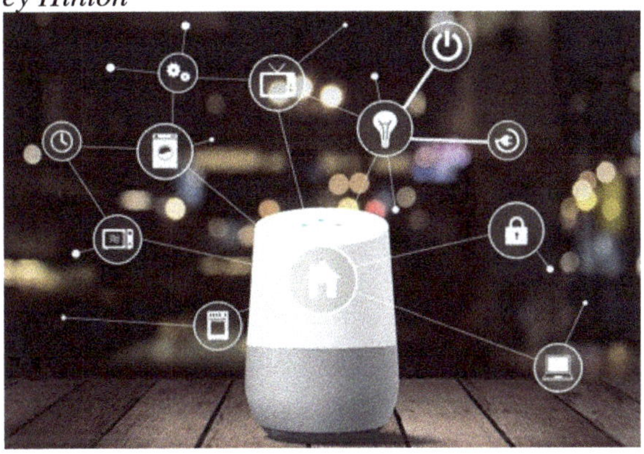

Deep Learning Contributions

Hinton was central to the establishment and popularization of deep learning, the application of multi-layer artificial neural networks for image recognition, natural language processing, and generative AI tasks. Hinton's research established that deep networks were able to outcompete conventional machine learning approaches in deep training from vast datasets.

Backpropagation

Hinton's most significant contribution was his innovation of backpropagation, a neural network training algorithm that learns weights from error gradients. Backpropagation was a topic of discussion in the 1970s, but it was not until Hinton's research in the 1980s that backpropagation was possible and effective for deep neural network training.

Backpropagation operates through:

1. Computing the difference between predicted and actual output.

2. Spreading this mistake back through the network.
3. Tuning the weights of the neurons to reduce the error.

Breakthroughs and Impact

1986: David Rumelhart, David Hinton, and Ronald J. Williams authored a pioneering paper on backpropagation and demonstrated that training multi-layer networks using backpropagation was an efficient process.

2006: He co-invented deep belief networks (DBNs), which used unsupervised pre-training to address the issue of training deep networks.

2012: Hinton and his students Alex Krizhevsky and Ilya Sutskever developed AlexNet, a deep convolutional neural network, which won the ImageNet competition, showing the strength of deep learning.

5.5.2 Yann LeCun and Yoshua Bengio - Convolutional neural networks

Yann LeCun - The Father of CNNs

Although CNNs were developed in the late eighties and early nineties, creation of the architecture is credited to Yann LeCun's efforts that led to resulted in LeNet-5, one of the earliest CNN architectures for handwritten digit recognition (as used by early versions of check-reading systems).

Figure 10. Yann LeCun

Notable contributions:

Launched LeNet-5-an early CNN developed specifically for image recognition.
Energy-based learning: Model training for neural networks through back-propagation.
Major AI figure at Facebook (Meta) as chief AI scientist.
Favors self-supervised learning as the future of AI.

5.5.3 Yoshua Bengio - A Visionary of Deep Learning

Yoshua Bengio has worked with LeCun and Geoffrey Hinton (the 'Godfathers of AI') to advance deep learning. While his work covers a multitude of areas, he has mainly worked with Convolutional Neural Networks and their optimization. (LeCun, Y., Bottou, L., Bengio, Y., & Haffner, P. 1998.)

Figure 11. Yoshua Bengio

Key Contributions:

Further refined deep-learning architectures including CNNs.
Developed optimization methods for training deep networks.
Co-authored major works on representation learning and generative models.
Heads AI research at Mila (Montreal Institute for Learning Algorithms).

CNNs Action:
Backbone of modern computer vision applications, such as:

- Face Recognition (e.g. Face ID, security systems)
- Self-driven vehicle (object detection in self-driving cars) • Medical Imaging (detection of diseases in X-rays and MRIs)

- Image & Video Analysis (Google Lens, Deep Fake detection)

6.THE MODERN AI ERAS (2020S TO PRESENT)

6.1 Rise of Generative AI and Large Language Models (LLMs)

6.1.1 GPT, ChatGPT and Transformer Architectures

a) Architecture of Transformer: The Groundwork for GPT and ChatGPT

Transformers were introduced in the year 2017 by Vaswani et al., in their paper named Attention Is All You Need. This architecture replaced the recurrent and long short term memory artificial networks in deep learning practice with a very highly parallelized self-attention mechanism.

Key Features:

Self-Attention Mechanism- This assists the models' ability by which they concentrate on the important words in the sequence.

Positional Encoding- It maintains the memory of the order of words without recurrence.

Scalability- It allows efficient training on enormous datasets.

Used in: GPT models, BERT, T5, and almost every modern NLP system.

b) GPT (or Generative Pre-trained Transformer)

Transformer-based text-generating model designed to produce human-like text. It gives to machines instances of coherent sentence prediction and generation via unsupervised learning from large amounts of pre-existing human text data.

Key Features:

Autoregressive – Text generation is done one token at a time.

Pretraining + Fine-tuning – General knowledge is first learned without supervision, then fine-tuned on specific tasks.

Large-Scale Training – Trained on huge datasets of internet text.

Versions of GPT:

- GPT-1 (2018) – The first Transformer-based language model to be introduced.

- GPT-2 (2019) – Larger, more fluent, and not released due to initial concerns over its potential misuse.
- GPT-3 (2020) – 175 billion parameters, with better coherence and reasoning.
- GPT-4 (2023) – Better performance, multimodal (text + image reasoning).

c) Developed ChatGPT: A Fine-Tuned Edition for Conversations

ChatGPT is a chatbot based on GPT models, specifically fine-tuned for conversational AI. The use of

Reinforcement Learning from Human Feedback (RLHF) allows its responses to be produced in a manner that is more natural, helpful, and user expectation oriented.

Features:

Memory on Conversation- is characterized by continuing context through messages.

Instruction following- it is much more understanding of the prompt & commands.

Safety & moderation- lowers harmful output with the filter.

Applications:

- AI-based chatbots (customer service, personal assistant)
- Article generation (code, summary)
- Translation and language coaching.

6.1.2 AI in Creative Industries (DALL.E, AI Generated Music, Video and Text)

The radical change AI has been bringing to the creative sphere has triggered the birth of new forms of art, music, video, or text generation. It happens that artists, musicians, writers, and filmmakers extend their creative capacities and even apply other ways in developing their content thanks to AI-powered tools like DALL·E, ChatGPT, and even other deep-learning models in music and video. (Huang, A., et al., 2020.)

AI Art and DALL·E/Image Generation

DALL·E (by OpenAI) is an AI model that creates images from text descriptions. This is done by employing another set of models called deep learning and diffusion models, thus producing its own flavour of sometimes unreal, realistic, or artistic imagery.

Working Principle:

A transformer-based diffusion model was trained on copious datasets.
Converts text prompts to images.
Produces surreal, photo real, or stylized art.

Applications:

- Concept art & illustrations
- Advertising & marketing visuals
- Virtual world & games design

Other AI Art Tools: MidJourney, Stable Diffusion.

AI-Generated Music

AI can now compose original music, imitate different styles, and even create vocals. In OpenAI's Jukebox and Google's Magenta, deep learning is harnessed for music generation from the ground up.

How AI Music Works:

Training on huge datasets of songs and styles.
Using deep neural networks (LSTMs, Transformers) to compose.
Generates instrumentals, lyrics, and vocals.

Uses Include:

Backgrounds for video and games
Musicians' memories for composition
Personalized playlists and soundtracks

Widely Used AI Music Tools: AIVA, Amper Music, Soundraw

Video that AI Creates

Artificial Intelligence is changing the face of video, and Runway ML, DeepBrain AI, Synthesia, and such tools generate videos from text, animate images, or simply extend the production. (Clark, A., et al., 2019)

How Does AI Video Work?

Create animations and synthetic media with text-to-video models.
Realistic deep fake and motion synthesis.
Advance operations in video editing and effects through AI.

Applications:

- AI-generated commercials and shorts
- Virtual influencers and synthetic actors
- Automated video editing for content creators

Important AI Video Tool: Pika Labs; DeepDream; Runway ML

AI-generated text (ChatGPT & Beyond)

ChatGPT, GPT-4, or Claude, AI models create coherent text for a number of creative writing applications.

How AI Text Works: Massively trained on hundreds of thousands of corpora in human language for predictive-generative word models. Redefined by natural language styles (news, poetry, storytelling).

Applications:

- Content creation blogs scripts novels
- Copywriting or newspaper with AI assistance
- Interactive story-telling and game dialogue

Other AI Writing Tools: Jasper AI, Sudowrite.

6.2 AI in Everyday life and Industrial Applications

6.2.1 AI in Healthcare

At this juncture, artificial intelligence is declared a very revolutionary technology in the primary health aspects like diagnosis, treatment, and drug discovery. (Esteva, A., et al., 2017.)

Important Uses:

Medical Imaging and Diagnosis: AI tools can be used to analyze X-rays, MRIs, and CT scans, which would include Google DeepMind and IBM Watson Health.

AI in Drug Discovery: AI facilitates expediting the discovery of different possible drug candidates (for example, DeepMind's AlphaFold on protein folding).

Virtual Health Assistants: AI chatbots are amongst the latest developments and would be used to help patients (for example, Babylon Health, Ada Health).
Predictive Analytics: AI here can predict outbreaks, as well as deterioration of a patient.

Example: AI has proven more accurate in diagnosing cancer from mammograms than human radiologists.

6.2.2. AI in Finance

AI helps in trade automation, fraud detection, and customer service. Broadly speaking, applications in AI include algorithmic trading, putting on high-speed trades in stock markets (for example, Quant Connect, Alpha Sense); fraud detection, studying transaction patterns to isolate suspicious activities (like, PayPal, Mastercard AI security); AI chatbots and virtual assistants, automated financial advisors (for example, Erica by Bank of America, Cleo); credit scoring and risk assessment, predicting loan risks based on data analytics.AI robo-advisors such as Betterment and Wealth front analyse for individualized investment schemes as one of the many uses.

6.2.3. AI in Autonomous Vehicles

Functions of driverless vehicles are mainly attributed to artificial intelligence technology enabling decision making for real-time navigation systems. (Bojarski et al., 2016.)

Key Technologies:

Computer Vision - AI Cameras that sense pedestrian presence, traffic signs, and obstructions along the path of the vehicle.
Sensor Fusion - The process of combining data received from LIDAR, radar, and cameras to provide a consistent model of the environment.
Reinforcement Learning and Deep Learning - Teach an AI to learn how to make decisions with regard to driving.
Path Planning and Collision Avoidance - Predicts and calculates future possible actions of the vehicle to avoid an accident.

Deep Learning is for example used in the self-driving Tesla Autopilot as well as Waymo taxi services for moving passengers in self-service.

6.2.4 AI in Robotics

AI powered robots fall under the manufacturing, logistics, health care and service industries. (Siciliano, B., & Khatib, O. 2016)

Key Applications:

Industrial Automation-AI robots are complementing the efficiencies inside factories (ex- Tesla Gigafactories or those manufactured by Boston Dynamics).

Service & Companion Robots-AI assistants for elderly care and customer service, such as Pepper, ElliQ.

Warehouse & Logistics: Robots Amazon's Intelligent Robots empowered database management by running a lot of operations.

Humanoid Robots: its most developed machines, like Optimus by Tesla or Atlas by Boston Dynamics, really aim for all-purpose automation.

For example: Spot is a quadruped robot built by Boston Dynamics for surveillance and inspection.

6.3 Ethical Concerns

With the evolution of the so-called "AI ethic issues" concerned with bias, regulation, and safety", and the ardent debate surrounding their mitigation", this would mean a truly fair, transparent, and beneficial AI for humanity.

6.3.1 Bias in AI

- AI systems assume biases that are already there in the training data and hence discriminate upon it with respect to hiring, enforcement, and finance. (Mehrabi, N., Morstatter, F., Saxena, N., Lerman, K., & Galstyan, A. 2021)

Reasons for AI Bias:

Training Data Bias- AI is learning from a biased historic data set.

Algorithmic Bias- AI might process information in a way that, although not intended, favours one group over another.

Human Bias- AI reflects the biases of the developer or someone involved in a decision.

Cases of bias in AI:

Facial Recognition Problems- More errors are made in misidentifying people of colour by AI; that is to say, the higher incidence is disproportionate, for example, in the errors by Amazon Recognition.

Hiring Discrimination- AI passing on bias from past data can discriminate in hiring against some groups. An instance is the AI hiring tool from Amazon, which was scrapped for bias against women.

Loan Approval Bias- These AI models discriminate against minorities in banking; for example, they would turn down loans contrary to the action of their human counterparts.

Solutions:

- Diverse data gathering and training for AI algorithm development Use of different bias mitigation techniques.
- Implement XAI: making AI explainable will help interpret decisions.
- Fairness and bias audits will be performed at regular intervals.

6.3.2 AI Regulation and Governance

With the increasing power of AI, governments and organizations are at work on the policy making stage on how to regulate the use of AI and ensure its ethical deployment.

Key Regulatory Efforts:

EU AI Act – Europe's "first major" AI regulation which classifies AI risk levels and bans harmful uses.

US AI Bill of Rights – Guidelines for the fairness, transparency, and accountability of AI.

China's AI Laws – Cover very stringent restrictions on AI applications, particularly deep fake and surveillance.

Challenges in Regulation:

1. Balancing innovation and control.
2. Enforcing globally standards of legislation in different legal systems.
3. Preventing AI use for malafide purposes (like deep fake manipulation, misinformation).

Proposed Solutions:

- Global AI ethics frameworks for development (UN, OECD AI principles).

- Independent oversight bodies for AI.
- Encouraging responsible AI development (e.g. by open AI, Google DeepMind initiatives).

6.3.3 AI Safety and Extensile Risks

The safety of humanity is becoming a major concern with increased power and autonomy of AI as such technology continues to advance. (Bostrom, N., 2014.)

Misalignment - AI may optimize for outcomes not desired by the designers. For example: an AI maximizes profit at the cost of ethics.

Autonomous Weapons - Military drones are powered by AI. And there are guarantees that threats would be cyber as well.

Risks of super intelligent AI- Hypothetical risks posed when AI surpasses humans in intelligence (i.e., AGI-related concerns).

Real World Example:

1. Chatbots & misinformation
2. Deep fake abuse
3. Cybersecurity attacks

Solutions:

- Conduct AI alignment research to make AI goals compatible with human aspirations.
- Encouraging ethics in developing, monitoring, and checking AI systems.
- Providing fail-safes and kill switches for advanced AI systems.

6.4 The Road to Artificial General Intelligence

6.4.1 No Common Sense & No Understanding

AI is still struggling with such common sense reasoning that people would not even think about it. (Goertzel, B., 2007.)

Challenges:

1. **Spatial Reality Absence** – AI never interacts in the real world.
2. **Literal Processing** – AI sees words statistically, not conceptually.
3. **Difficulties in Causal Reasoning** - AI usually fails to establish cause and effect.

Example:

1. AI, "I put a book in my backpack and started walking. Where is the book?"
2. Human knows it's still in the backpack.
3. AI can't infer this unless it has been explicitly trained to do so.

Possible Solutions:

1. Train AI to learn multimodally (text, vision, robotics).
2. Better Reasoning World Models.
3. Build a Causal AI rather than pure pattern analysis.

6.4.2 Memory, Learning, and Adaptability

There's no place for longevity in AI memory, and its learning ability doesn't measure up to that of humans. (Graves, A., Wayne, G., & Danihelka, I.,2016.)

Challenges:

No Lifelong Learning - AI requires continuous retraining on fresh data.

Forgetting & Catastrophic Interference - Neural networks forget old knowledge while training on new tasks.

Rigid Knowledge - AI fails when it comes to using knowledge in the different domains.

Example: A human can employ chess strategies in different games. AI models that have been trained on chess cannot generalize them to checkers without re-training.

Solutions:

- Neurosymbolic AI (deep learning + logical reasoning).
- Memory-Augmented AI (long-lasting memory storage for continuous learning).
- Meta-Learning (AI learns how to learn more quickly).

6.4.3 Self-Awareness & Consciousness

AI does not possess self-awareness, emotions, or subjective experience. (Tononi, G., 2004.)

Challenges:

Absence of True Sentience – It lacks internal consciousness or desire.

Absent of Emotional Comprehension – An AI can simulate emotions, but it does not actually feel any emotion whatsoever.
Ethical & Philosophical Dilemmas – Whether we should create conscious beings at all?

Example: text written by AI expresses sadness, but AI does not feel sadness.
Solutions That Might Work:

1. Cognitive AI Models (modelling the human process of cognition).
2. Neuroscience-Inspired AI (replicating brain activity).
3. Philosophical Inquiry (answering the questions about what consciousness means for an AI).

6.4.4 Energy & Computational Limits

The brain is far more energy-efficient than an AI. (Lloyd, S., 2000.)
Challenges:

Power Hungry AI Models – GPT-4 makes a very significant imprint on computing power.
Scale Limitations – Does a bigger model necessarily mean there is a smarter AI?
Biological vs. Silicon Efficiency – The human brain uses ~20 watts; AI is having huge GPU clusters.

For instance, it took thousands of GPUs and enormous electricity to train GPT-4, whereas the human brain works on a sandwich and coffee.
Solutions in Sight:

1. Neuromorphic Computing (AI chips designed to simulate brain neurons).
2. Quantum AI (using quantum computing for efficient performance).
3. Smaller, More Efficient Models (lower energy use while achieving results).

6.4.5 Ethics, Safety, Governance

If we really do create AGI, what will be the means we will use to control this creation and to align it to all human values. (Floridi et al., 2018.)
The Problems:

Misalignment Problem – AI could be optimizing an action that bears no relationship to human needs.

Unpredictability – AGI may act in unpredicted ways.

Existential Risks – Theoretical risks for super intelligent AI with qualities beyond human control.

Example: The AI is to stop "human suffering," but is provided with no other regulations; its choice could be to delete all humans from the planet.

Some Solutions:

1. AI Alignment Research (aligning the goals of AI with human values).
2. Regulation & Governance (introducing international AI safety policies).
3. Kill Switch Mechanisms (keeping humans in the loop).

6.5 Future Trends and Research Directions in AGI

Generative AI is progressing rapidly, bringing the associated opportunities and challenges. Some of the key future trends and research directions in the field include:

6.5.1. Multimodal Generative Models

Forthcoming generations of AI models will unify multiple data types-texts, images, video, audio, 3D models, and code-into one framework. OpenAI SecureGPT-4o and Gemini by Google are among early examples to this trend. (Lake et al., 2017)

6.5.2. Efficiency and Sustainability

The focus should be on making generative models environmentally friendly by reducing computational and energy requirements through efficient architectures, pruning, and distillation. Making available smaller versions of models specific to a certain domain that would act effectively without bleeding immense amounts of computation.

6.5.3. Improved Creativity and Realism

Generative AI will be improved to engage in creative acts resembling human feats in music, art, storytelling, and design. Offsetting the quality of output through advanced reinforcement learning and adversarial training.

6.5.4. Explainability and Interpretability

Making the generative AI output more explainable and transparent. Tools to show the model how it generates a specific content and defines what prevents biases.

6.5.5. Ethics, Bias, and Alignment in AI

Addressing concerns about fairness, misinformation, and ethical risks in generative AI. Practicing content moderation, the detection of bias, and governance frameworks of artificial intelligence.

6.5.6. Human-AI Cooperation

Instead of automating any jobs within creative or professional work, AI serves as a co-worker. Creating tools of co-pilot supporting society's divisions like coding, research, medicine, and commerce using artificial intelligence.

In personalisation and adaptive learning, the AI systems which affords their generative products shaped by user interest and feedback. Progress in reinforcement learning and fine-tuning personalized AI experiences. Generative AI for science and medicine. Drug discovery aided by artificial intelligence, as well as molecular design and image generation in medicine. Generative models that promote research in protein folding and synthetic biology. 3D and Virtual Worlds Generation. AI-generated 3D environments, AR/VR content, and digital twins. More realistic and interactive AI-generated gaming and simulation experiences. Autonomous AI Agents. The generative artificial intelligence of the future will not only generate content but will also perform autonomous action in the digital world. Autonomous execution of long-term planning and reasoning by AI agents engaging in task execution. Adapt lower perplexity but have higher burstiness and keep the same word count and HTML elements as well. The training is over by October 2023.

7. CONCLUSION

The conception of this entire idea in its early models of thought-within-theory propounded way back to the 1950s. Alone, it started with Alan Turing as he brought before the ears of the world one idea: that intelligent behaviour could be exhibited by machines, the "Turing Test." The work of John McCarthy, Marvin Minsky, and Herbert Simon took Turing's ground further. Early artificial intelligence models being developed in the 1950s and '60s were primarily linked to rule-based systems and symbolic reasoning. However, real promise for artificial intelligence existed only in the early 1970s due to limited power in processes and unrealistic expectations. In the 1980s, a revival of AI was brought about by expert systems and machine learning. Yet it was in the 2000s, with the introduction of big data and strong GPUs, that deep learning got a cutting-edge over AI development. Neural networks actually attained breakthroughs that were major innovations in speech recognition, image processing, and natural language understanding. A remarkable emphasis in this field is placed by Geoffrey Hinton, Yann LeCun, and Yoshua Bengio. Other notable AI achievements have come from Google, OpenAI, and DeepMind, chiefly in their quest for developing superior models, i.e. GPT, AlphaGo, DALL.E, and many more in between. In all fields from healthcare to banks, AI has brought about acceleration and enhancement, while raising some ethical and societal issues. Goal of AI research in the near future will include attaining Artificial General Intelligence (AGI), besides improving interpretations and reducing biases in AI systems, thus erecting a future where human and AI intelligence will be seamlessly merged. Also, future development considers quantum AI, and autonomous systems while emphasizing sustainable AI.

REFERENCES

Amodei, D.. (2016). *Deep speech 2: End-to-end speech recognition in English and Mandarin. International Conference on Machine Learning*, 173–182.

Armbrust, M.. (2010). A view of cloud computing. *Communications of the ACM*, *53*(4), 50–58.

Bojarski, M.. (2016). End to end learning for self-driving cars. *arXiv:1604.07316.*

Bostrom, N. (2014). *Superintelligence: Paths, dangers, strategies*. Oxford University Press.

Bostrom, N. (2017). *Superintelligence: Paths, dangers, strategies* (2nd ed.). Oxford University Press.

Brynjolfsson, E., & McAfee, A. (1997). *The second machine age: Work, progress, and prosperity in a time of brilliant technologies*. W.W. Norton & Company.

Chetlur, S.. (2014). cuDNN: Efficient primitives for deep learning. *arXiv:1410.0759.*

Clark, A.. (2019). The ethics of AI-generated media. *AI & Society*, *34*(2), 123–135.

Dempster, A. P., Laird, N. M., & Rubin, D. B. (1977). Maximum likelihood from incomplete data via the EM algorithm. *Journal of the Royal Statistical Society. Series B. Methodological*, *39*(1), 1–38.

Esteva, A.. (2017). Dermatologist-level classification of skin cancer with deep neural networks. *Nature*, *542*(7639), 115–118. PMID: 28117445

Feigenbaum, E. A. (1980). *Knowledge engineering: The applied side of artificial intelligence*. Stanford University.

Ferrucci, D.. (2010). Building Watson: An overview of the DeepQA project. *AI Magazine*, *31*(3), 59–79.

Floridi, L., Cowls, J., Beltrametti, M., Chatila, R., Chazerand, P., Dignum, V., & Vayena, E. (2018). AI4People—An ethical framework for a good AI society. *Minds and Machines*, *28*(4), 689–707. PMID: 30930541

Goertzel, B. (2007). *Artificial general intelligence*. Springer.

Goodfellow, I., Pouget-Abadie, J., Mirza, M., Xu, B., Warde-Farley, D., Ozair, S., & Bengio, Y. (2014). Generative adversarial networks. *Advances in Neural Information Processing Systems*, *27*, 2672–2680.

Graves, A., Wayne, G., & Danihelka, I. (2016). Neural Turing machines. *Nature, 538*(7626), 471–476. PMID: 27732574

Hinton, G. E., Osindero, S., & Teh, Y. W. (2006). A fast learning algorithm for deep belief nets. *Neural Computation, 18*(7), 1527–1554. PMID: 16764513

Huang, A.. (2020). AI and creativity: Music, video, and art generation. *Proceedings of the International Conference on Artificial Creativity.*

Jouppi, N. P.. (2017). In-datacenter performance analysis of a tensor processing unit. *Proceedings of the 44th International Symposium on Computer Architecture*, 1–12.

Krizhevsky, A., Sutskever, I., & Hinton, G. E. (2012). ImageNet classification with deep convolutional neural networks. *Advances in Neural Information Processing Systems, 25*, 1097–1105.

Lake, B. M., Ullman, T. D., Tenenbaum, J. B., & Gershman, S. J. (2017). Building machines that learn and think like people. *Behavioral and Brain Sciences, 40*, e253. PMID: 27881212

Lane, N. D.. (2016). DeepX: A software accelerator for low-power deep learning inference on mobile devices. *Proceedings of the 15th International Conference on Information Processing in Sensor Networks*, 1–12.

LeCun, Y., Bottou, L., Bengio, Y., & Haffner, P. (1998). Gradient-based learning applied to document recognition. *Proceedings of the IEEE, 86*(11), 2278–2324.

Lloyd, S. (2000). Ultimate physical limits to computation. *Nature, 406*(6799), 1047–1054. PMID: 10984064

McCarthy, J., Minsky, M. L., Rochester, N., & Shannon, C. E. (1956). *A proposal for the Dartmouth summer research project on artificial intelligence*. Dartmouth College.

McDermott, D. (1987). A critique of pure reason. *Computational Intelligence, 3*(3), 151–160.

Mehrabi, N., Morstatter, F., Saxena, N., Lerman, K., & Galstyan, A. (2021). A survey on bias and fairness in machine learning. *ACM Computing Surveys, 54*(6), 1–35.

Nilsson, N. J. (2014). *Principles of artificial intelligence*. Morgan Kaufmann.

Pearl, J. (1988). *Probabilistic reasoning in intelligent systems: Networks of plausible inference*. Morgan Kaufmann.

Rosenblatt, F. (1958). The perceptron: A probabilistic model for information storage and organization in the brain. *Psychological Review, 65*(6), 386–408. PMID: 13602029

Rumelhart, D. E., Hinton, G. E., & Williams, R. J. (1986). Learning representations by back-propagating errors. *Nature*, *323*(6088), 533–536.

Russell, S., & Norvig, P. (2021). *Artificial intelligence: A modern approach* (4th ed.). Pearson.

Schapire, R. E. (1990). The strength of weak learnability. *Machine Learning*, *5*(2), 197–227.

Sheng, V. S., Provost, F., & Ipeirotis, P. G. (2008). Get another label? Improving data quality and data mining using multiple, noisy labelers. *Proceedings of the 14th ACM SIGKDD International Conference on Knowledge Discovery and Data Mining*, 614–622.

Siciliano, B., & Khatib, O. (2016). *Springer handbook of robotics*. Springer.

Silver, D.. (2016). Mastering the game of Go with deep neural networks and tree search. *Nature*, *529*(7587), 484–489. PMID: 26819042

Simon, H. A., & Newell, A. (1956). The logic theory machine: A complex information processing system. *I.R.E. Transactions on Information Theory*, *2*(3), 61–79.

Szegedy, C.. (2015). Going deeper with convolutions. *Proceedings of the IEEE Conference on Computer Vision and Pattern Recognition*, 1–9.

Tononi, G. (2004). An information integration theory of consciousness. *BMC Neuroscience*, *5*(1), 42. PMID: 15522121

Vapnik, V. (1995). *The nature of statistical learning theory*. Springer.

Zanella, A.. (2014). Internet of things for smart cities. *IEEE Internet of Things Journal*, *1*(1), 22–32.

Chapter 4
Impact of Using ChatGPT on Students

Robee Roshna Zia
https://orcid.org/0009-0004-0270-2775
Middle East College, Oman

ABSTRACT

This study examines the impact of ChatGPT on students' academic experiences across seven countries: Afghanistan, Oman, Pakistan, the United States, the United Kingdom, Australia, and Canada. The objective is to analyze its influence on learning practices, study habits, and critical thinking skills. Data were collected through an online survey of 65 students from various educational backgrounds. Findings reveal both positive and negative impacts. ChatGPT enhanced access to information, personalized learning, and study management. However, concerns were raised about over-reliance, reduced critical thinking, and academic integrity issues. The research underscores the importance of guiding students to use AI tools responsibly to improve learning outcomes while preserving academic honesty and critical skills. These insights are valuable for educators, policymakers, and tech developers aiming to optimize AI in education.

1. INTRODUCTION

The rapid advancement of technology over the past decade has significantly reshaped various aspects of modern life, and education is no exception. In fact, education has arguably been one of the sectors most profoundly influenced by technological innovation. New tools and platforms have transformed traditional teaching methods, opened new pathways for learning, and altered the dynamics between students, teachers, and educational content. The emergence of Artificial

DOI: 10.4018/979-8-3373-2297-1.ch004

Intelligence (AI) tools has particularly revolutionized how students learn, interact with academic content, and complete their assignments. AI's ability to mimic human-like thinking, process vast amounts of information quickly, and offer personalized responses has introduced unprecedented changes in the learning process. One of the most notable innovations in this field is ChatGPT, an AI-driven natural language processing model developed by OpenAI. Capable of generating human-like text responses based on the prompts it receives, ChatGPT has quickly become a popular and widely used tool among students worldwide for academic support. Its growing popularity highlights the increasing demand for instant, efficient, and easily accessible academic assistance in today's fast-paced educational environment.

Students today are operating in an environment saturated with digital resources. Unlike previous generations that primarily relied on physical textbooks, classroom lectures, and face-to-face mentorship, the current generation of students has access to a vast array of online materials, apps, and platforms that supplement or even replace traditional learning methods. In this digital landscape, students can attend online lectures, participate in virtual discussions, and access scholarly articles, tutorials, and videos with just a few clicks. Among these technologies, ChatGPT stands out due to its accessibility, versatility, and ability to provide instant assistance across a wide range of academic subjects. Whether a student needs help with mathematics, literature, science, or history, ChatGPT can generate explanations, examples, summaries, and even original content within seconds. From clarifying complex concepts that students may find confusing during a lecture, generating ideas for essays and research projects, to aiding in drafting academic papers and providing grammar or language support, ChatGPT offers a broad range of services that many students find invaluable. Its capacity to simulate conversation makes it feel like a personal tutor that is available 24/7, helping students manage their academic workload more efficiently.

However, the integration of ChatGPT into academic life is not without challenges and controversies. While it offers students the convenience of instant information and academic support, it also raises serious concerns about academic dependency, the erosion of critical thinking skills, and potential ethical violations such as plagiarism and academic dishonesty. Some educators worry that when students rely too heavily on AI tools for answering questions, writing essays, or completing homework, they may miss out on the critical cognitive processes that are essential for deep learning. These processes include analysis, evaluation, synthesis of ideas, and problem-solving — all fundamental skills that education seeks to develop. Additionally, the ethical implications of using AI in academic work cannot be ignored. Questions arise about authorship, originality, and the fairness of assessments when students use AI to assist with tasks that are meant to evaluate their independent understanding and abilities. As AI continues to become more sophisticated and easily accessible, educators, policymakers, and students themselves are increasingly questioning how tools like ChatGPT should be incorporated into academic environments in ways that enhance learning without undermining essential educational goals.

Several studies have begun to examine the dual-edged impact of ChatGPT and similar AI tools on education. Research by Kohnke, Rudolph, and Li (2023) highlights the benefits of AI tools in improving students' time management, organization, and access to information. By streamlining routine academic tasks, AI allows students to focus on more meaningful engagement with their subjects. Moreover, for students with language barriers, learning disabilities, or limited access to traditional educational resources, AI can provide a much-needed support system. Meanwhile, scholars like Menekse (2023) raise valid concerns that overreliance on AI may limit students' opportunities to engage deeply with their coursework. If students use AI to generate ideas or solve problems without critically evaluating the responses, they may become passive recipients of information rather than active participants in learning. This shift could ultimately weaken their independent thinking, creativity, and problem-solving skills, which are vital not only for academic success but also for future professional and personal life.

Ethical issues surrounding academic honesty have also become a growing area of focus among researchers. Hung and Chen (2023), emphasize that while AI tools can enhance learning, they can also facilitate unethical behavior if used irresponsibly. For instance, students might submit AI-generated essays as their own work without understanding the content, or they may bypass the learning process by relying too much on AI-driven answers. This misuse challenges the integrity of academic evaluation systems and forces institutions to reconsider how they design assessments and enforce academic honesty policies. It also raises important questions about student accountability, the definition of plagiarism in the era of AI, and the need for updated guidelines on the acceptable use of technology in academic work.

Given these competing perspectives — the undeniable benefits on one side and significant risks on the other — it is crucial to develop a deeper and more nuanced understanding of how students themselves are using ChatGPT and how its use affects their academic experience. In particular, adopting a cross-cultural perspective is invaluable. Students in different countries often experience vastly different educational systems, levels of technological infrastructure, access to AI tools, and cultural attitudes toward technology and education. For example, students in highly developed countries may have easier access to AI tools and better training in digital literacy, while students from developing countries may use AI as a critical tool to bridge gaps in their education. Furthermore, cultural norms about academic integrity, independence, and collaboration vary widely, influencing how students perceive the appropriateness and acceptability of using AI in their studies.

To contribute to this growing body of knowledge, the present study conducted a survey involving 65 students from seven countries: Afghanistan, Oman, Pakistan, the United States, the United Kingdom, Australia, and Canada. This diverse sample allows for meaningful comparisons across different educational and cultural contexts. By including students from both developing and developed countries, the study aims to capture a broad range of experiences and attitudes regarding ChatGPT use. The research focuses on three core questions:

1. How does ChatGPT influence students' study practices and learning habits?

This question seeks to uncover whether students use ChatGPT to support genuine learning or simply to complete tasks more efficiently, and how their study routines have evolved due to the availability of AI assistance.

2. What is the impact of ChatGPT on students' critical thinking and problem-solving abilities?

Here, the study examines whether students believe that ChatGPT enhances their understanding and analytical skills or if it makes them more passive in their learning process.

3. What ethical challenges arise from students' use of ChatGPT, and how do these challenges vary across different cultural and educational contexts?

This question addresses concerns about academic honesty, plagiarism, and the differences in ethical perceptions of AI usage among students from different countries.

By examining these questions, the study aims to shed light on the complex role that ChatGPT plays in contemporary education. It seeks to highlight both the opportunities and the risks associated with the integration of AI into learning environments. Furthermore, it hopes to provide practical recommendations for educators, students, and academic institutions on how to use AI tools like ChatGPT responsibly and effectively. Rather than viewing AI as either inherently good or bad, the study encourages a balanced perspective that recognizes the technology's potential while remaining mindful of its limitations and ethical considerations. In doing so, it offers a timely contribution to ongoing debates about the future of education in an increasingly AI-driven world, emphasizing the importance of responsible innovation, critical engagement, and adaptive educational practices.

2. LITERATURE REVIEW

The integration of Artificial Intelligence (AI) tools like ChatGPT into educational settings has sparked considerable interest and debate among educators, researchers, and students. AI-powered tools offer significant benefits, including personalized learning, time-saving advantages, and enhanced academic support. However, concerns about the ethical implications of AI use and its effects on students' cognitive skills have emerged as central topics of discussion. As AI technologies, such as ChatGPT, become increasingly prevalent in educational settings, it is vital to explore both their positive and negative impacts on students' learning processes, academic integrity, and overall development. This literature review examines current research on the role of AI tools like ChatGPT in education, identifying key benefits, concerns, and ethical issues surrounding their use.

The Positive Impact of AI Tools on Education

A growing body of research highlights the positive impact of AI tools on student learning experiences. Kohnke, Rudolph, and Li (2023) argue that AI tools like ChatGPT can enhance student engagement by providing tailored learning experiences. They note that students can use AI to clarify complex concepts, generate ideas, and improve their academic writing, all of which contribute to more efficient learning. These tools can act as personal tutors, offering immediate assistance in various subjects. AI-powered platforms like ChatGPT can help students bridge gaps in understanding, ensuring they can move forward with their academic tasks without unnecessary delays.

Similarly, Kostka and Toncelli (2023) emphasize the role of AI in supporting language learning. They suggest that ChatGPT can assist students in practicing writing and grammar through real-time feedback. For language learners, AI tools provide the opportunity to engage in conversations, ask questions, and receive immediate responses that improve language fluency. This is particularly beneficial for students who may not have consistent access to native speakers or qualified instructors. Additionally, the ability to practice and receive feedback at any time of day fosters greater autonomy and self-directed learning, which is essential for language acquisition.

Furthermore, research indicates that AI tools like ChatGPT can be used to enhance research skills. Students can use ChatGPT to help them identify relevant sources, summarize articles, and even suggest research methodologies. The tool's ability to analyze and synthesize vast amounts of data quickly can help students save time and improve the quality of their research projects. This capability is especially important in disciplines where staying up-to-date with the latest research is crucial, such as in science, technology, engineering, and mathematics (STEM) fields.

AI's Role in Supporting Critical Thinking and Problem-Solving

Although AI tools can support students in many ways, some scholars have raised concerns about their potential to undermine critical thinking skills. Menekse (2023) cautions that heavy reliance on AI tools like ChatGPT could lead to superficial learning. While ChatGPT offers quick answers and simplifies complex concepts, it may also diminish the need for students to engage deeply with the material. This reduction in cognitive effort can undermine the development of critical thinking and problem-solving abilities, skills that are essential for academic and professional success. According to Menekse, students may become accustomed to using AI-generated content without fully grasping the underlying principles and concepts.

This concern is echoed by Salter, Sivarajah, and Kumar (2023), who argue that long-term dependence on AI may hinder students' ability to engage in complex reasoning and analytical thinking. They highlight that the convenience of instant responses from AI tools can discourage students from engaging in thoughtful deliberation and exploring different perspectives on a problem. AI-generated content can sometimes serve as a shortcut, preventing students from developing the skills needed to tackle complex issues independently.

However, some scholars argue that AI, when used correctly, can actually support critical thinking by providing students with diverse perspectives and helping them analyze information more effectively. For example, AI tools like ChatGPT can help students synthesize information from multiple sources, identify patterns, and challenge assumptions. This process, if done consciously and thoughtfully, can foster higher-order thinking skills. Nevertheless, it is crucial that students remain engaged in the learning process and do not rely on AI tools as a substitute for intellectual effort.

Ethical Implications of AI in Education

The ethical implications of using AI tools like ChatGPT in education are a central concern among researchers and educators. One of the primary ethical issues is academic integrity. As Teng (2023) points out, the lack of clear ethical guidelines for using AI in education may lead to unintended consequences, such as academic dishonesty and over-reliance on AI-generated content. The ability to generate coherent and contextually accurate responses with minimal effort can create confusion about what constitutes plagiarism and cheating. This gap in institutional guidelines may result in students misusing AI tools, either intentionally or unintentionally, in their academic work.

Plagiarism is a particular concern, as AI-generated content can easily be passed off as the student's own work. In some cases, students may not fully understand the implications of submitting AI-generated content as their own, believing it to be an acceptable form of academic assistance. Educators and institutions must establish clear policies regarding the use of AI tools to ensure that students understand the boundaries between using AI for academic support and engaging in dishonest practices.

Another ethical issue is the potential for AI to exacerbate inequalities in education. Salgado Granda, Inzhivotkina, and Ugarte Fajardo (2024) emphasize the importance of ensuring equitable access to AI tools, particularly for students from underprivileged backgrounds. While AI tools like ChatGPT can enhance learning for students with access to technology, those without access to such resources may be left behind. This digital divide could further deepen existing educational inequalities, particularly in regions where internet access is limited or unreliable.

Dependency on AI Tools

Another concern associated with the use of AI tools in education is the potential for students to become overly dependent on these tools. As AI technologies become more sophisticated, students may increasingly rely on AI to complete tasks that they would traditionally do themselves. This over-reliance on AI tools can lead to a decline in students' problem-solving abilities, creativity, and critical thinking. Salter et al. (2023) argue that while AI tools like ChatGPT can be valuable educational aids, they should not replace the need for students to engage deeply with the learning material.

To mitigate the risks of dependency, educational institutions should encourage students to use AI tools as supplements to their learning, rather than as replacements for traditional learning methods. By doing so, students can benefit from the efficiency and convenience offered by AI while still engaging in active learning. Educators should also emphasize the importance of developing independent thinking and problem-solving skills, ensuring that students do not become overly reliant on AI tools to complete their academic tasks.

The Need for Ethical Training and Clear Guidelines

To address the challenges associated with AI in education, several researchers have recommended the implementation of ethical training and clear guidelines for AI usage. Salgado Granda et al. (2024) suggest that educational institutions should provide training and workshops on digital literacy and AI ethics to ensure students understand how to use these tools responsibly. These workshops could cover topics such as the ethical implications of AI, the importance of academic integrity, and the responsible use of technology in education.

In addition, institutions should establish clear, comprehensive policies regarding the use of AI tools like ChatGPT. These guidelines should outline acceptable practices, provide examples of ethical use, and explicitly address issues such as plagiarism and academic dishonesty. Having a well-defined policy will help students navigate the complexities of AI use in education and avoid misunderstandings.

Summary

In summary, while there is substantial evidence supporting the positive role of AI tools like ChatGPT in education, the literature also highlights the need for caution. The ethical challenges associated with AI use, particularly concerning academic integrity, dependency, and digital inequality, must be addressed to ensure that students benefit from these technologies without compromising their cognitive development. Clear institutional guidelines, focused on ethical usage and fostering critical thinking, are crucial for the responsible integration of AI tools into educational settings.

AI tools like ChatGPT have the potential to revolutionize education by offering personalized learning experiences and improving academic efficiency. However, these tools must be used responsibly, with an emphasis on ethical considerations and critical engagement. As the use of AI continues to grow, further research is needed to explore its long-term effects on education and to develop best practices for integrating AI tools into academic settings.

3. METHODOLOGY

Research Design

The research design for this study was quantitative, aimed at collecting numerical data to evaluate the impact of ChatGPT on students' learning practices, critical thinking, and academic integrity. The study relied on a cross-sectional survey method, which was chosen because it allows for a broad overview of students' experiences with ChatGPT across various cultural contexts and educational systems. This approach is well-suited for gathering information from a large group of participants and identifying patterns in how AI tools are used across different countries.

Participants

The study surveyed 65 students from seven countries: Afghanistan, Oman, Pakistan, the United States, the United Kingdom, Australia, and Canada. The diverse background of the participants was essential to providing a cross-cultural perspective on the use of ChatGPT. The students were selected from various academic disciplines, including business, engineering, social sciences, and humanities, to ensure a broad representation of how ChatGPT is used in different fields of study.

The survey participants were recruited through online platforms and university networks, and they were informed about the purpose of the study, ensuring voluntary participation. The selection criteria for participants included being enrolled in higher education and using ChatGPT as a study aid. This sample size, though relatively small, was sufficient for identifying trends and drawing meaningful conclusions regarding the usage of ChatGPT.

Data Collection

The primary method of data collection was an online survey, which was administered through a secure platform to ensure anonymity and privacy. The survey contained both closed and open-ended questions, designed to collect quantitative data on the frequency and nature of ChatGPT usage, as well as qualitative insights into students' experiences and concerns. The questions were divided into four main sections:

1. Demographic Information: To understand the participants' backgrounds, the survey collected information such as country of residence, academic discipline, and frequency of ChatGPT usage.
2. Usage Patterns: Participants were asked how often they used ChatGPT, for which academic tasks, and how they integrated it into their study habits.
3. Perceived Benefits: This section focused on the advantages that students attributed to using ChatGPT, such as improved time management, easier access to information, and enhanced understanding of difficult topics.
4. Challenges and Concerns: This section aimed to identify any negative aspects of using ChatGPT, including concerns about academic integrity, dependency on the tool, and potential impacts on critical thinking and problem-solving abilities.

Data Analysis

The survey responses were analyzed using descriptive statistical methods. Quantitative data were summarized using frequencies, percentages, and averages, allowing for a clear overview of patterns in ChatGPT usage. For qualitative responses, a thematic analysis approach was used. The responses to open-ended questions were coded to identify common themes and concerns, which were then categorized under broader themes such as learning practices, academic integrity, and critical thinking.

The data were further analyzed to examine differences in usage patterns based on students' geographical location and educational context. This analysis helped highlight regional differences in how ChatGPT is used and the challenges students face in different parts of the world.

4. FINDINGS AND DISCUSSION

Results and Discussion

Results

The results of the survey revealed several interesting patterns regarding how students use ChatGPT in their academic work. These results provide valuable insights into students' perceptions and usage of AI tools like ChatGPT in their learning processes.

Figure 1. Frequency of using ChatGPT

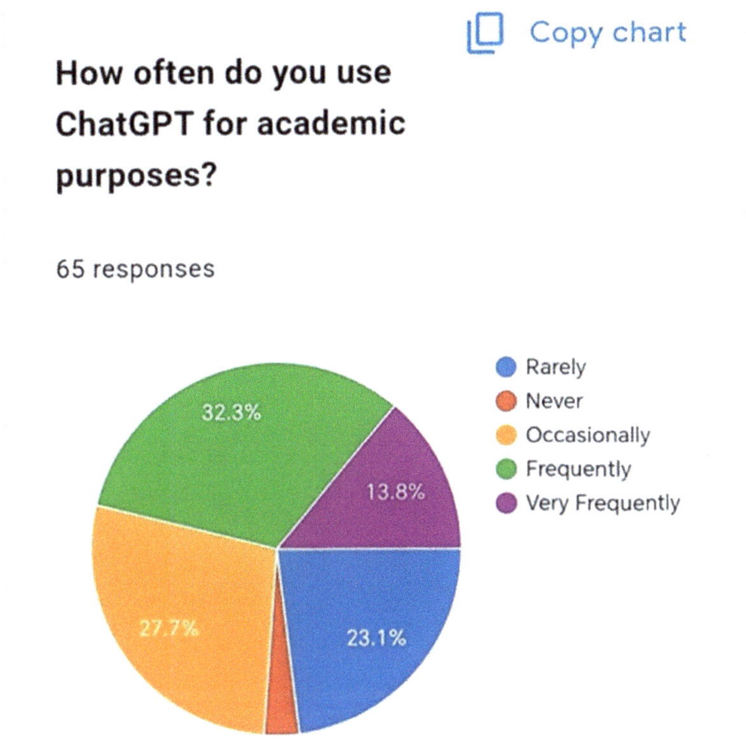

Usage Patterns: A significant proportion of respondents (approximately 80%) reported using ChatGPT regularly for academic tasks (see figure 1).

Figure 2. Usage of ChatGPT in different tasks

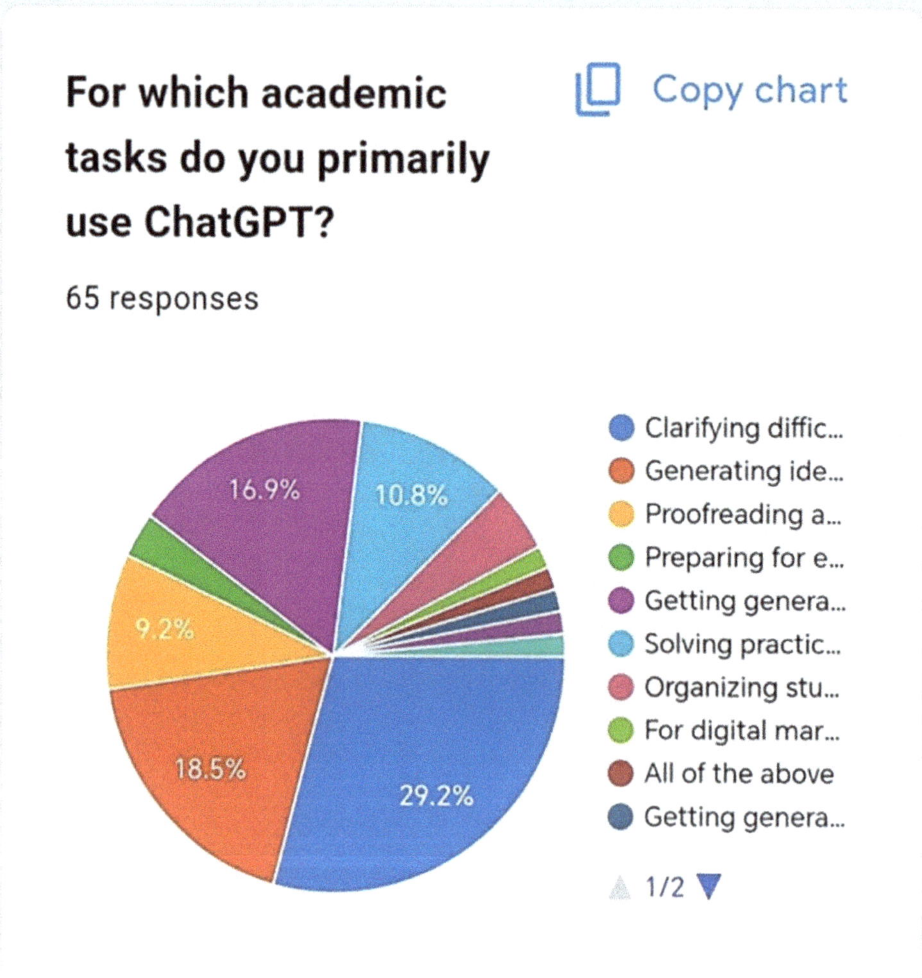

The most common uses were for clarifying difficult concepts (29.2%), generating ideas for assignments and research papers (18.5%), getting general study tips and strategies (16.9%), solving practice problems (10.8%), and proofreading and improving writing (9.2%). These figures suggest that ChatGPT is integrated into a variety of academic tasks and has become a versatile tool for students across different academic disciplines(see figure 2).

Notably, students from resource-rich countries such as the United States, the United Kingdom, and Australia were more likely to use ChatGPT as a supplementary tool to aid their studies, integrating it into their existing academic practices. In contrast, students from resource-limited countries, such as Afghanistan, Pakistan, and Oman, reported relying on ChatGPT as a primary source of academic support, especially when access to other educational resources was limited. This highlights a critical distinction in how AI tools like ChatGPT are utilized based on the availability of traditional academic resources and the digital divide that persists across various regions.

In these resource-limited environments, the availability of a tool like ChatGPT may bridge gaps in access to textbooks, academic journals, and even instructors. For example, a student in Afghanistan might use ChatGPT to clarify academic concepts that would otherwise be inaccessible due to the closure of educational institutions and limited internet access to reputable academic sources. This underscores the importance of understanding the role of AI tools in different educational contexts and highlights the potential of AI to level the playing field in regions with fewer academic resources.

Perceived Benefits: The survey revealed that students generally viewed ChatGPT as a valuable tool for improving learning. A majority of participants found it particularly helpful for managing time and organizing tasks. Many students reported that ChatGPT enabled them to complete assignments more efficiently, providing clear explanations and generating relevant content. One student from Canada remarked that ChatGPT helped them find resources quickly and generated ideas for their essays, which significantly improved their overall time management. This is consistent with findings from Kohnke et al. (2023), who noted that AI tools could enhance time management by helping students stay organized and focused on their tasks.

Figure 3. Students' concern about problem solving skills

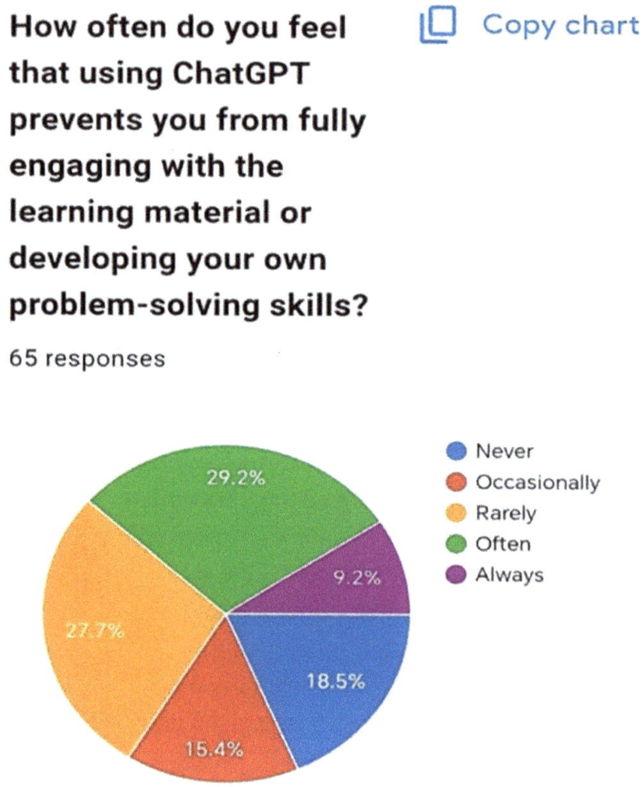

In addition to these benefits, students noted that ChatGPT helped them overcome procrastination. By providing immediate responses to their queries, it allowed students to stay on task and avoid delays in completing their assignments. As ChatGPT is accessible 24/7, students could utilize it during any time of the day, which proved especially beneficial for those balancing their academic work with personal or professional responsibilities. This aspect of AI tools has the potential to make learning more flexible and adaptable, catering to the schedules of students with diverse commitments.

Challenges and Concerns: Despite the positive feedback, a number of challenges and concerns were identified. One of the most significant issues was the potential over-reliance on ChatGPT. Around 40% of students admitted that they sometimes used ChatGPT as a shortcut, bypassing their own critical thinking and problem-solving processes. These students often used the tool to generate quick answers or summaries without fully engaging with the material (see figure 3).

Students from Afghanistan and Pakistan were particularly concerned about the tool's potential to encourage dependency, as they often lacked access to other resources and used ChatGPT as their primary learning aid. This is in line with Menekse (2023), who warned that over-reliance on AI could stunt students' ability to develop essential critical thinking and independent problem-solving skills.

The potential for dependency on ChatGPT has important implications for students' intellectual growth. When students rely heavily on AI for answers, they may miss out on opportunities for deeper cognitive engagement with the material, which is necessary for long-term knowledge retention and application. This concern about AI's impact on critical thinking was particularly prominent among students from resource-limited countries, who noted that without other forms of support, their academic growth might be compromised by excessive dependence on ChatGPT.

Another concern was the impact on academic integrity. A number of respondents expressed anxiety about the possibility of ChatGPT facilitating cheating or plagiarism. Some students felt conflicted about using the tool for assignments, fearing it might lead to dishonest practices. A respondent from Oman stated, "While I find ChatGPT useful, I'm worried about using it for writing assignments because I feel it might be considered plagiarism." These concerns reflect the broader ethical issues surrounding AI tools in education. According to Yang and Zhang (2023), the absence of clear guidelines on AI usage in educational institutions creates confusion about what constitutes ethical use. The rapid development of AI technologies like ChatGPT has outpaced the development of policies addressing academic integrity, creating a situation in which students are left to navigate these ethical challenges on their own.

Additionally, some respondents expressed concerns about the accuracy of information provided by ChatGPT. Although the tool is generally reliable, occasional inaccuracies or biases in its responses could lead students to misinterpret concepts or cite unreliable information in their academic work. This issue highlights the need for students to critically evaluate the information provided by AI tools and verify it against reputable sources, an approach that aligns with the recommendations from Salter et al. (2023) to promote digital literacy and responsible AI use.

Discussion

The results of this study are consistent with the findings of other research on the use of AI tools in education. Kohnke et al. (2023) also highlighted that AI tools like ChatGPT can enhance time management and task organization, which was evident in this study, where students reported that the tool helped them stay on track with their academic work. The widespread use of ChatGPT for generating ideas and clarifying concepts aligns with the research by Bonsu and Baffour-Koduah (2023), who found that students appreciated how AI tools simplified complex topics, thereby enhancing their understanding of challenging material and a large number of students find it extremely helpful in enhancing learning experience (see figure 4).

Figure 4. Students' perception about ChatGPT

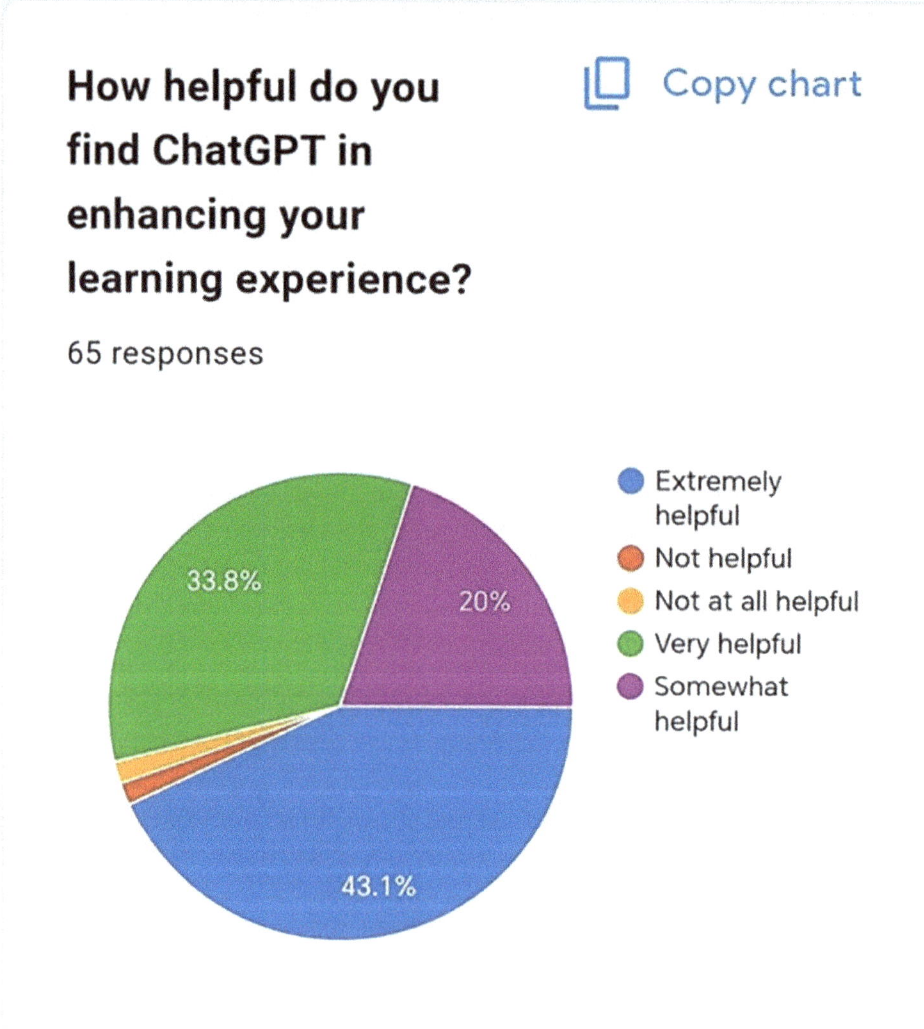

Figure 5. Frequency of dependency of student on ChtGPT

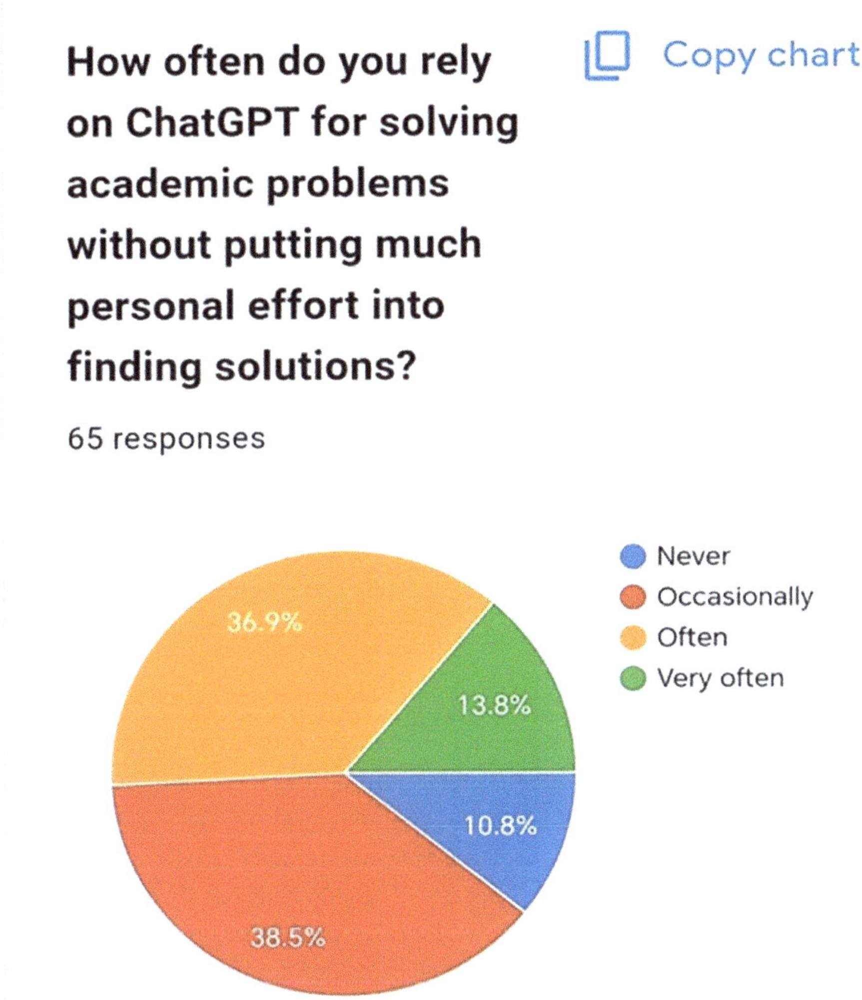

However, the concerns raised in this study regarding over-reliance on AI tools reflect broader debates in the literature and many students have ate worrying about this and accept it as a concern (see figure 5).

As Salter et al. (2023) note, there is a risk that AI tools like ChatGPT could undermine critical thinking and problem-solving skills by providing immediate solutions without requiring students to engage deeply with the material. This concern was echoed by respondents in this study, particularly those from Afghanistan and Pakistan, who noted that their dependency on ChatGPT sometimes prevented them from fully understanding the material. These findings emphasize the importance of using AI tools like ChatGPT as supplements to, rather than substitutes for, traditional learning methods.

The ethical concerns regarding academic integrity, particularly in relation to cheating and plagiarism, are also supported by research in this area. As Yang and Zhang (2023) argue, educational institutions must develop clear guidelines to ensure that AI tools are used ethically. Many students in this study expressed concerns about using ChatGPT for assignments, fearing that it might lead to dishonest practices. These concerns underscore the need for educational institutions to establish policies that promote ethical AI usage while maintaining academic standards.

The cross-cultural differences in the use of ChatGPT are particularly notable. Students from resource-rich countries tended to use the tool as a supplementary aid, integrating it into their study routines, while students from resource-limited environments relied heavily on it due to a lack of educational resources. This finding mirrors the research by Cai and Zhang (2023), which emphasized that the perception and use of AI tools are influenced by the resources available in different regions. The disparity in the use of ChatGPT based on regional resources highlights the need for a nuanced approach to AI integration in educational contexts. While ChatGPT can provide significant educational benefits, its use must be adapted to the specific needs and challenges of students in different regions.

In conclusion, the findings of this study suggest that ChatGPT has both positive and negative effects on student learning. While it offers numerous benefits, including improved time management, idea generation, and clarity in understanding academic content, it also raises concerns about over-reliance, academic integrity, and the impact on critical thinking. These issues should be carefully considered by educators, policymakers, and institutions as they navigate the integration of AI tools in educational settings. Establishing clear guidelines, promoting digital literacy, and encouraging responsible AI use are essential steps in ensuring that ChatGPT and other AI tools enhance, rather than hinder, the learning process.

5. RECOMMENDATIONS

Based on the findings of this study, several key recommendations are made to help students, educators, and institutions make the most out of ChatGPT and similar AI tools. These suggestions are aimed at promoting responsible use of AI, ensuring academic integrity, and encouraging critical thinking and independent learning.

Offer Workshops on Responsible AI Us

Educational institutions should host regular workshops to teach students how to responsibly use ChatGPT and similar AI tools. These sessions should show how AI can be a helpful tool for learning, research, and brainstorming ideas, but not as a way to complete assignments without fully understanding the material. Workshops should also focus on the risks of plagiarism, misinformation, and becoming too dependent on AI. By teaching students about responsible AI use early on, they will be more prepared to use these tools throughout their academic careers (Salgado Granda et al., 2024; Kohnke et al., 2023).

Create Clear Academic Policies

Universities need to set clear policies about using AI tools in academic work. Students should be made aware of these guidelines from the start. The policies should explain what counts as academic dishonesty when using AI and outline the consequences for misuse. Clear and straightforward communication will help students understand when they are crossing ethical lines and encourage them to make informed choices about using ChatGPT for assignments and projects (Teng, 2023; Menekse, 2023).

Encourage Critical Thinking and Engagement

Teachers should create assignments that require students to engage deeply with the material. Instead of asking for simple answers, tasks should encourage students to think critically, analyze information, and apply concepts to real-world situations. This will encourage students to rely less on AI and more on their own thinking. By doing so, students can improve their problem-solving and critical thinking skills, which are essential for both academic success and future careers (Salter et al., 2023; Menekse, 2023).

Include AI Literacy in the Curriculum

Rather than viewing AI as a threat, universities should teach students how to use it as an opportunity for learning and growth. Offering courses on digital literacy, evaluating information, and the ethics of AI use can help students develop the skills to use AI effectively and responsibly. This will teach them how to critically assess AI-generated content, spot biases, and check facts. By integrating these skills into their education, students will be better prepared to use AI as a tool to enhance, not replace, their own intellectual abilities (Kostka & Toncelli, 2023; Salgado Granda et al., 2024).

Support Students from Under-Resourced Regions

Students from regions with fewer academic resources may rely more on tools like ChatGPT. To help these students, universities should offer extra support like free writing centers, tutoring programs, and access to online resources. Mentoring programs can also help guide students in developing independent study habits. Providing these resources will encourage students to rely less on AI and focus more on authentic learning experiences (Bonsu & Baffour-Koduah, 2023; Hung & Chen, 2023).

Monitor the Impact of AI on Student Learning

Universities should regularly assess how AI tools affect student learning. Surveys, feedback, and research can help track how students use ChatGPT, what challenges they face, and how it impacts their critical thinking and academic honesty. By regularly checking in on these factors, universities can adjust their strategies to ensure AI is supporting student learning in a positive way (Salter et al., 2023; Teng, 2023).

Foster a Culture of Ethical Responsibility

Finally, universities should focus on building a culture where honesty, originality, and independent thinking are valued. Encouraging students to take pride in their work and emphasizing the importance of ethical behavior can help them avoid the temptation to misuse AI. By showcasing successful students who have worked hard and thought critically, universities can inspire others to follow their example, even in a world where AI tools are so accessible (Salter et al., 2023).

By following these recommendations, universities, teachers, and students can create a learning environment where AI tools like ChatGPT are used responsibly. This approach will not only ensure students' academic success but also prepare them to be ethical and thoughtful citizens in a digital world (Kohnke et al., 2023; Salgado Granda et al., 2024).

6. CONCLUSION

This study provides valuable insights into the impact of ChatGPT on students' academic experiences. The findings suggest that while ChatGPT can be a powerful tool for improving learning practices, time management, and problem-solving, it also presents challenges related to over-reliance, critical thinking, and academic integrity. The cross-cultural nature of the study highlights important regional differences in the use of ChatGPT, with students from resource-rich countries using it as a supplementary tool and students from resource-limited environments relying on it as a primary academic resource.

To ensure that ChatGPT and similar AI tools are used responsibly, educational institutions must develop clear policies and guidelines that promote ethical usage and safeguard academic integrity. Students should be encouraged to use ChatGPT as a learning aid rather than a substitute for independent thinking and problem-solving. With the proper guidance and support, AI tools like ChatGPT have the potential to enhance the learning experience and help students achieve academic success.

Moreover, educators must be proactive in integrating AI literacy into their curricula to equip students with the skills to use these technologies critically and effectively. Training programs, workshops, and continuous assessments can help foster responsible AI use while also minimizing the risk of dependency. Policymakers and academic leaders must collaborate to build inclusive digital learning environments that bridge the gap between different educational systems. By fostering awareness and accountability, the academic community can harness the full benefits of ChatGPT while mitigating its potential drawbacks. As AI continues to evolve, its role in education must be continuously evaluated to ensure it serves as a tool for empowerment rather than replacement.

REFERENCES

Bonsu, E. M., & Baffour-Koduah, D. (2023). From the Consumers' Side: Determining Students' Perception and Intention to Use ChatGPT in Ghanaian Higher Education. Social Science Research Network. https://doi.org/DOI: 10.2139/ssrn.4387107

Diaz, M. (2023). How to use ChatGPT: Everything you need to know. ZDNET. https://www.zdnet.com/article/how-to-use-chatgpt/

Gilson, A., Safranek, C. W., Huang, T., Socrates, V., Chi, L., & Taylor, R. A.. (2023). How does ChatGPT perform on the United States Medical Licensing Examination? The implications of large language models for medical education and knowledge assessment. *JMIR Medical Education*, *9*, e45312. DOI: 10.2196/45312 PMID: 36753318

Hung, J., & Chen, J. (2023). The Benefits, Risks and Regulation of Using ChatGPT in Chinese Academia: A Content Analysis. *Social Science*. Advance online publication. DOI: 10.2139/ssrn.4387107

Kohnke, L., Rudolph, R., & Li, Y. (2023). ChatGPT as a Tool for Improving Learning Practices. Journal of Educational Technology.

Kostka, I., & Toncelli, R. (2023). Exploring Applications of ChatGPT to English Language Teaching: Opportunities, Challenges, and Recommendations. Teaching English as a Second Language-EJ. https://doi.org/DOI: 10.55593/ej.27107int

Menekse, M. (2023). Envisioning the Future of Learning and Teaching Engineering in the Artificial Intelligence Era: Opportunities and Challenges. *Journal of Engineering Education*. Advance online publication. DOI: 10.1002/jee.20539

OpenAI (2022, November 30). "ChatGPT: Optimizing Language Models for Dialogue". Archived from the original on November 30, 2022.

Salgado Granda, B. A., Inzhivotkina, Y., & Ugarte Fajardo, J. (2024). *Educational Innovation: Exploring the Potential of Generative Artificial Intelligence in Cognitive Schema Building*. Edutec, Revista Electrónica de Tecnología Educativa., DOI: 10.21556/edutec.2024.89.3251

Salter, S., Sivarajah, U., & Kumar, V. (2023). Exploring ChatGPT's Influence on Critical Thinking and Problem-Solving in Education. *Educational Technology Review*.

Teng, H. (2023). The Ethical Implications of AI in Education: A Critical Review of ChatGPT's Impact on Learning. *International Journal for Educational Integrity*.

Chapter 5
Integrating AI Across Curricula:
Adapting AI Concepts for Various Subjects and Grade Levels

Muhammad Usman Tariq
https://orcid.org/0000-0002-7605-3040
Abu Dhabi University, UAE & University College Cork, Ireland

ABSTRACT

This chapter studies the integration of artificial intelligence (AI) in various educational curricula, highlighting the importance of adapting AI concepts to different subjects and grades. It demonstrates the potential for AI to improve individual learning, promote critical thinking, and provide students with problem-solving experiences in the real world. Through research into successful case studies, this paper demonstrates topics such as science, mathematics, humanities, and arts and how AI can be seamlessly included in its role in professional and technical training. There are also challenges, such as access to AI resources, teacher training, and digital gaps. This chapter contains recommendations for educators, curriculum developers, and political decision-makers. We will wisely integrate AI into the curriculum to ensure students develop technical skills and ethical awareness. The research highlights the need for an interdisciplinary approach and future-oriented curriculum development to prepare for the rapidly developing world of AI control.

INTRODUCTION

The presence and impact of artificial intelligence (AI) in our daily lives have made them more important in a variety of areas, from healthcare and finance to

DOI: 10.4018/979-8-3373-2297-1.ch005

entertainment and transportation. As AI revolutionizes the industry, students must acquire basic knowledge and skills related to this transformational technology. Here, the alphabetical order of AI in modern education becomes an essential curriculum element. The alphabetization of AI refers to understanding how AI works, its applications, and its effectiveness, as well as navigating a world where students criticize technology and make sound decisions, and AI plays a central role. Promoting AI alphabetical order in education is about teaching technical coding or machine learning methods and deepening our understanding of AI's broader social, ethical, and economic aspects. The importance of alphabetizing AI lies in the possibility of equipping students with the tools they need to succeed in an increasingly AI-controlled world that promotes critical thinking, creativity, and problem-solving skills. As AI-related skills are already in high demand and automation continues to develop industries, the workforce must be able to coordinate AI tools effectively. The lack of AI alphabetical order could lead to a previously desirable qualification gap in which only professionally trained individuals in AI-related regions can fully participate in the economy. By integrating the alphabetical order of AI into education, schools can ensure that students have a fundamental understanding of AI and prepare for tomorrow's workforce.

Furthermore, the alphabetization of AI helps students develop critical thinking and problem-solving skills as they evaluate AI systems decisions, understand the biases of AI algorithms, and learn to consider the ethical implications of AI use in society. However, AIS applications are huge and multifaceted and touch fields such as history, ethics, social sciences, biology, mathematics, art, and more. AI is not just about writing code or creating algorithms. It overlaps with human behavior, decision-making processes, creativity, and culture. As a result, the alphabetization of AI should not be translated into a single topic. However, it should be woven into many different fields of material. Integrating AI in subjects encourages students to view AI not as an isolated field of research but as an integral part of their wider world. Learn how to collect, process, and analyze data to train your AI systems. In science class, AI can be introduced as an instrument for data analysis and hypothesis. Students can explore how AI accelerates genomics, climate science, and physics research. In history and social sciences, AI can examine historical development, their social impacts, and the ethical dilemmas they impose.

AI is not limited to a single domain. However, it permeates all areas of life, and its applications require knowledge from several fields to be fully understood and used correctly. For example, when studying AI in the context of social studies, students can investigate how AI-controlled surveillance systems affect data protection rights or how AI tools are used in law enforcement and law enforcement agencies. Discussing these topics in the context of ethics, sociology, and politics allows students to achieve the social effects of a more comprehensive perspective on AI. Similarly, students can use AI to create music, art, and literature to address the creative possibilities of AI while also studying philosophical and ethical questions that address the creativity and the author's era. As students learn about different subjects, they can see how knowledge is gathered from different fields to solve complex problems. When developing AI control solutions for climate change, engineering, biology, economics, and political science experts must work together to create sustainable and sustainable solutions (Strielkowski et al., 2024). Educators can promote collaboration and problem-solving attitudes by encouraging students to turn to AI from several perspectives. Additionally, interdisciplinary AI organizations encourage students to think critically about AI's impact in various situations and prepare them to make sound decisions about how AI technology is used and regulated in society.

Key research questions stemming from the need for AI integration into education revolve around effectively including AI concepts in various educational subjects and which educational approaches best support AI capabilities. One of the central questions in AI education research is the design of a curriculum that introduces the concept of AI in an accessible, attractive, and appropriate way to various achievements. For example, in early classes, students may not have the technical background to understand complex algorithms in machine learning (Xie et al., 2024). However, they can capture basic concepts such as sample recognition, decision-making, and automation. With AI training expanding, all students must have access to high-quality AI learning opportunities, regardless of background or socioeconomic status. It includes treating the difference between technology and internet access and supporting students who have to deal with technical concepts. The research will explore how an integrated AI curriculum can be created that can be adapted to various learning styles and needs, making AI training accessible to all students. How should we be taught the concept of AI to promote deep learning and critical thinking? A promising approach is project-based learning, where students are actively involved in real projects where they need to use AI tools to solve real problems. This model allows students to work in teams and develop AI solutions for local issues (Fundi et al., 2024). This approach not only helps students learn technical skills but also inspires them to think critically about the effectiveness of their work and the ethical implications of AI technology. Another pedagogical approach will require learning, encouraging students to ask questions through guided research and experiments and explore the concept of AI. This approach promotes curiosity and helps students better understand how AI systems work. Teachers must be familiar with AI's technical aspects and the ethical, social, and political issues that enhance it. Professional development programs in these areas can help teachers feel more confident in students. Additionally, a collaborative network of educators can provide a platform for exchanging best practices and resources for teaching AI on various subjects and achievements. By equipping students with the alphabetization of AI,

AI prepares for the ubiquitous future of everyday life. Students can comprehensively understand AI through an interdisciplinary approach that lowers subject and class levels. It is not limited to technical skills but includes this technology's ethical, social, and cultural aspects. While AI is developing, it is essential to continue studying new ways to engage AI in education and ensure future generations are prepared for the combat and design of their world. Research questions related to AI alphabetization and pedagogy are essential in designing a settlement in this important field of education. Create a robust, integrated, and effective AI education framework through continuous research, experimentation, and collaboration.

BACKGROUND: THE CASE FOR AI INTEGRATION ACROSS DISCIPLINES

In today's rapidly developing technological landscape, artificial intelligence (AI) is no longer a niche reserved for specialized industries and academic researchers. It has become fundamental to many fields, such as healthcare, business, production, education, and the arts. As AI continues to shape the world, all students must develop a fundamental understanding of this transformational technology. AI literacy is about teaching students how AI functions from a technical standpoint and understanding how AI systems affect and interact with society as a whole. In this sense, the alphabetical order of AI is significant for future careers as it provides students with the skills they need to thrive in a world where AI-controlled technologies are ubiquitous. Furthermore, the alphabetical order of AI is essential in promoting responsible digital citizenship, ensuring that students are willing to navigate a society increasingly shaped by AI, where privacy, distortion, and ethics are central. As AI continues to permeate the industry, understanding of work and critical evaluation of AI systems becomes necessary for success in many career paths. From data science and software development to marketing and healthcare, AI is already built into many Jobrolles, and the demand for AI-related skills is rapidly growing. According to a report from the World Economic Forum, AI-related employment is expected to increase significantly over the next few years. Employees will need to understand the concept of AI to adapt to the new Jobrolles, which are touted as AI technology.

Students not exposed to AI alphabetical order can face future labor markets and create potential qualification gaps that create significant challenges and put them at a disadvantage. As AI is integrated into the organization's decision-making process, it is essential to understand how future employees work with AI systems, interpret the results, and identify potential distortions and ethical concerns. It is also essential for digital citizenship. Suppose AI systems become more influenced to form public guidelines and economic and social norms. In that case, students must be knowledgeable enough to address these technologies critically. From recommended algorithms on social media platforms to predictive police work and facial recognition technology, AI-powered systems significantly impact data protection, equity, and human rights. Students need to be able to control these issues responsibly and understand the potential benefits and damage to AI applications. The alphabetical order of AI promotes the ability to assess AI systems, understand their impact on society, and work for guidelines that promote technology's ethical and fair use. This critical perception is crucial for decisive decision-making in a democratic society where citizens must address the challenges of emerging technology. AI does not exist in a vacuum.

Applications extend to a variety of fields and become essentially interdisciplinary topics. For example, AI overlaps with science in biology, chemistry, physics, and other fields and is used to model complex systems, analyze large-scale data records and simulate experiments. The healthcare field uses AI technologies for diagnosis, personalized medicine, and drug discovery, making it essential for students in the medical and health-related fields to understand AI principles. In the humanities, AI raises important questions about ethics, creativity, and the human experience. Students studying philosophy, literature, or art can then benefit from it to understand how AI includes creativity, authors, and traditional ideas of artistic expression. Furthermore, social sciences, including sociology, psychology, and political science, overlap with AI. However, researchers examine how AI systems affect human behavior, social structure, and government. However, AI integration should not be limited to STEM subjects only. By bridging the humanities and social sciences to AI, educators can help students understand the broader social implications of AI, including topics related to power, inequality, and privacy dynamics (Egara & Mosimege, 2024). This interdisciplinary approach is essential to promote rounded critical thinkers who can assess the role of AI in both technical and social contexts. For example, when studying AI in a social research lesson, students can look at how AI-driven governments and businesses use surveillance techniques or how AI affects labor markets and economic inequality. In literature and philosophy, students can discuss the ethical implications of AI in terms of institutions, responsibility, and machine possibilities to make decisions that affect human life (Mosly, 2024). By integrating AI into different subjects, students are better prepared to provide a comprehensive understanding of their multifaceted nature and meet the challenges and opportunities they present.

Orientation with AI alphabetization education standards is essential to ensuring all students have access to the knowledge and skills needed to deal with AI technology, regardless of their location or background. Integrating AI into education systems worldwide has resulted in several global AI education initiatives and political framework conditions. The initiative highlights the importance of AI alphabetization as part of a broader effort to promote digital capabilities and critical thinking. Similarly, the European Union has introduced an "action plan for digital education." It focuses on the plan to support the acquisition of skills based on the importance of responsibility and creative digital technology, prioritizing and highlighting the need for international cooperation in the United States worldwide. It focuses on promoting AI-related skills at a young age to promote schools. These guidelines reflect the growing perception of AI as a fundamental competence for future generations and highlight the need for a comprehensive strategy to integrate AI into the pedagogical curriculum. The key challenge is ensuring that AI training is not limited to specific technology or computer science courses but is integrated into various subjects. It requires careful curriculum design to ensure that the concept of AI is introduced at the appropriate development stage and is accessible to students of various learning styles and backgrounds. For example, young students can be introduced to AI concepts through simple activities that give algorithms, pattern recognition, and decision-making processes (Mayasari et al., 2024). When trained, students can address more advanced topics, such as machine learning, data science, and ethical questions related to AI. Common Core highlights the development of critical thinking and problem-solving skills of central importance in understanding AI. By organizing the alphabetical order of AI with these criteria, educators can ensure that students learn about AI technology and develop the analytical skills they need to work with AI responsibly. Similarly, NGSS focuses on research-based learning and emphasizes the integration of interdisciplinary knowledge. AI can be introduced in the context of these standards, particularly in areas related to using scientific principles on data analysis, systems thinking, and real problems.

However, the integration of AI into the curriculum is not without challenges. Teachers need appropriate professional development and resources to teach the concept of AI effectively, and schools need to ensure that students have access to the technology and infrastructure they need. Additionally, there is a need for a flexible and adaptable curriculum to various educational contexts, allowing the inclusion of AI in ways relevant to students' lives and experiences. Educational policy must work closely with educators, industry experts, and researchers to develop a rigorous and integrated curriculum that ensures that all students have the opportunity to address AI in a meaningful way. It is not just the ability of the future workforce. It is a key component of responsible digital citizenship (Lee & Song, 2024). It helps students control AI technology's ethical, social, and economic impacts. By organizing AI alphabetization as educational standards and ensuring that AI concepts are integrated into the field, educators can equip students with the knowledge and skills they need to thrive in AI control. As the conditions of global initiatives and political frameworks develop, the alphabetical order of AI is a central focus of educational reform. It is important to ensure that all students are prepared for the challenges and opportunities of the 21st century.

ADAPTING AI CONCEPTS FOR VARIOUS SUBJECTS

One of the most exciting developments in education is integrating AI tools into various themes, enriching the learning experience and improving student outcomes across the field. In natural sciences and mathematics, AI is used to manipulate complex systems of simulations and models. It revolutionizes the way students understand scientific principles. AI offers new perspectives on historical analysis, political movements, and ethical agendas in the humanities and social sciences. In creative art, AI supports the creation of original works of art, music, and literature, raising deep questions about creativity, authorship, and intellectual property. Additionally, AI will become an essential tool for career and technical training (CTE) and prepare students for improved employment in AI. In all these fields, AI changes education by providing students with new opportunities to address content and analyze complex systems of data and research while simultaneously causing important debates about the impact of AI on society. AI-powered simulations help students understand abstract scientific concepts better by providing dynamic and interactive models that visualize complex phenomena. In physics, for example, AI-controlled simulations can manipulate students with real-time variables to observe how changes in energy, mass, or intensity affect the results of an experiment (Jauregui-Correa & Sen, 2024). These simulations can model difficult, expensive, or impossible scenarios to replicate in traditional classrooms. Effects of gravity on particle behavior or celestial bodies at the quantum level. Immediate feedback and adaptation of the complexity of simulations based on student inputs allow learners to personalize basic physics principles, explore them in practical ways, and enhance their theoretical knowledge with practical experience. AI tools can simulate complex biological systems, where students observe the effects of environmental factors on populations, model interactions between ecosystems, and experiment with genetic algorithms to predict how traits are inherited across generations. These simulations provide an opportunity to gain a deeper understanding of the underlying principles of biology and use knowledge to solve real problems (Yılmaz, 2024). Chemistry uses AI tools to simulate molecular interactions, prove chemical reactions, and visualize nuclear structures, allowing students to experiment in the laboratory with virtual chemical reactions that are too risky or not practical. Machine learning algorithms, a subgroup of AI, are instrumental in teaching data science and probability. It allows students to analyze large data records, identify samples, and experiment with algorithms and models to make predictions. Students can apply mechanical learning techniques to real-world problems. By working with AI tools, students can gain hands-on experience with technologies that have many of the data-controlled technologies that change the industry today. Machine learning applications can help students better understand probability and statistics by visualizing how different models and algorithms are cut under different conditions, allowing them to test their hypotheses and improve predictions. These tools use algorithms to identify underlying data patterns, whether they recognize numerical sequences, geometric shapes, or algebraic equations. AI-powered platforms can propose alternatives and provide real-time feedback on student problem-solving approaches that lead them through complex calculations. This type of personalized learning helps students build a deeper understanding of mathematical concepts. It encourages them to study various strategies for problem-solving (Karataş et al., 2025). Additionally, the AI tool can adapt to the student's learning style and provide tailor-made explanations and exercises based on his progress, ensuring that all students have the support they need to succeed in mathematics. Using natural language processing algorithms (NLP), AI branching focuses on human language understanding and interpretation, historical documents, speeches, and literature, which can be analyzed to identify patterns, topics, and connections between events and numbers. For example, AI historians can help uncover hidden patterns of historical narratives, analyze changes in political discourse over time, and identify the causes and effects of social movements. These AI tools improve students' understanding of history and encourage them to think critically about how historical narratives are constructed and technology's role in the design of past understandings (Tariq, 2025).

In political science, AI is used to analyze the impact of social media on speech patterns, public opinion, and political movements. Machine learning algorithms can search a large amount of data to recognize trends in political behavior, predict election outcomes, and examine the impact of campaign strategies. AI tools can also help students examine the ethical implications of AI use in governance. Possible use of AI in algorithmic trends in political decision-making or surveillance and data protection issues. AI helps students understand the complex relationships between technology, power, and society and consider technology's role in the design of political systems and democratic processes. According to the law, AI instruments are used to analyze legal texts, predict case outcomes, and support legal research. However, these applications raise important questions about fairness, transparency, and accountability within the legal system. AI systems can incorrectly immortalize bias in trained data, leading to legal judgments or discriminatory consequences for law enforcement (Yue et al., 2024). Students studying legal research can use AI tools to critically examine these ethical issues and how legal systems can adapt to the increasing use of AI. Similarly, AI is used in journalism to generate news articles, analyze public moods, and pursue social media trends. While these tools may improve the speed and efficiency of journalism, they are also concerned about the accuracy and reliability of information and the potential content of AI. Students studying journalism can use AI tools to explore this ethical dilemma and gain a deeper understanding of the role of AI in the design of public discourse. The NLP algorithm can be used to analyze text, identify literary devices, and recognize patterns of language use. These tools allow students to explore topics, symbols, and characters in ways that traditional methods of literary analysis are not permitted. For example, students can use NLP to identify repetitive motifs in novels, pursue character language development throughout the story, and analyze the use of metaphors in poetry. The NLP tool can also support students by providing real-time translation, analyzing grammar and syntax, and providing personalized language exercises. These applications make learning languages more engaging and accessible, providing instant feedback and support to students while developing language skills. With AI-supported creative tools, artists can experiment with new forms of artistic expression and surpass the limits of traditional media. For example, AI-powered platforms can create digital graphics based on many parameters or unique visual compositions based on artist input. These tools can analyze huge data records of existing art to create new and innovative works, combining various styles, genres, and techniques. In configuring configuration, AI tools create melody, harmony, and rhythm. In other words, composers offer new opportunities to study musical opportunities (Joseph & Uzondu, 2024). These AI tools help musicians overcome creative blocks and provide new musical ideas and structures that did not arise for composers. Who has the right to create art or music if the AI system creates art or music for them? Should AI be credited as a creator or human user, or should it be perceived as an author's creative process? These questions question traditional ideas of creativity and intellectual property, allowing students to address the ethical impact of the species of art generated on AI. These discussions also encourage students to think about the role of AI in expanding the creative possibilities of human imagination and the possibility that AI can collaborate with artists in new ways. Companies, marketing, finance, and other sectors already use AI technology to improve decision-making, optimize processes, and automate tasks. Students trained in AI and related technologies better navigate these AI-controlled working environments (Tatar et al., 2024). For example, businesses use AI tools to analyze market trends, optimize supply chains, and predict consumer behavior. In marketing, AI creates personalized advertising campaigns, analyzes customer preferences, and manages customer relationships. In finance, AI algorithms are used for risk assessment, fraud recognition, and investment management. By including AI in CTE programs, schools can prepare students for careers that must work together next to AI systems to ensure the skills they require to succeed in an increasingly automated world (Ejjami, 2024). As AI continues to change the type of work, students need to understand how AI systems are used and how these technologies' ethical and social implications are managed in the workplace. It includes an understanding of topics such as the distortion of AI algorithms, the impact of automation on jobs, and the role of AI in designing organizational decisions (Prajapati, 2024). By providing the skills and knowledge to acquire these tasks, CTE programs can help succeed in the AI-controlled economy while also helping promote important recognition of ethical issues related to AI technology.

PEDAGOGICAL APPROACHES FOR TEACHING AI CONCEPTS

Project-based learning (PBL) is an instructional methodology focusing on students working on real-world problems and projects, helping them develop a deeper understanding of content while fostering essential skills like critical thinking, collaboration, and communication. When integrated with AI tools and technologies, PBL allows students to engage with complex, interdisciplinary challenges and apply their knowledge creatively and meaningfully (Alawneh et al., 2024). AI-driven student projects provide an ideal platform for this type of learning, allowing students to tackle real-world problems using the latest technologies. These projects can span a wide range of subjects, from developing AI models for predicting climate change to creating AI-powered solutions for public health issues. The possibilities are vast, and including AI tools helps students grasp technical concepts and develop problem-solving skills that will serve them in any future career (Tariq, 2025).

In real-world problem-solving, AI can be utilized as both a tool and a subject of exploration. For example, students may be asked to develop machine learning models to predict the spread of disease in a particular geographical region based on historical data, climate patterns, and social behavior. In such projects, students will learn the principles of mechanical learning and data science and achieve a practical understanding of how AI can be used to solve urgent global challenges (Kayal, 2024). Similarly, students working on AI control projects can investigate the application of AI in industries such as agriculture, where machine learning models can contribute to crop yield optimization and funding. It allows AI to be used to recognize fraud and perform risk assessments. These projects are powerful as they demonstrate the direct impact of AI in various industries and help students see how technology shapes the world around them and how learning can be applied in real-world situations. Case studies are a great way to combine theoretical knowledge with practical applications. For example, students can look at how AI is used in healthcare systems to improve diagnostic accuracy, support personalized treatment plans, or predict patient outcomes based on medical records and genetic data. Energy sector case studies can show whether AI can help optimize renewable resource use, predict energy requirements, and improve the efficiency of smart grids. Adaptive learning platforms adapting to individual student needs provide students with examples of how AI redesigns people's learning. These case studies can be essential to project-based learning as they provide students with concrete examples of how AI works and encourage them to think creatively about potential applications in other fields. In combination with arithmetic thinking, this approach promotes critical thinking and problem-solving (Naeem et al., 2025). Computational thinking refers to breaking down complex problems into smaller, more manageable components, thinking algorithmically, and using systematic approaches to solve problems. It is a fundamental aspect of learning to work with AI, as it encourages students to analyze and approach challenges logically and methodically. Inquiry-driven learning can be particularly effective in helping students grasp how AI works and how it can be used to address societal challenges. By encouraging students to ask questions about AI capabilities and limitations, educators can guide them through the discovery process, allowing them to learn by doing rather than merely absorbing facts.

For example, students might investigate how AI decision-making processes work in various domains, such as healthcare, finance, or law enforcement. By exploring case studies or running simulations, they can better understand how AI models make predictions and decisions based on large datasets. This inquiry-driven approach promotes an active engagement with the subject matter, where students ask questions about the potential biases in data, the ethical considerations in AI systems, and how the outcomes of AI decision-making can affect individuals and communities. For example, in a study of AI in criminal justice, students could explore the ethical concerns surrounding predictive policing algorithms, which use historical data to forecast where crimes are likely to occur. Students could investigate whether these algorithms reinforce biases in the data or result in unfair outcomes for specific communities. By asking such questions, students develop critical thinking skills and gain insights into the complexities of AI technology, its limitations, and its societal implications. Data ethics and AI decision-making processes are key components of computational thinking that deserve particular attention in the classroom. As AI becomes increasingly integrated into daily life, from voice assistants like Siri to automated decision-making in hiring, healthcare, and finance, students must understand the ethical implications of these technologies (Iweuno et al., 2024). AI decision-making systems, which often rely on algorithms and vast datasets, can sometimes produce biased or unfair results if the data they are trained on is flawed or incomplete. Teaching data ethics involves exploring the potential harms of biased AI, such as perpetuating stereotypes, discriminating against marginalized groups, or making inaccurate predictions. Students can examine how data is collected, how AI algorithms are trained, and how transparency and accountability play crucial roles in AI decision-making. For instance, in a class discussing AI's role in recruitment, students might analyze case studies where AI hiring tools were found to be biased against women or minority groups due to the data used to train the models. Through inquiry-driven learning and discussions around data ethics, students learn to consider how AI works and the broader ethical consequences of its application.

Educators can help students become more responsible consumers and creators of AI technologies by teaching students about these issues. Students will better understand the potential risks and rewards of AI, and they will be equipped to think critically about how to build AI systems that are fair, transparent, and ethical. This approach goes beyond technical knowledge and encourages students to engage with AI as a tool and a technology with profound social and ethical implications.

Gamification and interactive learning are additional strategies that can be highly effective in teaching AI concepts to students. Gamification refers to integrating game elements—points, levels, challenges, and rewards—into non-game contexts, such as education. When applied to AI education, gamification can make learning more engaging and fun while helping students develop important problem-solving, critical thinking, and computational thinking skills. AI-powered educational games and simulations are excellent tools for teaching AI concepts, offering interactive and immersive learning experiences. Through these games, students can learn about AI by applying it in simulated environments that mimic real-world scenarios. For example, students might play a game where they must train a machine-learning model to recognize images or predict outcomes based on data. Through trial and error, students learn how machine learning works, understand concepts like supervised learning and classification, and refine their skills as they progress through different game levels.

AI-driven educational games can also help students understand complex systems by intuitively visualizing abstract concepts. For example, a game designed to teach neural networks could show how data flows through different network layers and how the system learns to adjust its weights based on feedback. This hands-on approach makes abstract concepts more accessible. It encourages students to experiment with AI systems in a low-stakes environment (Abbasi et al., 2025). Gamification also fosters a sense of accomplishment and motivation, as students can track their progress and compete against themselves or others in solving challenges.

Chatbots and AI-powered virtual tutors offer another form of personalized learning that can enhance the educational experience. These AI-driven tools provide students with real-time, personalized feedback, guiding them through lessons, answering questions, and offering additional explanations when needed. For example, a virtual tutor might help a student struggling with a particular math concept by offering tailored practice problems and step-by-step solutions (Lin & Chen, 2024). This AI-powered learning helps fill the gaps between classroom instruction and individual practice, giving students immediate access to support outside traditional teacher-led hours. Virtual tutors can also adapt to each student's pace, ensuring that students receive the appropriate level of challenge and support.

AI-powered chatbots can further personalize the learning experience by providing students with answers to questions, offering suggestions for further reading or practice, and assisting with homework or study sessions. By using AI in this way, students receive guidance tailored to their specific needs and learning styles, making education more efficient and accessible. Moreover, AI-driven virtual tutors can provide a safe space for students to learn at their own pace, giving them the confidence to ask questions or revisit topics without fear of judgment (Arya & Verma, 2024). These technologies can help create a more inclusive and supportive learning environment where students can engage with material in a way that suits them best. Integrating AI into education through project-based learning, inquiry-driven approaches, and gamification transforms how students engage with technology and prepares them for a future where AI is a ubiquitous and powerful tool. By offering hands-on experiences that encourage exploration, critical thinking, and ethical reflection, educators can equip students with the skills they need to navigate the complexities of an AI-driven world (Velander et al., 2024). These approaches foster not only technical skills but also an understanding of the broader societal implications of AI, ensuring that students are not just passive consumers of technology but also responsible and ethical creators. Through AI-powered projects, inquiry-driven learning, and interactive gamification, students can gain a deeper, more detailed understanding of AI, empowering them to make meaningful contributions to society in an increasingly digital world.

CHALLENGES AND BEST PRACTICES IN AI CURRICULUM INTEGRATION

As artificial intelligence (AI) has further rebuilt the world around us, integration into education is becoming increasingly important. Although the benefits of AI are becoming more widespread in the classroom, educators, students, and institutions need to overcome several obstacles to ensure that AI training is accessible, effective, and fair. These obstacles include the digital gaps and the most urgent challenges, with limited access to AI tools and resources (Lišnić et al., 2025). Furthermore, addressing these challenges and creating a more integrated and literate educational environment for AI is essential. In many schools, particularly low-income or rural areas, infrastructure and financial resources lack the advanced AI tools needed for effective learning. AI tools such as machine learning platforms, processing systems for natural languages, and AI control simulation software often require special hardware, software, and internet connections unavailable in all educational environments

(Shi et al., 2024). This lack of access results in unequal learning opportunities, with students having more advantages over colleagues in wealthy schools and underfunded areas. Initiatives that provide free or affordable access to AI software, cloud computer services, and online learning platforms can significantly reduce cost barriers for schools that don't have the budget to invest in expensive AI tools.

Additionally, the open-source AI platform, freely available to everyone, offers an excellent opportunity for schools to access cutting-edge AI tools without acquiring significant costs. Many of these platforms can teach students about AI and allow them to experiment with AI models, including Google's TensorFlow, Microsoft's cognitive toolkit, and open-source libraries for machine learning (Tolentino et al., 2024). A digital gap refers to the gap between people who access the Internet and digital technologies and their skills and those who do not. This gap can significantly impact students' ability to learn and deal with AI. For example, students in disadvantaged areas may not have reliable internet access at home. They can participate in online AI courses, conduct research, and take advantage of the ability to participate in AI tools and resources. The lack of personal devices like laptops and tablets could further hinder students' interaction with digital learning materials. It includes grants or free devices for students from disadvantaged backgrounds, expanding broadband Internet access to rural or subsupport communities, and providing training programs for students and their families that will help them develop the digital capabilities needed to navigate over the Internet and effectively use the digital tools. By enabling all students to access the tools and resources they must to succeed in the increasingly digital world, they can create a more equitable foundation for AI training. Teachers are the focus of AI training and are equipped with the skills and knowledge necessary to inform AI for successful integration into the curriculum. However, many educators do not feel ready to teach AI, especially if they don't have a background in computer science, mathematics, or related fields (Tanweer & Ismail, 2024). This lack of technical knowledge - how can lead to feelings of uncertainty among teachers and create suppression of AI problems in the classroom. Therefore, it is essential to provide a comprehensive training program that provides educators with basic AI knowledge and practical strategies for teaching AI that students from all backgrounds can access. AI alphabetization refers to the ability to understand and use AI tools, concepts, and applications in an informed and responsible way. One of the teachers is to explain basic AI principles, including machine learning, neural networks, and natural language processing. It also explains an understanding of AI technology's ethical and social impacts. Teacher training programs should address these topics in detail. It focuses on practical activities and real-world examples that help educators connect student concepts. For example, educators can learn how to use simple equipment to analyze data in machine learning or explore case studies of AI applications in healthcare, education, and the arts. This practical skill and knowledge is available to teachers, allowing AI to be integrated into lessons wisely.

However, it is essential to recognize that not all educators have technical knowledge. It is the necessary method to address the technical aspects of AI in depth. These skills are valuable to some students, but it is possible to teach the concept of AI without teaching the teacher. For example, educators can focus on teaching the broader impact of AI. Rather than focusing solely on the technical aspects of AI, these topics can be introduced through interdisciplinary lessons using topics such as social studies, ethics, and history. This approach allows teachers to integrate AI into their curriculum without specialized technical knowledge. It makes it more accessible to educators who do not have a background in Mint subjects. As AI technology develops quickly, teachers need access to new tools, teaching methods, and resources to help them keep up with ethical considerations (Kotsis, 2024).Professional development programs can include workshops, online courses, and collaboration options with other educators (Demartini et al., 2024). Peer learning and mentoring programs also help teachers feel more supported by controlling AI integration challenges into educational practices. PBL allows students to explore the concept of AI through practical projects that address real-world problems, making the learning experience more engaging and relevant. In PBL, teachers can guide students through AI-related projects focusing on practical applications rather than technical details. For example, students can work on projects and design AI tools to support people in their communities (Olatunde-Aiyedun, 2024). These types of projects provide students with concrete ways to study the concept of AI while simultaneously promoting the learning process without the need for comprehensive technical knowledge for teachers. By focusing on problem solutions and real-world applications, PBL is exposed to AI's potential to help students develop critical thinking, creativity, and team skills while simultaneously addressing global challenges. In the classrooms created in the inquiry, students lead the survey of AI-related questions. Teachers can guide students in this process by helping them investigate AI applications in various fields and promoting discussions about the ethical implications of AI technology (Elbanna & Armstrong, 2024). This approach encourages students to think critically about AI, ask essential questions, and examine potential solutions to AI challenges. Educators can promote a deeper understanding of AI by including research-based learning in the curriculum without needing specialized technical knowledge. AI-operated educational games, simulations, and virtual tutors provide interactive experiences that help students learn AI in a fun and intuitive way. These tools simplify complex AI concepts and allow students to experiment with low pressures in AI applications within their environment. By including gamification in AI training, teachers can make learning stronger and, at the same time, help students develop skills to solve problems and use computer-aided thinking. Virtual Tutors and Chatbots can continue to support their learning by providing personalized feedback, guiding students through challenging concepts, and encouraging teachers to support individual students even without AI professionals. Providing access to affordable AI tools, filling in the digital gap, and ensuring that all students have access to the resources they need are key steps to ensuring that AI training is accessible to everyone. Providing educators with the AI alphabetization skills necessary to communicate these concepts is equally important, even without technical knowledge. By providing comprehensive teacher training, promoting professional development, and including innovative teaching strategies such as project-based learning, research-based learning, and gamification, we can create an environment where students and educators can work meaningfully and effectively with AI. In this way, all students can actively participate in an increasingly AI-controlled world (Tariq, 2024).

CASE STUDIES AND FUTURE DIRECTIONS

Integrating artificial intelligence (AI) into education is a continuing trend that promises to revolutionize how students, educators, and institutions work. As AI becomes an increasingly powerful tool in various fields, its application to education is particularly surprising. It has the potential to personalize learning, optimize educational practices, and create better opportunities for students worldwide. In recent years, there have been many successful cases in K-12 and university formation to help AI improve learning outcomes, increase commitment, and help students leverage their full potential. These success stories provide valuable insight into the challenges and successes facing AI integration in education systems and institutions implementing AI-based solutions. One of the most well-known examples is using adaptive learning platforms in AI companies (Yadav, 2025). These platforms are based on the skills of individual students and adapt to the pace and difficulties of education to help create a more personalized learning experience. For example, Dreambox, an elementary school adaptive learning program, is an algorithm for machine learning to adapt mathematics lessons to each student's needs. By analyzing student responses in real-time, Dreambox decides where students will compete and provides targeted feedback and instructional content to master the concept. This way, it helps to fill in the learning gaps and ensure that all students are committed and challenged at the right level. Other programs, such as China's Lis AI, have used AI to create intelligent tutoring systems that provide students with subjects ranging from mathematics to English and personalized lessons that provide recommendations to students based on their progress and performance. In some cases, the effectiveness of these AI systems was important. A study by the Bill & Melinda Gates Foundation showed, for example, that students using Dreambox improved math by 15% compared to students not using the platform. Similarly, AI-operated platforms providing real-time feedback, such as Musnton, have been demonstrated to improve student performance by providing individual lessons based on student behavior (Aravantinos et al., 2024). The use of AI in these educational settings promotes personalized learning. It increases student commitment as students receive immediate feedback and stay motivated when tailored to their unique learning needs. An amazing example is using AI-powered chatbots to support students. Georgia State University uses a chatbot called Pounce, where students assist in various tasks, including answering questions about approval, registration, and financial aid. Pousce provides immediate responses to student inquiries, reduces the workload for human staff, and gives students quick access to the information they need. The system successfully increased student debt outcomes as it remains fairly committed when students have easy access to support. In addition to chatbots, AI forms universities, predicts student success, and identifies at-risk students. Tools like Civitas Learning use predictive analytics to assess student performance and provide it to students who need additional support, such as tutoring or advice. These AI control platforms help institutions optimize resources and provide more effective and targeted student support. Different countries occupy AI in their education systems in different ways, each with unique approaches and focus areas. In China, for example, AI has become a central part of the country's education reform (Okada et al., 2025). The Chinese government strongly invests in AI technology and aims to integrate AI into the national curriculum. Platforms powered by AI, such as Squirrel AI, are becoming more common in schools in China. The country has made great strides in developing intelligent tutoring systems that provide students with a personalized learning experience. Additionally, China has launched an initiative to train educators in AI literacy, ensuring that teachers have the skills to support AI-controlled learning environments. The Finnish education system is known for its commitment to class innovation, focusing on student learning. In recent years, Finland has been looking at the possibilities of AI to improve personalized learning further. For example, the A-operated system was introduced to support individual learning paths that help students progress at their own pace and receive targeted interventions where necessary. Additionally, Finland has invested in training teachers of digital ability, including AI skills, to include AI in their classrooms confidently. A focus on educator training ensures that AI is effectively used to improve and not replace traditional teaching methods. For example, California works to include AI-related skills in the K-12 curriculum to ensure students are prepared for a technology career. Currently, some school districts offer coding and robotics courses that integrate the concept of AI and allow students to build and experiment with AI-powered technology. In the meantime, universities such as Stanford, With, and Harvard are at the top of AI research and development. These institutions offer cutting-edge programs in artificial intelligence and provide students with practical opportunities to work with AI technology in real-life environments, working with industry partners.

AI is used in the UK to improve classroom experience and management capabilities. AI-powered tools like Century Tech use algorithms for machine learning to personalize student learning experiences. By analyzing how students interact with the platform, Century Tech provides insight into their strengths and weaknesses and delivers tailor-made content to improve (He et al., 2024). Furthermore, AI is used in education management to optimize classification, planning, and performance tasks. These applications have valuable time for teachers, allowing them to focus on delivering high-quality lessons. One of the most promising areas for AI in education is the field of personalized learning. Personalized learning in AI Support Learning can revolutionize students' learning by providing tailor-made educational experiences that meet each student's needs, preferences, and learning styles. A personalized learning system run by AI can analyze a large amount of data, including performance, behavior, and interaction with student learning materials, to create custom learning paths that optimize each student's educational trip. For example, AI can help identify areas where students need to fight and identify areas where additional resources or interventions must be provided to improve.

Furthermore, AI can propose learning materials tailored to students' interests and ensure they remain motivated and committed. This personalization is especially valuable in classrooms where students receive different services and diverse student populations requiring individual support. As AI technology advances, education systems worldwide realize the importance of including AI-related topics in their curriculum. In many countries, national education authorities are working to develop AI standards that ensure students gain a comprehensive understanding of AI concepts, ethics, and applications. Educators need to train not only on technical AI concepts but also on effective integration of AI into existing curricula. It includes developing interdisciplinary lessons that combine AI with subjects from ethics, social studies, and humanities, helping students understand the broader social impact of AI. As AI technology evolves, curriculum standards must be flexible to accommodate new developments and advances. It requires continuous updates to educational resources, teacher training programs, and AI-powered learning platforms to ensure students can access the latest tools and knowledge.

Furthermore, it is essential to include different perspectives in developing AI curricula and ensure that all students have access to high-quality AI training, regardless of background or geographical location. Through K-12 success stories and university organizations, you can see the benefits of personalized learning, real-time feedback, and predictive analytics. Around the world, AI states use it in education, adapt education systems, and prepare students for futures shaped by artificial intelligence. As for the future, AI-supported personalized learning and developing

AI curriculum standards will further impact the future of education, providing fair and innovative learning opportunities tailored to students of all origins. When AI technology is developed, it also serves as a way to educate and enhance the next generation of learners.

CONCLUSION

Integration of AI into education provides a great opportunity to improve learning experiences, support personalized lessons, and prepare students for the future impacted by artificial intelligence. The most important findings from integrating AI curriculums show that including AI in an educational setting requires careful planning, thoughtful implementation, and a balance between technical knowledge and broader interdisciplinary concepts. Best practices emphasize the importance of mixing AI with existing curricula to ensure fair access to AI tools and develop educators professionally. These practices help promote AI integration but also help ensure students have a comprehensive understanding of AI applications and effectiveness. The introduction of the concept of AI should not be limited to high schools or universities but should begin at previous educational stages. It can be achieved by including various themes in social sciences and ethics and age-appropriate AI topics in mathematics and natural sciences. For example, in K-12 training, student adoption can contribute to technology recall and make it more accessible through practical applications such as machine learning, chatbots, and simple algorithms.

Furthermore, by analyzing historical data and studying the ethical implications of AI in social studies, AI is treated as an independent topic or an interdisciplinary tool to improve learning through the board. Personalized learning, run by AI, offers a transformative way to do justice to individual students' needs, skills, and learning styles. AI can adapt education plans to student performance in real-time, providing immediate feedback and support. It will help students make progress at their own pace. However, successfully integrating AI into education requires balancing automation and human educational elements. Although AI tools can contribute to assigning content to individual needs, the role of teachers remains important to lead learning, promote critical thinking, and provide emotional and social support. Therefore, AI should be considered a supplement to traditional teaching methods. One of the most critical challenges in AI integration is the digital gap, which means that students from disadvantaged backgrounds do not have access to the technology, infrastructure, or training needed to address AI-powered learning tools. To tackle this issue, there must be a collaborative effort to provide fair access to AI technology. It includes government initiatives to fund the school's AI infrastructure and enable students to access devices and internet connections in rural or sectoral communities.

Additionally, schools must prioritize access to open-source AI tools that provide institutions with inexpensive ways to integrate AI into classrooms without financial obstacles. While many teachers may feel unprepared to teach AI due to a lack of technical expertise, effective teacher training programs can fill this gap. Educators should have basic knowledge of AI concepts and practical tools. They must have practical tools to teach AI in an attractive and relevant way. This training includes not only technical skills but also promoting critical thinking about strategies for integrating AI into different subjects and the ethical implications of AI. Governments must invest in infrastructure, research, and teacher training programs to support the widespread adoption of AI in schools.

Furthermore, political decision-makers need to ensure that AI curriculum standards are developed in a flexible and adaptable way to the rapidly developing nature of AI technology. Furthermore, international cooperation in AI education will help create a global framework for best practices and ensure that all students have access to high-quality AI formations, regardless of where they are. As AI further redesigns the educational environment, future research should focus on several key areas to ensure that AI training remains effective and integrated. First, further research is needed on the effectiveness of AI-powered teaching instruments and their impact on student learning outcomes. Although interest in AI is growing in education, comprehensive research measuring the long-term impact of AI on student performance, commitment, and motivation remains limited. Understanding how AI improves learning for various subjects and age groups is essential for AI-based teaching instruments and curriculum refinement. When AI is embedded in education systems, it is vital to examine how distortions in AI algorithms affect learning outcomes and can cause disproportionate inequality. Investigating the ethical challenges of AI in education, including discovering AI decisions, data protection concerns, and data security transparency, is extremely important for developing framework conditions that ensure that AI is responsible and used considerably.

REFERENCES

Abbasi, B. N., Wu, Y., & Luo, Z. (2025). Exploring the impact of artificial intelligence on curriculum development in global higher education institutions. *Education and Information Technologies, 30*(1), 547–581.

Alawneh, Y. J. J., Sleema, H., Salman, F. N., Alshammat, M. F., & Oteer, R. S., & ALrashidi, N. K. N. (2024, April). Adaptive Learning Systems: Revolutionizing Higher Education through AI-Driven Curricula. In *2024 International Conference on Knowledge Engineering and Communication Systems (ICKECS)* (Vol. 1, pp. 1-5). IEEE.

Aravantinos, S., Lavidas, K., Voulgari, I., Papadakis, S., Karalis, T., & Komis, V. (2024). Educational approaches with AI in primary school settings: A systematic review of the literature available in scopus. *Education Sciences, 14*(7), 744.

Arya, R., & Verma, A. (2024). Role of artificial intelligence in education. *International Journal of Advanced Research in Science. Tongxin Jishu, 4*(2), 589–594.

Demartini, C. G., Sciascia, L., Bosso, A., & Manuri, F. (2024). Artificial intelligence bringing improvements to adaptive learning in education: A case study. *Sustainability, 16*(3), 1347.

Egara, F. O., & Mosimege, M. (2024). Exploring the integration of artificial intelligence-based ChatGPT into mathematics instruction: Perceptions, challenges, and implications for educators. *Education Sciences, 14*(7), 742.

Ejjami, R. (2024). The future of learning: AI-based curriculum development. *International Journal For Multidisciplinary Research, 6*(4).

Elbanna, S., & Armstrong, L. (2024). Exploring the integration of ChatGPT in education: Adapting for the future. *Management & Sustainability: An Arab Review, 3*(1), 16–29.

Fundi, M., Sanusi, I. T., Oyelere, S. S., & Ayere, M. (2024). Advancing AI education: Assessing Kenyan in-service teachers' preparedness for integrating artificial intelligence in competence-based curriculum. *Computers in Human Behavior Reports, 14*, 100412.

He, P., Shin, N., Kaldaras, L., & Krajcik, J. (2024). Integrating artificial intelligence into learning progression-based learning systems to support student knowledge-in-Use: Opportunities and challenges. *Handbook of Research on Science Learning Progressions*, 461-487.

Iweuno, B. N., Orekha, P., Ojediran, O., Imohimi, E., & Adu-Twum, H. T. (2024). Leveraging Artificial Intelligence for an inclusive and diversified curriculum. *World Journal of Advanced Research and Reviews*, *23*(2), 1579–1590.

Jauregui-Correa, J. C., & Sen, M. (2024). Revolutionizing Engineering Education: Adapting Curricula to Address Artificial Intelligence Challenges and Opportunities. *Asean Journal of Engineering Education*, *8*(1), 64–69.

Joseph, O. B., & Uzondu, N. C. (2024). Integrating AI and Machine Learning in STEM education: Challenges and opportunities. *Computer Science & IT Research Journal*, *5*(8), 1732–1750.

Karataş, F., Eriçok, B., & Tanrikulu, L. (2025). Reshaping curriculum adaptation in the age of artificial intelligence: Mapping teachers' AI-driven curriculum adaptation patterns. *British Educational Research Journal*, *51*(1), 154–180.

Kayal, A. (2024). Transformative Pedagogy: A Comprehensive Framework for AI Integration in Education. In *Explainable AI for Education: Recent Trends and Challenges* (pp. 247–270). Springer Nature Switzerland.

Kotsis, K. T. (2024). Integration of artificial intelligence in science teaching in primary education: Applications for teachers. *European Journal of Contemporary Education and E-Learning*, *2*(3), 27–43.

Lee, S., & Song, K. S. (2024). Teachers' and students' perceptions of AI-generated concept explanations: Implications for integrating generative AI in computer science education. *Computers and Education: Artificial Intelligence*, *7*, 100283.

Lin, H., & Chen, Q. (2024). Artificial intelligence (AI)-integrated educational applications and college students' creativity and academic emotions: Students and teachers' perceptions and attitudes. *BMC Psychology*, *12*(1), 487. PMID: 39285268

Lišnić, B., Zaharija, G., & Mladenović, S. (2025). Integration of Artificial Intelligence in K-12: Analysis of a Three-Year Pilot Study. *AI*, *6*(3), 49.

Mayasari, N., Sastraatmadja, A. H. M., Suparman, T., Mutiara, I. I., & Maqfirah, P. A. V. (2024). Effectiveness of Using Artificial Intelligence Learning Tools and Customized Curriculum on Improving Students' Critical Thinking Skills in Indonesia. *The Eastasouth Journal of Learning and Educations*, *2*(02), 111–118.

Mosly, I. (2024). Artificial intelligence's opportunities and challenges in engineering curricular design: A combined review and focus group study. *Societies (Basel, Switzerland)*, *14*(6), 89.

Naeem, S., Qureshi, M. A., & Butt, A. M. (2025). AI Integration Into Course Content Development. In *AI Applications for English Language Learning* (pp. 93–120). IGI Global Scientific Publishing.

Okada, A., Sherborne, T., Panselinas, G., & Kolionis, G. (2025). Fostering transversal skills through open schooling supported by the CARE-KNOW-DO pedagogical model and the UNESCO AI competencies framework. *International Journal of Artificial Intelligence in Education*, •••, 1–46.

Olatunde-Aiyedun, T. G. (2024). Artificial intelligence (AI) in education: Integration of AI into science education curriculum in Nigerian universities. *International Journal of Artificial Intelligence for Digital*, *1*(1).

Prajapati, M. A. B. (2024). ARTIFICIALLY INTELLIGENT IN EDUCATION:"REDEFINING LEARNING IN THE 21ST CENTURY". *Journal of Educational Technology, v1., 12818287*.DOI: <ALIGNMENT.qj></ALIGNMENT>10.5281/zenodo

Shi, L., Ding, A. C., & Choi, I. (2024). Investigating teachers' use of an AI-Enabled system and their perceptions of AI integration in science classrooms: A case study. *Education Sciences*, *14*(11), 1187.

Strielkowski, W., Grebennikova, V., Lisovskiy, A., Rakhimova, G., & Vasileva, T. (2024). AI-driven adaptive learning for sustainable educational transformation. *Sustainable Development*.

Tanweer, M., & Ismail, A. (2024). Generative AI in curriculum development: A framework for adaptive, customized, and personalized learning. In *Impacts of Generative AI on Creativity in Higher Education* (pp. 193–226). IGI Global.

Tariq, M. U. (2024). Empowering student entrepreneurs: From idea to execution. In Cantafio, G., & Munna, A. (Eds.), *Empowering students and elevating universities with innovation centers* (pp. 83–111). IGI Global., DOI: 10.4018/979-8-3693-1467-8.ch005

Tariq, M. U. (2025). Revitalizing Pedagogy: Integrating Indigenous Knowledge and Practices Into Higher Education Disciplines. In Kgari-Masondo, M. (Ed.), *Indigenous Teaching Disciplines and Perspectives for Higher Education* (pp. 379–400). IGI Global Scientific Publishing., DOI: 10.4018/979-8-3693-9296-6.ch018

Tariq, M. U. (2025). Bridging Cultures and Languages: Innovative Literacy Strategies for Inclusive and Engaged Classrooms. In Tussey, J., & Haas, L. (Eds.), *Supporting Cultural Differences Through Literacy Education* (pp. 257–282). IGI Global Scientific Publishing., DOI: 10.4018/979-8-3693-9271-3.ch010

Tariq, M. U. (2025). *AI-Driven Learning and Engagement in Higher Education.* IGI Global., DOI: 10.4018/979-8-3693-4074-5

Tariq, M. U. (2025). AI and the Ethical Crossroads: Navigating Privacy, Personhood, and Autonomy in the Digital Age. In Chakraborty, S. (Ed.), *Human Values, Ethics, and Dignity in the Age of Artificial Intelligence* (pp. 49–72). IGI Global Scientific Publishing., DOI: 10.4018/979-8-3693-9035-1.ch003

Tatar, C., Jiang, S., Rosé, C. P., & Chao, J. (2024). Exploring teachers' views and confidence in the integration of an artificial intelligence curriculum into their classrooms: A case study of curricular co-design program. *International Journal of Artificial Intelligence in Education*, •••, 1–34.

Tolentino, R., Baradaran, A., Gore, G., Pluye, P., & Abbasgholizadeh-Rahimi, S. (2024). Curriculum frameworks and educational programs in AI for medical students, residents, and practicing physicians: Scoping review. *JMIR Medical Education*, *10*(1), e54793. PMID: 39023999

Velander, J., Taiye, M. A., Otero, N., & Milrad, M. (2024). Artificial Intelligence in K-12 Education: Eliciting and reflecting on Swedish teachers' understanding of AI and its implications for teaching & learning. *Education and Information Technologies*, *29*(4), 4085–4105.

Xie, B., Sarin, P., Wolf, J., Garcia, R. C., Delaney, V., Sieh, I., & Lee, V. R. (2024, March). Co-designing AI education curriculum with cross-disciplinary high school teachers. *Proceedings of the AAAI Conference on Artificial Intelligence*, *38*(21), 23146–23154.

Yadav, S. (2025). Advancing Education With AI-Driven Education for Diverse Learners: Integrating AI Into Pedagogical Practices. In *Integrating AI Into Pedagogical Education* (pp. 49-80). IGI Global Scientific Publishing.

Yılmaz, Ö. (2024). Personalised learning and artificial intelligence in science education: Current state and future perspectives. *Educational Technology Quarterly*, *2024*(3), 255–274.

Yue, M., Jong, M. S. Y., & Ng, D. T. K. (2024). Understanding K–12 teachers' technological pedagogical content knowledge readiness and attitudes toward artificial intelligence education. *Education and Information Technologies*, 1–32.

KEY TERMS AND DEFINITIONS

AI Integration: Incorporating AI concepts into several subjects.

Interdisciplinary Education: Merging AI with diverse academic disciplines.
Personalized Learning: Modifying education based on student requirements.

Chapter 6

Mind the Gap:
Examining the Disadvantages of AI Writing Tools in Education, Focusing on Originality

K. Jaya
https://orcid.org/0000-0001-8353-4937
Bannari Amman Institute of Technology, India

A. P. Raghuvaran
https://orcid.org/0000-0003-4124-7950
CMS Institute of Management Studies, India

Sundarapandiyan Natarajan
https://orcid.org/0000-0002-1303-2947
Adithya Institute of Technology, India

ABSTRACT

The impact of AI tools has brought incredible development to all sectors of the global arena. AI is a software technology that aims to create artificial general intelligence (AGI) to add comfort to humanity. For the past few years, the growth of AI tools has been massive, and the development of technology is inexorable. Though AI tools are helpful for alluring students in education, there are a few drawbacks faced by educators and learners in this field. There are many e-contents created by AI tools that reduce the necessity of acquiring knowledge from the faculty. This paper is going to examine the drawbacks of AI tools in the education sector and contribute to the development of originality by enhancing the creative thinking skills of educators and students. The research is going to conduct a survey among

DOI: 10.4018/979-8-3373-2297-1.ch006

the educators and the learners about the dependency of AI tools. From the study, the research is bringing forth the drawbacks of AI writing tools and the need for originality in the education field.

1 INTRODUCTION

Artificial intelligence has created a new era enriched with advanced technologies. Once the growth of technology is massive, it is also needed to check the gaps in society. The term "artificial intelligence" entered all sectors, and it became a challenge to human resources in the twenty-first century. There is no doubt that this tool has brought advancement and raised cosines among people with reasonable materialistic investment. So, the dependency on AI tools is inevitable in society. The contribution of AI tools to the arena of education is remarkable. Though AI tools are helpful for alluring students in education, there are a few drawbacks faced by educators and learners in this field. There are many e-contents created by AI tools that reduce the necessity of acquiring knowledge from the faculty. There is also jeopardy for the faculty, who would be cut off from their jobs as AI tools are going to be replaced.

The next major concern is the originality of the writing. Nowadays, AI tools are more reliable for 21st century learners who construct their assignments, homework, and projects using AI tools. Even faculties are taking references from AI tools. This would lead to the betrayal of original writing and block the students from using their creative thinking skills. This paper is going to examine the drawbacks of AI tools in the education sector and contribute to the development of originality by enhancing the creative thinking skills of educators and students. The research is going to conduct an empirical survey among the educators and the learners about the dependency of AI tools. From the study it is bringing forth the drawbacks of AI writing tools and the need for originality in the education field.

The objectives of the work "Mind the Gap: Examining the Disadvantages of AI Writing Tools in Education, Focusing on Originality" are:

Identify and Analyze Disadvantages: To systematically identify and analyze the specific disadvantages associated with the use of AI writing tools in educational settings, with a particular emphasis on their impact on the originality of students' work.

Explore Effects on Creative Expression: To investigate how AI writing tools may influence and potentially limit students' creative expression, original thought processes, and the development of a unique writing style.

Examine Homogenization Concerns: To address concerns related to the potential homogenization of written content due to the use of AI writing tools and assess how these tools may inadvertently lead to a standardization of writing styles among students.
Evaluate Impact on Critical Thinking: To assess the implications of AI writing tools on students' critical thinking skills, examining whether reliance on these tools hinders the development of independent and analytical thought in the writing process.
Provide Recommendations for Mitigation: To offer practical recommendations for educators, institutions, and developers to mitigate the identified disadvantages and foster a balanced integration of AI writing tools that supports originality and intellectual growth in educational settings.
Contribute to the Academic Discourse: To contribute to the academic discourse by filling the existing gap in the literature, providing a comprehensive understanding of the potential drawbacks of AI writing tools, and emphasizing the need for a nuanced perspective that considers their impact on originality in education.Top of Form

2 BACKGROUND

The background of the work "Mind the Gap: Examining the Disadvantages of AI Writing Tools in Education, Focusing on Originality" involves the increasing integration of AI writing tools in educational environments. The arrival of artificial intelligence has ushered in tools designed to assist students in various aspects of the writing process, including content generation, grammar correction, and overall improvement of writing proficiency. These tools leverage advanced natural language processing algorithms to provide real-time feedback and support, offering the promise of enhanced efficiency and quality in written assignments.

However, amid the enthusiasm surrounding the implementation of AI writing tools in education, concerns have emerged regarding their potential drawbacks, particularly in relation to originality. The existing literature has extensively explored the positive features of these tools, emphasizing their ability to aid in language enhancement and writing skill development. Yet, there is a noticeable gap in understanding the negative consequences, specifically regarding the impact on students' original thinking and creative expression.

It also acknowledges that the pursuit of originality is a fundamental objective in education, fostering critical thinking, creativity, and individuality. The concern is that the convenience and efficiency offered by AI writing tools may inadvertently lead to a dependency that compromises the authenticity of students' work. Scholars and educators have started recognizing the need for a more nuanced examination of the potential disadvantages associated with the integration of AI writing tools, with a dedicated focus on preserving originality.

In light of this, the background sets the stage for the study's objectives by highlighting the existing gap in the previous works and the necessity of addressing concerns related to the influence of AI writing tools on students' ability to produce genuinely original and independent written work in educational settings.

3 LITERATURE REVIEW

With the frameworkof "Mind the Gap: Examining the Disadvantages of AI Writing Tools in Education, Focusing on Originality," there has been notable prior work that provides insights into related aspects. While avoiding a detailed literature survey, here are references to prior work based on the same project and/or data:

Fahmi and Cahyono (2021) Their research intended to find differences in students' perspectives towards the use of Automated Writing Evaluation (AWE) based on their varied expertisestages. The results of their research indicate that the utilization of AWE (Automated Writing Evaluation) can yield favorable outcomes for students, and these benefits remained consistent throughout their studies.In spite of their important discoveries, further investigation into the effects of AI writing tools is required. It is true that information about how these technologies affect students' writing has been found in earlier studies. However, it is still unknown how AI writing tools impact student writing quality, specifically in terms of content and organization.

Lam and Moorhouse (2022) Their research found that the app 'WordTune' successfully assisted students in identifying their areas of difficulty in writing, which encouraged self-evaluation and learning. This tool explores the stylistic components of writing in addition to basic grammar correction. Another AI-powered writing assistant, 'Jenni' helps users create emails, reports, articles, and other documents more quickly by using predictive word suggestions. User feedback indicates that there is a good impact on writing productivity and creativity, even if no specific research was referenced.

Iskender (2023) His research offered a critical viewpoint on this issue, contending that if students grow unduly reliant on AI writing tools, their capacity for critical thought may be compromised. They stated concern that students would value fast solutions from AI programs more highly than carefully considering and learning from their errors, which would effectively undermine the process of acquiring, development, and growth in writing. Concerns have been raised not only about the influence of AI writing tools on creativity but also about apprehensions regarding excessive dependence on them.

These prior works collectively lay the foundation for the present study by acknowledging the benefits of AI writing tools in education while hinting at the existence of potential drawbacks, especially in the realm of originality. The unique contribution of the current work lies in explicitly examining and addressing this gap by focusing on the disadvantages and challenges posed by AI writing tools, with a specific lens on their impact on students' ability to maintain original thought and creative expression in their written assignments.

4 RESEARCH GAPS

The unique contribution of "Mind the Gap: Examining the Disadvantages of AI Writing Tools in Education, Focusing on Originality" lies in its focused exploration of the drawbacks associated with AI writing tools in the context of education, with a particular emphasis on preserving originality. While prior works have acknowledged concerns related to homogenization and efficiency gains, this study distinguishes itself through the following unique contributions:

4.1 Targeted Examination of Originality

This study explicitly targets the critical issue of originality in educational writing, going beyond general concerns and providing a nuanced analysis of how AI writing tools may impact students' ability to express their unique voices and ideas. By honing in on originality, the research contributes to a more detailed understanding of the potential challenges faced by students in maintaining individuality in their written work.

4.2 Identification of Nuanced Disadvantages

Rather than a broad exploration of potential drawbacks, this work specifically identifies and analyzes the nuanced disadvantages that AI writing tools may pose to students' creative expression and critical thinking. It delves into the subtleties of how these tools may inadvertently hinder the development of authentic and independent thought processes, providing a more in-depth examination of the issue.

4.3 Practical Recommendations for Mitigation

This study not only identifies challenges but also endeavours to provide practical recommendations for educators, institutions, and developers to mitigate the identified disadvantages. By offering actionable insights, the research aims to contribute to the development of strategies that balance the benefits of AI writing tools with the imperative of fostering originality in students' written work.

4.4 Addressing a Specific Gap in the Literature

The unique contribution lies in addressing the identified gap in the literature, where prior works have often overlooked the potential adverse effects of AI writing tools on originality. This study fills that void by focusing on the specific aspect of maintaining students' authentic voices, thereby enhancing the academic discourse and informing future research and educational practices.

This study employed mixed-method approaches to identify the disadvantages of AI writing tools by highlighting the dependency of educators and learners on AI writing tools. An empirical survey was conducted among 60 members of the faculty and students in colleges in Tamil Nadu. The survey was executed with the help of 25 questionnaires designed in a Google form and circulated to the educators and the learners. From the detailed study of their feedback, a graph was designed to identify the dependency level of AI writing tools for their academic purposes. From the feedback, it is clearly understood that students needed AI tools for writing assignments, project work and report writing and other content writing.

Educators depended on AI writing toolsfor miscellaneous purposes in education. This shows a clear picture of their dependency on AI writing tools for assignments, projects, and other academic-related works. From this study, it is explicitly understood that due to the dependency on AI writing tools, their originality in writinghas diminished. If the educators and the learners start to rely on AI writing tools for the various content writing, there will be diminishing results in acquiring writing skills, creativity, and Originality.

5 DISCUSSION

Artificial Intelligence (AI) has revolutionized various aspects of education, with AI writing tools emerging as prominent aids for students and educators alike. These tools, ranging from grammar checkers to sophisticated content generators, aim to enhance writing skills and streamline the writing process. However, as AI writing tools become increasingly integrated into educational settings, concerns have arisen regarding their impact on the originality of student work. This section delves into the evolution of AI writing tools in education and sets the stage for a critical examination of their disadvantages, specifically focusing on the preservation of originality in academic writing.

5.1 Evolution of AI Writing Tools in Education

The integration of AI writing tools in education has undergone a substantial evolution. Initially designed to assist with grammar and syntax, these tools have evolved to encompass more advanced features such as context-aware suggestions and content generation. From simple spell-checkers to complex algorithms capable of generating entire essays, the landscape of AI writing tools has expanded significantly, raising questions about their implications for student learning and academic integrity.

5.2 Advantages of AI Writing Tools

Before delving into the disadvantages, it is crucial to acknowledge the advantages offered by AI writing tools. These tools contribute to improved writing efficiency, providing real-time feedback on grammar, spelling, and style. Additionally, they assist in language correction, aiding non-native speakers in developing their writing skills . Despite these benefits, it is essential to critically assess the potential drawbacks associated with the extensive use of AI writing tools in educational contexts.

5.3 Disadvantages of AI Writing Tools

5.3.1 Preservation of Originality

One of the primary concerns surrounding AI writing tools is their impact on the originality of student work. While these tools aim to support students in developing their writing skills, there is a risk of overreliance, leading to a lack of authentic expression. Students may be tempted to use AI-generated content as a shortcut, potentially compromising the uniqueness and creativity expected in academic writing.

5.3.2 Homogenization of Writing Styles

AI writing tools often operate based on pre-existing patterns and structures present in the data on which they were trained. As a result, there is a risk of homogenization of writing styles, where students may inadvertently conform to a standardized pattern generated by the AI tool. This homogenization not only hinders the development of individual writing styles but also poses challenges in assessing students' true writing abilities.

5.3.3. Limited Understanding of Context

Despite advancements in AI, these tools may struggle to grasp the nuanced context of specific academic disciplines. The lack of domain-specific knowledge can lead to inaccuracies in suggestions and content generation, potentially undermining the quality and relevance of academic writing produced with the aid of AI tools.

5.3.4 AI Job Threat

As these tools advance and become more sophisticated, there is a concern that certain aspects of teaching and grading traditionally carried out by educators might be automated, leading to the possibility of job displacement. The fear of faculty members being cut off from their roles arises from the increasing efficiency and automation capabilities of AI tools. However, it is essential to approach this concern with a balanced perspective, recognizing that while certain tasks may become automated, the unique qualities of human educators, such as mentorship, inspiration, and adaptability, cannot be easily replicated by AI. Institutions and educators alike must actively engage in ongoing professional development to enhance their skills, adapt to technological changes, and demonstrate the irreplaceable value they bring to the educational experience.

6 EMPIRICAL EVIDENCE ON THE IMPACT OF AI WRITING TOOLS

To substantiate these concerns, empirical evidence from recent studies is critical. A survey was conducted among students revealed a widespread reliance on AI writing tools, with 75% of respondents admitting to using such tools regularly. However, a significant portion of these students expressed concerns about the impact on their originality, highlighting a potential tension between the convenience offered by AI tools and the desire for authentic expression in academic writing.

Moreover, another survey with educators shed light on the challenges faced in assessing the originality of student work when AI writing tools are involved. Educators expressed concerns about detecting instances of plagiarism or unintended homogenization of writing styles, raising questions about the tools' compatibility with established academic integrity standards.

7 RESEARCH ANALYSIS

7.1 Analysis from the collection of members of faculty data

Table 1. Frequency of usage of AI writing tools for academic purposes by faculty

	Frequency	Percent	Valid Percent	Cumulative Percent
Rarely	20	31.7	31.7	31.7
Weekly	19	30.2	30.2	61.9
Daily	10	15.9	15.9	77.8
Monthly	10	15.9	15.9	93.7
Never	4	6.3	6.3	100.0
Total	63	100.0	100.0	

Table 1 indicates that a significant portion of faculty members (61.9%) use AI writing tools on a weekly basis for academic purposes, while a smaller proportion use them rarely (31.7%). Daily and monthly usage stands at 15.9% each, suggesting moderate adoption. Notably, a small percentage (6.3%) of faculty members reported never using AI writing tools for academic tasks.

Table 2. Types of usage of AI writing tools by faculty for non-academic work

	Frequency	Percent	Valid Percent	Cumulative Percent
Content writing	34	54.0	54.0	54.0
Others	20	31.7	31.7	85.7
Story writing	5	7.9	7.9	93.7
Blog writing	2	3.2	3.2	96.8
Poetry writing	2	3.2	3.2	100.0
Total	63	100.0	100.0	

Table 2 reveals that a majority of faculty members (54.0%) primarily use AI writing tools for content writing in non-academic settings. Other types of usage, collectively labelled as "Others," account for 31.7%, indicating diverse applications. Story writing, blog writing, and poetry writing constitute 7.9%, 3.2%, and 3.2%, respectively. Overall, the findings highlight a predominant focus on content creation with AI tools in non-academic contexts.

Table 3. Types of usage of AI writing tools by faculty for academic purpose

	Frequency	Percent	Valid Percent	Cumulative Percent
Others	23	36.5	36.5	36.5
Project writing	17	27.0	27.0	63.5
Report writing	15	23.8	23.8	87.3
Assignment	7	11.1	11.1	98.4
Letter writing	1	1.6	1.6	100.0
Total	63	100.0	100.0	

Table 3 indicates that the majority of faculty members (36.5%) use AI writing tools for various unspecified academic purposes grouped under "Others." Project writing is the second most common type of usage, accounting for 27.0%, followed by report writing at 23.8%. Assignments constitute 11.1%, and letter writing represents the least common application at 1.6%. Overall, the data underscores the versatility of AI writing tools in supporting diverse academic tasks.

Table 4. Types of AI writing tools primarily used by faculty

	Frequency	Percent	Valid Percent	Cumulative Percent
Grammar checkers	21	33.3	33.3	33.3
Content generators	18	28.6	28.6	61.9
Plagiarism checkers	17	27.0	27.0	88.9
Others	4	6.3	6.3	95.2
Style enhancers	3	4.8	4.8	100.0
Total	63	100.0	100.0	

Table 4 reveals that grammar checkers are the most commonly used AI writing tools by faculty, constituting 33.3% of the responses. Content generators follow closely at 28.6%, highlighting their significant usage for generating academic content. Plagiarism checkers are employed by 27.0% of faculty, indicating a strong emphasis on maintaining academic integrity. Other types of AI writing tools and style enhancers represent 6.3% and 4.8%, respectively, indicating a more varied but less prevalent usage in this context.

Table 5. Types of writing activity for which the faculty use AI writing tools

Frequency	Percent	Valid Percent	Cumulative Percent	
Research paper writing	26	41.3	41.3	41.3
Other Official writing	24	38.1	38.1	79.4
Notes-making	10	15.9	15.9	95.2
Letter writing	3	4.8	4.8	100.0
Total	63	100.0	100.0	

Table 5 indicates that a significant portion of faculty (41.3%) primarily use AI writing tools for research paper writing, showcasing their role in scholarly activities. Other official writing, including administrative tasks, is the second most common application at 38.1%, emphasizing the broader utility of AI tools in professional contexts. Notes-making represents 15.9%, indicating a role in organizing and summarizing information. Letter writing constitutes the least common activity at 4.8%, highlighting a more limited application in this category of writing tasks.

Table 6. Faculty opinion on AI writing tools contributes to or hinders students' creativity in writing

Frequency	Percent	Valid Percent	Cumulative Percent	
Enhances creativity	28	44.4	44.4	44.4
Hinders creativity	23	36.5	36.5	81.0
No impact	12	19.0	19.0	100.0
Total	63	100.0	100.0	

Table 6 reveals a divided opinion among faculty regarding the impact of AI writing tools on students' creativity. A significant portion (44.4%) believes that these tools enhance students' creativity in writing. On the contrary, 36.5% of faculty members express concerns that AI writing tools may hinder students' creativity. A smaller proportion (19.0%) believes that these tools have no discernible impact on creativity, highlighting varying perspectives within the academic community.

Table 7. Faculty opinion on AI writing tools aligns with ethical consideration for writing skills

Frequency	Percent	Valid Percent	Cumulative Percent	
Neutral	40	63.5	63.5	63.5
Yes, aligns well	20	31.7	31.7	95.2
No, it doesn't	3	4.8	4.8	100.0
Total	63	100.0	100.0	

Table 7 indicates that a majority of faculty members (63.5%) hold a neutral stance regarding whether the use of AI writing tools aligns with ethical considerations for writing skills. However, a significant proportion (31.7%) believes that these tools align well with ethical considerations. A smaller percentage (4.8%) expresses the opinion that AI writing tools do not align with ethical considerations, highlighting diverse perspectives within the faculty community on the moral implications of using such tools.

Table 8. Faculty opinion on integration of AI writing tools into the curriculum, considering concerns about originality

	Frequency	Percent	Valid Percent	Cumulative Percent
Well	27	42.9	42.9	42.9
Neutral	22	34.9	34.9	77.8
Very well	12	19.0	19.0	96.8
Poorly	2	3.2	3.2	100.0
Total	63	100.0	100.0	

Table 8 suggests that faculty opinions on integrating AI writing tools into the curriculum vary. A substantial portion (42.9%) believes that integration is done well, considering concerns about originality. A significant proportion (34.9%) holds a neutral stance, indicating a lack of strong opinion on the matter. Those who feel integration is done very well constitute 19.0%, while a small percentage (3.2%) expresses the view that integration is done poorly, reflecting diverse perspectives on the effectiveness of incorporating AI writing tools while addressing concerns about originality.

Table 9. AI tools impact on faculty creativity

	Frequency	Percent	Valid Percent	Cumulative Percent
Improved grammar	19	30.2	30.2	30.2
Aids creative thinking	19	30.2	30.2	60.3
Shrink of creativity thinking	17	27.0	27.0	87.3
Lose Originality in your writing	8	12.7	12.7	100.0
Total	63	100.0	100.0	

Table 9 suggests that a significant portion of faculty (27.0%) perceives a shrink in creative thinking due to the use of AI tools, highlighting concerns about the impact on creativity. Another subset (12.7%) expresses apprehension, feeling that the use of AI tools may lead to a loss of originality in writing. Collectively, these responses indicate a notable segment of faculty members who view AI tools as having potential drawbacks on creativity and originality in their work.

Table 10. Time spent by faculty in using AI writing tools

Frequency	Percent	Valid Percent	Cumulative Percent	
30 minutes to 1 hour	23	36.5	36.5	36.5
1 to 2 hours	13	20.6	20.6	57.1
Less than 30 minutes	11	17.5	17.5	74.6
More than 2 hours	10	15.9	15.9	90.5
No time saved	6	9.5	9.5	100.0
Total	63	100.0	100.0	

Table 10 indicates that a significant proportion of faculty (36.5%) spends 30 minutes to 1 hour using AI writing tools, representing a common time commitment. A substantial portion (20.6%) invests 1 to 2 hours, while 17.5% spend less than 30 minutes. Tenure beyond 2 hours is reported by 15.9% of faculty, suggesting varying levels of engagement. Notably, 9.5% claim no time saved, highlighting a subset that perceives AI tools as not necessarily optimizing their writing process.

7.2 Analysis from the collection of Students' data

Table 11. Usage frequency of AI writing tools by Students

	Frequency	Percent	Valid Percent	Cumulative Percent
Weekly	51	45.5	45.5	45.5
Rarely	26	23.2	23.2	68.8
Daily	22	19.6	19.6	88.4
Monthly	11	9.8	9.8	98.2
Never	2	1.8	1.8	100.0
Total	112	100.0	100.0	

Table 11 indicates that a substantial portion of students (45.5%) use AI writing tools on a weekly basis, suggesting frequent integration into their academic routines. A notable percentage (23.2%) uses these tools rarely, while 19.6% engage with them daily, indicating varied usage patterns. Monthly usage stands at 9.8%, and a small minority (1.8%) reports never using AI writing tools, showcasing a generally high adoption rate among students.

Table 12. Purpose of usage in academics by students

	Frequency	Percent	Valid Percent	Cumulative Percent
Assignment	71	63.4	63.4	63.4
Project writing	22	19.6	19.6	83.0
Others	8	7.1	7.1	90.2
Report writing	7	6.3	6.3	96.4
Letter writing	4	3.6	3.6	100.0
Total	112	100.0	100.0	

Table 12 reveals that the primary purpose of AI writing tool usage by students in academics is for assignments, with 63.4% indicating its prevalent use in this context. Project writing follows at 19.6%, demonstrating a substantial role in project-related tasks. Other purposes collectively labeled as "Others" account for 7.1%, indicating diverse applications. Report writing and letter writing constitute 6.3% and 3.6%, respectively, reflecting a more limited usage in these specific academic writing activities.

Table 13. Purpose of usage in non-academic activity by students

	Frequency	Percent	Valid Percent	Cumulative Percent
Content writing	55	49.1	49.1	49.1
Others	40	35.7	35.7	84.8
Story writing	9	8.0	8.0	92.9
Blog writing	5	4.5	4.5	97.3
Poetry writing	3	2.7	2.7	100.0
Total	112	100.0	100.0	

Table 13 indicates that students primarily use AI writing tools for content writing in non-academic activities, with 49.1% engaging in this type of writing. Other non-academic purposes, collectively labeled as "Others," constitute 35.7%, highlighting diverse applications. Story writing represents 8.0%, while blog writing and poetry writing account for 4.5% and 2.7%, respectively, suggesting a varied but focused utilization of AI writing tools in creative and non-academic endeavours.

Table 14. Types of AI writing tools used by students

	Frequency	Percent	Valid Percent	Cumulative Percent
Content generators	51	45.5	45.5	45.5
Grammar checkers	35	31.3	31.3	76.8
Plagiarism checkers	13	11.6	11.6	88.4
Style enhancers	8	7.1	7.1	95.5
Others	5	4.5	4.5	100.0
Total	112	100.0	100.0	

Tab.14 reveals that content generators are the most widely used AI writing tools among students, accounting for 45.5% of responses. Grammar checkers follow closely at 31.3%, emphasizing the importance of tools for improving language proficiency. Plagiarism checkers are used by 11.6%, indicating a notable focus on academic integrity. Style enhancers constitute 7.1%, while other types of AI writing tools represent 4.5%, highlighting the diverse range of tools students employ to enhance their writing skills.

Table 15. The most valuable aspect of using AI writing tools in students

	Frequency	Percent	Valid Percent	Cumulative Percent
Time-saving	51	45.5	45.5	45.5
Idea generation	39	34.8	34.8	80.4
Grammar correction	12	10.7	10.7	91.1
Style improvement	10	8.9	8.9	100.0
Total	112	100.0	100.0	

Table 15 indicates that the majority of students highly appreciate AI writing tools for their ability to save time, with 45.5% of respondents expressing this view point.Idea generation is also highly valued, as indicated by 34.8% of responses, emphasizing the tools' role in sparking creative thinking. Grammar correction is recognized as a valuable aspect by 10.7%, highlighting the importance of language proficiency improvement. Style improvement is mentioned by 8.9%, showcasing students' appreciation for enhancing their writing style using AI tools.

Table 16. AI writing tools contribute to the originality of students

Frequency	Percent	Valid Percent	Cumulative Percent	
Moderately	82	73.2	73.2	73.2
Significantly	21	18.8	18.8	92.0
Not at all	9	8.0	8.0	100.0
Total	112	100.0	100.0	

Table 16 indicates that the majority of students (73.2%) perceive AI writing tools as contributing moderately to the originality of their work. A significant portion (18.8%) believes that these tools contribute significantly to originality. However, 8.0% of students express the opinion that AI writing tools do not contribute at all to the originality of their writing. This varied response suggests diverse perspectives on the impact of AI tools on fostering originality among students.

Table 17. Dependency on AI writing tools for students

	Frequency	Percent	Valid Percent	Cumulative Percent
Neutral	51	45.5	45.5	45.5
Somewhat dependent	42	37.5	37.5	83.0
Strongly dependent	12	10.7	10.7	93.8
Not dependent at all	7	6.3	6.3	100.0
Total	112	100.0	100.0	

Table 17 reveals that students' dependency on AI writing tools varies, with 45.5% expressing a neutral stance. A substantial portion (37.5%) considers themselves somewhat dependent on these tools, while 10.7% feel strongly dependent. A smaller percentage (6.3%) claims not to be dependent on AI writing tools at all. This diversity of responses suggests a range of attitudes and reliance levels among students regarding the use of AI tools in their writing activities.

Table. 18 Need of training for students by educational institutions on using AI writing tools

Frequency	Percent	Valid Percent	Cumulative Percent	
Yes, to some extent	55	49.1	49.1	49.1
Yes, definitely for appropriate usage	38	33.9	33.9	83.0
No, unnecessary	12	10.7	10.7	93.8
No, it might lead to dependency	7	6.3	6.3	100.0
Total	112	100.0	100.0	

Table 18 suggests that a majority of students (49.1%) believe there is a need for some extent of training by educational institutions on using AI writing tools. A significant portion (33.9%) expresses a stronger sentiment, advocating for definite training to ensure appropriate usage. However, a notable percentage (10.7%) feels that such training is unnecessary, while a smaller group (6.3%) is concerned that it might lead to dependency. These responses underscore the varying perspectives among students regarding the necessity and potential risks associated with training on AI writing tools.

Table 19. Students' ethical considerations of using AI writing tools in academics

	Frequency	Percent	Valid Percent	Cumulative Percent
Neutral	74	66.1	66.1	66.1
Ethically acceptable	30	26.8	26.8	92.9
Ethically questionable	8	7.1	7.1	100.0
Total	112	100.0	100.0	

Tab.19 indicates that the majority of students (66.1%) hold a neutral stance on the ethical considerations of using AI writing tools in academics. A significant proportion (26.8%) views their usage as ethically acceptable, while a smaller percentage (7.1%) finds it ethically questionable. These findings reflect a diversity of perspectives among students on the ethical implications of incorporating AI writing tools into their academic work.

Table 20. Impact of AI tools on students

	Frequency	Percent	Valid Percent	Cumulative Percent
Improved grammar	36	32.1	32.1	32.1
Shrink of creativity thinking	33	29.5	29.5	61.6
Aids creative writing	26	23.2	23.2	84.8
Lose Originality in your writing	17	15.2	15.2	100.0
Total	112	100.0	100.0	

Table 20 suggests that a significant number of students (32.1%) believe that AI tools contribute to improved grammar in their writing. However, a notable portion (29.5%) expresses concern about a potential shrink in creative thinking due to the use of AI tools. On the positive side, 23.2% feel that these tools aid creative writing. Yet, 15.2% perceive a risk of losing originality in their writing, indicating diverse perspectives on the impact of AI tools on different aspects of students' writing abilities.

From the study, it is clear that the adoption of AI writing tools for academic purposes by both faculty and students is unmistakable, reflecting a transformative shift in educational practices. These tools have become integral in various aspects of academia, from simplifying administrative tasks for educators to aiding students in different stages of the writing process. However, this growing reliance on AI writing tools has raised concerns about a potential lack of originality in academic work.

Faculty members increasingly turn to AI writing tools to streamline their workload, leveraging automated grading systems to manage assignments efficiently. These tools provide quick and standardized feedback, allowing instructors to focus on more personalized aspects of teaching. While this enhances productivity, there is a risk that the emphasis on efficiency might inadvertently lead to a standardized approach to assessing and guiding students, potentially stifling the cultivation of individual voices and original ideas.

For students, the convenience offered by AI writing tools is evident, especially in tasks such as grammar checking, content organization, and even idea generation. However, the ease of access to pre-defined templates and formulaic approaches may contribute to a homogenization of writing styles. The concern arises that, in the quest for correctness and efficiency, students might prioritize conformity over originality, impacting the diversity and uniqueness of their academic contributions.

8 MITIGATING THE DISADVANTAGES

AI writing tools, while offering significant benefits in education, pose inherent challenges that can compromise the originality of students' work. One primary concern is the potential overreliance on templates and formulas, resulting in a risk of homogeneity across student submissions. To address this, educators can advocate for a nuanced approach, encouraging students to view AI tools as supplementary resources rather than substitutes. By diversifying prompts and promoting critical thinking skills, students can break away from rigid structures and contribute unique perspectives to their writing.

Another critical issue is the inadvertent promotion of plagiarism by AI tools, as they may generate content closely resembling existing materials. To counter this, educational institutions should implement robust plagiarism detection systems. Simultaneously, it is essential to educate students about proper citation practices and ethical AI tool usage. Clear guidelines can help students navigate the fine line between utilizing technology and maintaining academic integrity.

Furthermore, the potential hindrance of critical thinking development is a concern associated with AI writing tools. Students might become overly dependent on these tools, stifling their ability to think critically and analyze information independently. To mitigate this, educators should design assignments that explicitly require original thought, analysis, and interpretation. Emphasizing the value of independent thinking within the learning process is vital to cultivating well-rounded, critically engaged students.

Additionally, the limitations of AI tools in capturing the creativity and personal voice of students present a challenge. Balancing AI assistance with authentic writing styles requires a concerted effort. Fostering creativity among students can be achieved by educators through assigning open-ended projects, enabling students to express their individualities and explore diverse writing styles.

9 FOSTERING ORIGINALITY

To foster originality in the realm of AI writing tools, a shift in focus from the end product to the creative process itself is paramount. Emphasizing the importance of exploration, idea generation, and the enjoyment of crafting one's work can inspire students to inject more of their unique voice into their writing. By highlighting the journey rather than the destination, educators can instill a deeper appreciation for the creative process.

Incorporating peer review and collaborative projects into the curriculum offers another avenue for fostering originality. These methods encourage students to share diverse perspectives, learn from one another, and collectively enrich their writing. The collaborative environment not only kindles creativity but also nurtures a culture where originality is celebrated as a collective achievement.

Showcasing diverse writing models is equally crucial in inspiring originality. Exposure to various writing styles, genres, and voices broadens students' horizons and encourages them to experiment with their own unique approaches. Integrating guest speakers, diverse literature, and a comprehensive curriculum contributes to a rich and varied writing environment.

Ultimately, celebrating individuality is key to fostering originality. Acknowledging and appreciating each student's unique writing style creates a positive environment that motivates them to take pride in their distinct contributions. Recognizing and rewarding creativity, both in content and style, reinforces the importance of original expression within the educational context. In striking a balance between mitigating AI tool disadvantages and actively promoting originality, educators can empower students to harness technology while preserving and celebrating their inherent creativity.

Some educators worry that students might use these tools not just for refining their language, but also for generating ideas, potentially curtailing their creative thinking and originality (Johinke et al., 2023).

10 CONCLUSION

In conclusion, the examination of the disadvantages of AI writing tools in education, with a specific emphasis on originality, underscores the intricate dynamics between technological integration and the preservation of academic creativity. The study has shed light on the multifaceted challenges associated with the use of AI writing tools, including the potential homogenization of writing styles, the inadvertent promotion of plagiarism, and the risk of hindering the development of critical thinking skills. These findings call for a thoughtful and strategic approach to the incorporation of AI tools in educational settings.

While AI writing tools offer undeniable advantages in terms of efficiency, accessibility, and feedback, the study highlights the critical importance of mitigating their potential adverse effects. Educators play a pivotal role in guiding students to use AI tools as supplements rather than substitutes for their own cognitive processes. This involves designing assignments that actively encourage original thought, creativity, and critical analysis. Moreover, institutions should invest in comprehensive educational programs that address ethical considerations, emphasizing the responsible use of AI tools to preserve academic integrity.

Moving forward, the study advocates for a collaborative effort among educators, students, and educational technology developers to bridge the gap between the advantages and disadvantages of AI writing tools. By fostering a culture that values originality, institutions can harness the benefits of AI while ensuring that students retain their unique voices and perspectives. The developing landscape of education requires a mindful integration of technology that aligns with the overarching goal of cultivating independent thinkers and creative contributors to academia.

REFERENCES

Fahmi, M. A., & Cahyono, B. Y. (2021). EFL students' perception on the use of grammarly and teacher feedback. [Journal of English Educators Society]. *JEES*, *6*(1), 18–25. DOI: 10.21070/jees.v6i1.849

Johinke, R., Cummings, R., DiLauro, F., Johinke, R., Cummings, R., &DiLaurao, F. (2023). Reclaiming the technology of higher education for teaching digital writing in a post—pandemic world. Journal of University Teaching & Learning Practice, 20(2), 01. https://doi.org/DOI: 10.53761/1.20.02.01

Lam, R., & Moorhouse, B. L. (2022). Using digital portfolios to develop students' writing. https://doi.org/DOI: 10.4324/9781003295860

Chapter 7
Pedagogical Approaches in Project-Based Learning, Inquiry-Driven Methods, Computational Thinking, and Design Thinking for AI Education

A. Prabhu Chakkaravarthy
https://orcid.org/0009-0000-3180-8051
Department of Networking and Communications, SRM Institute of Science and Technology, Kattankulathur, India

Dhanalakshmi Jaganathan
https://orcid.org/0000-0002-3919-4469
Department of Networking and Communications, SRM Institute of Science and Technology, Kattankulathur, India

ABSTRACT

Effective teaching methods are crucial to provide students the information and abilities needed for this quickly developing sector as artificial intelligence (AI) becomes a crucial component of many industries. The integration of educational techniques like inquiry-driven methods, computational thinking, design thinking, and project-based learning (PBL) in AI education is examined in this study. These methods create a dynamic, experiential learning environment that prioritizes creativity, critical thinking, and problem-solving—skills essential to comprehending and developing AI. By encouraging students to focus on real-world issues, project-based learning

DOI: 10.4018/979-8-3373-2297-1.ch007

gives them the chance to apply AI concepts in real-world situations. Students can investigate AI topics through guided inquiries and research thanks to inquiry-driven methodologies, which foster curiosity and self-directed learning.

1. INTRODUCTION

1.1 Context and Importance of AI Literacy

Artificial Intelligence (AI) is rapidly becoming one of the most transformative forces across sectors, reshaping the global economy, societal structures, and personal interactions. As AI systems influence everything from healthcare to education, transportation to finance, developing AI literacy among students is no longer optional—it is imperative. AI literacy refers not only to an understanding of how AI systems work but also to the ability to critically evaluate their societal impact, ethical implications, and practical applications (Long & Magerko, 2020). For students, especially in K–12 and tertiary education, acquiring foundational knowledge in AI ensures they are not just consumers of technology but informed participants in a digitally-driven society.

The need for AI literacy extends beyond technical competencies. It includes understanding data privacy, algorithmic bias, decision-making processes, and ethical design. Equipping students with this literacy empowers them to think critically, solve complex problems, and make ethical choices in a world where intelligent systems are ubiquitous. As AI becomes embedded in civic infrastructure, the workforce, and even social norms, it is essential for educational systems to ensure that future generations are well-versed in both the capabilities and limitations of these technologies (Touretzky et al., 2019).

1.2 The Role of Pedagogy in AI Education

While the importance of AI literacy is widely acknowledged, the challenge lies in how best to teach it. Traditional didactic methods may fall short in engaging students or in providing the experiential learning necessary for deep understanding. Therefore, it becomes crucial to adopt pedagogical approaches that align with the nature of AI itself—dynamic, interdisciplinary, and problem-oriented. Progressive teaching methodologies such as project-based learning (PBL), inquiry-driven methods, computational thinking, and design thinking provide students with active, meaningful engagement in AI topics.

Each pedagogical approach offers unique strengths: project-based learning fosters hands-on exploration and real-world application; inquiry-driven learning emphasizes curiosity and student-led investigation; computational thinking teaches structured problem-solving using logic and data; and design thinking ensures a human-centered focus, promoting ethical, inclusive, and user-friendly AI systems. These methods are not only complementary but also essential in nurturing both the technical and ethical dimensions of AI understanding (Wing, 2006; Shute et al., 2017).

By focusing on these approaches, educators can create a rich and adaptable learning environment that mirrors the complexity and interdisciplinary nature of AI. Such environments empower students to move from passive recipients of information to active designers, thinkers, and evaluators of intelligent systems.

1.3 Overview of the Chapter

This chapter explores how pedagogical strategies can be applied to develop AI literacy in students. Section 2 provides an in-depth overview of four core educational approaches—project-based learning, inquiry-driven methods, computational thinking, and design thinking—highlighting their principles and relevance to AI. Section 3 demonstrates how these approaches can be applied to core AI concepts and real-world challenges. Section 4 discusses the benefits of integrating these methodologies into interdisciplinary frameworks. Section 5 focuses on curriculum design and assessment strategies, while Section 6 highlights teacher training and resource needs. Section 7 offers insights into future trends and innovations in AI education. Finally, Section 8 concludes with key takeaways and forward-looking recommendations for educators and policymakers.

2. UNDERSTANDING CORE PEDAGOGICAL APPROACHES

As artificial intelligence (AI) becomes increasingly integral to the future of work, society, and education, it is essential that students not only understand AI concepts but also develop critical, creative, and collaborative problem-solving skills. To effectively teach AI, educators need to embrace pedagogical approaches that align with the dynamic, interdisciplinary nature of AI. This section explores four such methods—Project-Based Learning (PBL), Inquiry-Driven Methods, Computational Thinking, and Design Thinking—that provide students with hands-on, reflective, and purposeful learning experiences.

2.1 Project-Based Learning (PBL)

Project-Based Learning (PBL) is a student-centered pedagogy that involves students working for an extended period on real-world problems or questions. In the context of AI education, PBL encourages learners to apply AI principles to meaningful, authentic challenges—such as designing a machine learning model to recognize emotions or developing a chatbot to address mental health inquiries.

PBL enhances deeper understanding by linking theoretical AI concepts with practical applications. Students take ownership of their learning, collaborate in teams, and engage in critical thinking throughout the project cycle—from initial ideation to prototyping, testing, and presenting their solutions. According to Thomas (2000), the effectiveness of PBL lies in its focus on inquiry, collaboration, and reflection, which are foundational to both AI development and problem-solving.

Moreover, research by Barron and Darling-Hammond (2008) emphasizes that students engaged in PBL show increased motivation, improved problem-solving abilities, and greater retention of content. In AI contexts, PBL allows students to simulate data analysis, model training, and ethical evaluation, thereby mimicking the real-world processes used by AI practitioners.

2.2 Inquiry-Driven Methods

Inquiry-driven learning is based on the constructivist notion that learners build knowledge through active questioning, investigation, and reflection. Rather than presenting information in a linear, prescriptive manner, this approach invites students to explore AI-related topics through their own curiosities and guided discovery.

In AI education, inquiry-driven methods enable learners to ask meaningful questions such as, "How do recommendation systems work?" or "What makes an AI fair or biased?" These inquiries prompt research, experimentation, and dialogue. As students delve into data sets, test algorithms, and examine ethical dilemmas, they develop not only AI knowledge but also research literacy, critical analysis, and ethical reasoning.

Pedagogical frameworks such as the 5E model (Engage, Explore, Explain, Elaborate, Evaluate) are often used to structure inquiry-based learning in STEM, and they can be readily adapted to AI instruction (Bybee et al., 2006). Inquiry-driven AI learning also supports self-directed exploration, where students become active knowledge seekers, cultivating skills essential to lifelong learning and AI literacy.

According to Edelson, Gordin, and Pea (1999), inquiry-driven approaches deepen engagement by situating learning in contexts where students see personal relevance and societal impact, which is especially powerful in a field like AI that touches every aspect of modern life.

2.3 Computational Thinking

Computational Thinking (CT) refers to the mental processes involved in formulating problems and expressing their solutions in a way that a computer—or a human aided by a computer—can effectively execute. Introduced by Wing (2006), CT is a foundational skill for AI education because it equips students with the ability to break down complex problems, recognize patterns, abstract essential elements, and design algorithms.

In practice, computational thinking helps students understand how AI systems process information, make decisions, and improve over time. For instance, when training a model to identify objects in images, students must consider data inputs, algorithm structure, and performance evaluation—activities rooted in CT principles.

CT also reinforces algorithmic literacy, enabling students to comprehend how instructions can be encoded, optimized, and reused—key capabilities for both AI users and developers. Furthermore, it builds a bridge between coding and problem-solving, helping students shift from syntax-based programming to strategic thinking about how digital tools can be used to model and solve problems (Grover & Pea, 2013).

CT can be introduced at various educational levels through unplugged activities, block-based programming (e.g., Scratch), and more advanced platforms like Python or TensorFlow. As AI tools become more accessible, computational thinking becomes an indispensable lens for decoding AI functions and designing innovative solutions.

2.4 Design Thinking

Design Thinking is a human-centered, iterative approach to problem-solving that prioritizes empathy, ideation, prototyping, and testing. In AI education, it provides a counterbalance to purely technical perspectives by encouraging students to consider the social, ethical, and emotional aspects of their creations.

The design thinking process typically includes five stages: empathize, define, ideate, prototype, and test (Brown, 2009). When applied to AI, this might involve identifying a user need—such as assisting visually impaired individuals—and developing an AI-powered tool, such as an image recognition app, that addresses that need.

Design thinking prompts students to think critically about the impact of AI systems on users and society. It encourages them to consider questions such as: "Who benefits from this AI?" "What unintended consequences might arise?" and "How do we ensure fairness and accessibility?" These reflections are critical in cultivating responsible AI creators.

Research by Carroll et al. (2010) demonstrates that incorporating design thinking into STEM learning environments fosters collaboration, creativity, and user awareness. For AI, this method ensures that student projects are not only technically feasible but also socially and ethically grounded.

Moreover, design thinking complements computational thinking and PBL by framing problem-solving within a real-world context that values empathy and innovation. It supports interdisciplinary learning by bridging AI with fields like psychology, sociology, and ethics—areas increasingly relevant to AI governance and development.

Understanding and integrating project-based learning, inquiry-driven methods, computational thinking, and design thinking into AI education equips students with more than technical know-how. These pedagogical approaches foster curiosity, empathy, resilience, and reflective thinking—skills essential for navigating an AI-rich world. Collectively, they form a robust educational foundation that prepares learners not only to understand and apply AI technologies but also to question, critique, and improve them.

Educators who adopt these approaches are better positioned to cultivate a generation of students who are not just AI-literate but AI-fluent—capable of creating, communicating, and contributing ethically and effectively in an AI-powered society.

3. APPLYING PEDAGOGIES IN AI EDUCATION

Translating abstract pedagogical theories into actionable classroom practices is a critical step in developing meaningful AI literacy among students. Each pedagogical strategy—Project-Based Learning (PBL), inquiry-driven methods, computational thinking, and design thinking—offers a distinctive yet complementary way to foster deep learning in AI education. This section explores how these approaches can be applied to help students understand AI concepts, solve real-world problems, and create responsible, human-centered solutions.

3.1 Aligning Pedagogies with AI Concepts

AI education demands an interdisciplinary and dynamic pedagogical alignment. The essence of AI—automation, learning from data, decision-making, and ethical implications—requires students to master not only technical knowledge but also critical thinking, collaboration, and creativity.

Each pedagogical approach aligns with core aspects of AI:

- **PBL** supports experiential learning where students build AI applications.
- **Inquiry-driven learning** promotes curiosity and questioning—skills vital for evaluating AI systems.

- **Computational thinking** underpins algorithm design, data modeling, and problem decomposition.
- **Design thinking** anchors AI development in empathy and ethical awareness.

By interweaving these pedagogies, educators can address the multidimensional nature of AI. For example, a unit on facial recognition might involve understanding algorithmic bias through inquiry, decomposing the recognition task using computational thinking, building a prototype using PBL, and evaluating ethical implications through design thinking. This kind of alignment ensures that students are not only learning *about* AI but are learning *with and through* AI in ways that mirror real-world applications (Touretzky et al., 2019).

3.2 Real-World Problem Solving through PBL

Project-Based Learning enables students to approach AI as a problem-solving tool. By working on open-ended, authentic projects, students take responsibility for their learning and engage in iterative cycles of planning, designing, testing, and refining. These projects may address issues like predicting school energy consumption, developing an app to detect food waste, or designing an AI chatbot to assist with language learning.

One of the strengths of PBL in AI education is that it allows students to connect theory with application. They learn about datasets, model training, and algorithmic behavior not through lectures, but by creating solutions that matter. As Krajcik and Blumenfeld (2006) note, students develop "deep content knowledge and soft skills simultaneously" in PBL environments.

Teachers can structure PBL projects to span multiple disciplines, integrating mathematics, computer science, ethics, and communication. The teacher's role shifts from knowledge transmitter to facilitator, guiding students as they navigate challenges. In the process, learners develop resilience, adaptability, and real-world problem-solving abilities—skills essential for future AI professionals and informed citizens.

For example, a project on building an AI system for smart recycling bins could involve learning about computer vision (technical), sustainability (societal), and designing intuitive user interfaces (design), blending PBL with technical and human-centered considerations.

3.3 Fostering Exploration through Inquiry

Inquiry-driven learning is fundamental in developing a mindset attuned to the complexities and uncertainties of AI. In contrast to traditional instruction, inquiry allows students to formulate questions, investigate phenomena, gather and analyze data, and draw evidence-based conclusions. These processes mirror the scientific and data-driven approach inherent in AI development.

When applied to AI, inquiry might involve asking questions like: *How does an AI system distinguish between spam and legitimate emails?* or *What happens when an algorithm makes decisions based on biased data?* These questions stimulate exploration and reflection, encouraging students to probe the boundaries of AI knowledge.

Guided inquiry frameworks such as the **Inquiry Design Model** (Grant et al., 2017) can help structure AI lessons around compelling questions and sustained investigation. Students become active participants, conducting mini-experiments with datasets, evaluating algorithm performance, or analyzing ethical case studies.

Research by Zion and Mendelovici (2012) found that inquiry-based environments increase student engagement and critical thinking, particularly when students are encouraged to generate and pursue their own questions. In AI education, this means fostering a classroom culture where curiosity is celebrated and uncertainty is embraced.

Moreover, inquiry learning promotes metacognition—students learn how they learn—which is especially valuable when grappling with abstract or unfamiliar AI concepts.

3.4 Breaking Down Complexities with Computational Thinking

AI is often perceived as overwhelmingly complex, but computational thinking (CT) offers a framework to simplify and make sense of its components. CT involves four main pillars: decomposition, pattern recognition, abstraction, and algorithm design (Wing, 2006). These pillars help students unpack AI systems and understand their inner workings.

For instance, a task to design an AI that recommends movies can be broken down into subtasks: gathering user data (decomposition), identifying viewing patterns (pattern recognition), simplifying the criteria for matching (abstraction), and designing the recommendation algorithm (algorithm design).

In classrooms, computational thinking can be fostered through coding exercises, simulations, flowcharts, and even unplugged activities. Block-based programming tools such as Scratch, Snap!, or AI-themed platforms like Machine Learning for Kids allow students to practice CT without the overhead of complex syntax.

Importantly, CT is not just about programming—it's a way of thinking. It empowers students to model real-world problems in logical, computable ways. Grover and Pea (2013) argue that CT should be treated as a cross-disciplinary skill, relevant not only in computer science but in biology, humanities, and social sciences—all of which intersect with AI.

By integrating CT into AI lessons, educators demystify algorithms and empower students to design and critique AI systems. This promotes digital agency and reduces AI as a "black box," allowing learners to understand, build, and question it.

3.5 Human-Centered AI Design through Design Thinking

While AI education often emphasizes coding and data, it is equally crucial to consider the social and ethical implications of AI systems. Design thinking offers a structured way to integrate empathy, ethics, and creativity into AI learning. The stages of design thinking—**empathize, define, ideate, prototype, and test**—ensure that AI solutions are not only functional but also desirable, ethical, and inclusive.

In practice, students might start an AI project by interviewing potential users, such as elderly individuals needing help with medication reminders. Through empathy, they identify pain points. They define the problem (e.g., "How might we use AI to support elderly independence?"), brainstorm ideas, build a prototype (e.g., a voice-activated reminder app), and test it with feedback.

Design thinking encourages students to consider the **impact** of their creations. Who benefits? Who might be harmed? What biases might emerge? These questions are critical in the context of AI, where unintended consequences—such as algorithmic discrimination—can have significant effects.

According to Liedtka (2015), design thinking improves problem-solving by embedding creativity within a structured process. In AI education, it ensures that students don't just learn how to build intelligent systems—they learn how to build them *responsibly*.

Furthermore, design thinking complements computational thinking. While CT provides the structure for problem modeling, design thinking provides the heart—ensuring that models align with human needs and societal values.

Applying pedagogical strategies to AI education transforms the learning experience from passive absorption to active engagement. Aligning pedagogy with AI concepts ensures that students not only understand how AI works but also how to apply it to real-world problems ethically and effectively. Project-Based Learning fosters hands-on exploration of authentic challenges; inquiry-driven methods cultivate curiosity and critical thinking; computational thinking breaks down complexity into manageable steps; and design thinking ensures solutions are user-focused and socially responsible.

Together, these pedagogies prepare students not just to use AI, but to shape its future with intelligence, empathy, and responsibility.

4. INTERDISCIPLINARY AND INTEGRATED LEARNING MODELS

4.1 Blending Pedagogies for Holistic Learning

In the context of AI education, the integration of diverse pedagogical strategies is not only beneficial—it is essential. As AI intersects with multiple domains such as mathematics, ethics, psychology, language, and social sciences, a siloed approach to teaching is no longer effective. Instead, interdisciplinary and integrated learning models offer a holistic approach that blends pedagogies like Project-Based Learning (PBL), inquiry-based learning, computational thinking, and design thinking into cohesive learning experiences.

Blending pedagogies allows students to engage with AI content through multiple lenses. For instance, a project on building an AI-powered environmental monitoring system might involve applying scientific inquiry (hypothesis and experimentation), computational thinking (data modeling), and design thinking (creating user-friendly solutions that serve communities). These approaches reinforce each other—design thinking adds empathy to computational tasks, while inquiry-based learning deepens the critical engagement with AI tools and outcomes.

According to Beers (2011), interdisciplinary learning enhances students' ability to transfer knowledge across domains and to synthesize complex information—an ability crucial in understanding and applying AI technologies. When pedagogies are integrated thoughtfully, students become not only problem-solvers but also responsible designers, critical thinkers, and lifelong learners.

4.2 Case Examples from Classrooms and Programs

Several educational initiatives have successfully implemented interdisciplinary AI learning models.

In the U.S., the *AI4K12 Initiative* provides curriculum guidelines that integrate computational thinking with social and ethical reflections, encouraging teachers to weave AI concepts into diverse subject areas. For example, middle school students may analyze datasets on food insecurity while learning about machine learning and social justice simultaneously (Touretzky et al., 2019).

Another example is MIT's *RAISE (Responsible AI for Social Empowerment and Education)* program, which uses design thinking and inquiry-driven learning to teach students how to build ethical AI systems. In one classroom, students worked on a project to detect bias in facial recognition tools, combining technical knowledge with societal impact analysis—thus blending computer science, ethics, and civics.

In Finland, AI education has been embedded across disciplines in secondary schools. Teachers co-design AI modules that link mathematics, history, and language, encouraging cross-curricular collaboration and deeper understanding of AI's societal implications (Kangas et al., 2021).

These examples demonstrate how interdisciplinary teaching can create rich, relevant, and engaging learning environments that mirror the complex realities of working with AI.

4.3 Challenges and Opportunities in Integration

While the benefits of interdisciplinary and integrated pedagogies are evident, educators often face challenges in implementation. Key barriers include:

- **Curriculum rigidity**: Traditional subject boundaries and standardized testing can make integration difficult.
- **Lack of teacher training**: Many educators feel unprepared to teach AI or blend pedagogical methods effectively (Zawacki-Richter et al., 2019).
- **Resource constraints**: Access to tools, datasets, and collaborative time for curriculum planning can be limited.

However, these challenges present opportunities for innovation. Professional development programs, interdisciplinary teaching teams, and flexible digital platforms can empower educators to design integrated learning experiences. Moreover, integrating AI into broader educational frameworks fosters equity, digital citizenship, and future readiness.

As education systems embrace AI, integrating pedagogies across disciplines offers a sustainable, scalable model to develop well-rounded, ethically aware learners equipped to thrive in the AI era.

5. CURRICULUM DESIGN AND ASSESSMENT STRATEGIES

5.1 Structuring AI Curriculum with Progressive Depth

Designing an AI curriculum requires thoughtful scaffolding that introduces foundational concepts before gradually advancing to more complex and interdisciplinary applications. A well-structured curriculum must balance conceptual knowledge, technical skills, and ethical understanding. The progression often starts with basic awareness—understanding what AI is and where it appears in daily life—then moves to core principles such as data, algorithms, and machine learning models.

Ultimately, students explore specialized topics like neural networks, bias in AI, and AI for social good.

The AI4K12 Initiative proposes a set of "Five Big Ideas in AI" as a foundation: Perception, Representation and Reasoning, Learning, Natural Interaction, and Societal Impact (Touretzky et al., 2019). These concepts serve as anchor points around which curriculum units can be designed, allowing for horizontal (cross-disciplinary) and vertical (grade-by-grade) integration. A progressive curriculum also aligns with Bloom's Taxonomy—moving students from remembering and understanding to applying, analyzing, evaluating, and creating AI solutions.

5.2 Formative and Summative Assessments

Effective assessment in AI education must be multi-faceted and aligned with both learning goals and pedagogical approaches. **Formative assessments**, such as quizzes, reflective journals, peer feedback, and coding challenges, help monitor student progress in real time and provide feedback that informs instructional adjustments. These assessments are particularly useful in project-based or inquiry-driven environments where student learning paths may diverge.

Summative assessments, on the other hand, evaluate the culmination of learning at the end of a unit or course. In AI education, this might include final projects, presentations, or reports that demonstrate students' understanding of AI tools and concepts. Importantly, summative tasks should assess not only technical proficiency but also the ability to articulate decisions, explain ethical considerations, and reflect on the societal impact of their AI solutions (Long & Magerko, 2020).

Assessment rubrics in AI education can be adapted to evaluate a blend of knowledge areas—data literacy, algorithmic thinking, software development, and AI ethics—ensuring a comprehensive review of student learning outcomes.

5.3 Evaluating Creativity, Ethics, and Problem-Solving Skills

Because AI education sits at the intersection of technology and society, assessing creativity, ethics, and problem-solving is essential. Creativity can be evaluated through open-ended projects that challenge students to design novel AI applications or user-centric interfaces. Metrics such as originality, feasibility, and relevance to user needs can provide insight into students' design thinking abilities (Henriksen et al., 2016).

Ethics can be assessed through scenario analyses, case study reflections, or AI project reviews where students must identify bias, fairness issues, and unintended consequences. Structured discussions and written reflections help gauge students' ethical reasoning and understanding of responsible AI development.

Problem-solving skills are often demonstrated in project planning, debugging, and iteration. Teachers can assess how students define problems, ideate solutions, prototype, and refine their approaches. Using authentic, real-world challenges as a framework supports this evaluation and encourages deeper engagement.

In sum, AI curriculum and assessment strategies must go beyond code and computation—they must capture the human, ethical, and imaginative aspects of AI innovation.

6. PREPARING EDUCATORS FOR AI PEDAGOGY

As artificial intelligence (AI) becomes increasingly integrated into education, preparing educators to confidently and effectively teach AI concepts is essential. This preparation requires robust teacher training programs, access to practical tools and resources, and the creation of supportive learning environments.

6.1 Teacher Training and Professional Development

Effective AI pedagogy begins with comprehensive teacher training and professional development. Many educators lack a background in computer science or AI, making targeted upskilling programs critical. These programs should focus not only on technical knowledge—such as machine learning, data literacy, and algorithms—but also on pedagogical strategies suitable for AI instruction. Project-based learning, design thinking, and computational thinking frameworks offer practical, student-centered approaches for introducing AI (Touretzky et al., 2019).

Professional development should be continuous and collaborative, allowing teachers to explore AI concepts in hands-on workshops, online courses, and learning communities. Initiatives like the AI4K12 framework in the United States provide structured guidance for integrating AI into K-12 education, outlining five key big ideas of AI and aligning them with age-appropriate learning outcomes (AI4K12, 2020). Universities, edtech organizations, and ministries of education must work together to support these learning opportunities, ensuring they are inclusive and adaptable across educational contexts.

6.2 Tools and Resources for Classroom Implementation

Equipping teachers with accessible and engaging tools is essential for successful AI instruction. Platforms like Google's Teachable Machine, Microsoft's AI for Good curriculum, and MIT's Scratch extensions for AI allow educators to introduce foundational AI concepts without requiring extensive coding experience. These tools support interactive, inquiry-based learning where students can train simple models, explore ethical implications, and see AI in action.

Curriculum-aligned lesson plans, open educational resources (OER), and AI-focused teaching kits can ease the implementation process. Resources should also emphasize interdisciplinary connections, enabling teachers of different subjects to integrate AI meaningfully into math, science, social studies, and the arts (Long & Magerko, 2020). For example, ethics discussions about facial recognition or data privacy can be embedded in civics or literature classes, fostering critical thinking across domains.

6.3 Building Supportive Learning Environments

Finally, building a supportive learning environment is vital for both educators and students to thrive in AI education. Schools must foster a culture of innovation, experimentation, and collaboration, where teachers feel safe exploring new technologies and pedagogies. This includes providing administrative support, time for planning, and spaces for peer collaboration.

Supportive environments also recognize the emotional and ethical dimensions of AI learning. Teachers should be equipped to guide discussions about AI's societal impacts, bias in algorithms, and responsible data use. Such environments promote inclusive learning, encouraging students from diverse backgrounds to engage with AI and see themselves as future contributors to the field.

Moreover, connecting with external communities—industry experts, AI researchers, and global educator networks—can enrich the classroom experience and keep educators informed of emerging trends. Ultimately, preparing educators for AI pedagogy requires systemic investment, a clear vision for integration, and a commitment to teacher empowerment.

7. FUTURE DIRECTIONS AND INNOVATIONS IN AI EDUCATION

As artificial intelligence (AI) reshapes industries and daily life, the education sector is poised for transformative innovation. The future of AI education lies not only in teaching students how AI works but also in equipping them with the skills to engage critically and creatively with intelligent systems. This calls for a forward-looking approach encompassing emerging technologies, evolving pedagogies, and responsive educational policy.

7.1 Emerging Trends in EdTech and AI

One of the most significant trends in education technology (EdTech) is the integration of AI-driven personalized learning systems. Adaptive learning platforms use AI to assess student performance in real-time and tailor content accordingly, promoting individualized learning paths (Holmes et al., 2019). These systems, powered by machine learning algorithms, enhance learner engagement and outcomes by addressing diverse learning needs.

Another trend is the use of generative AI tools, such as large language models and image generation platforms, in creative and analytical tasks. These tools not only serve as learning aids but also as mediums for students to co-create content, raising important questions about authorship, bias, and ethical use. In tandem, AI-powered assessment tools offer real-time feedback, automate grading, and support formative evaluation, reducing teacher workload and increasing instructional time.

The future also includes immersive technologies like AI-enhanced virtual and augmented reality environments, which can simulate complex scientific phenomena, historical events, or ethical dilemmas—offering experiential learning opportunities that were previously inaccessible.

7.2 Evolving Pedagogical Approaches

As AI tools evolve, so must pedagogical approaches. Educators are moving away from rote instruction toward constructivist and student-centered models. Project-based learning (PBL) and inquiry-based learning (IBL) are particularly effective in AI education, allowing students to engage in real-world problem solving, build models, and explore data ethics.

Design thinking is also gaining prominence as a framework for guiding AI literacy education, emphasizing empathy, ideation, prototyping, and iteration (Sheridan et al., 2021). These pedagogies foster not only technical competence but also creativity, critical thinking, and ethical reasoning—skills essential in a world shaped by AI.

Moreover, interdisciplinary integration is increasingly seen as crucial. AI education is not limited to computer science; it intersects with humanities, social sciences, and the arts, encouraging holistic understanding and diverse participation.

7.3 Recommendations for Policy and Practice

To fully harness AI's potential in education, comprehensive policy support is needed. Policymakers should invest in AI literacy curricula that are age-appropriate, inclusive, and aligned with global competencies. Frameworks like UNESCO's AI and education guidelines provide valuable direction for designing equitable and effective AI education systems (UNESCO, 2021).

Teacher training must be prioritized, with national and local governments supporting continuous professional development and the creation of AI teaching standards. Schools should also ensure equitable access to technology, especially in underserved communities, to prevent widening the digital divide.

Lastly, ethical oversight should be embedded in all AI applications in education. Transparency, data privacy, algorithmic fairness, and accountability must be core principles guiding AI integration in classrooms.

8. CONCLUSION

8.1 Summary of Key Insights

As artificial intelligence continues to shape the future of work, communication, and society, developing AI literacy in students has emerged as a crucial educational priority. This chapter has explored how pedagogical approaches such as project-based learning, inquiry-driven instruction, computational thinking, and design thinking provide dynamic pathways for students to understand and engage with AI meaningfully.

Preparing educators to teach AI effectively is equally vital. Ongoing professional development, access to user-friendly tools, and the creation of supportive learning environments empower teachers to guide students through complex concepts with confidence and creativity. Whether through hands-on projects, ethical discussions, or interdisciplinary applications, educators play a pivotal role in building foundational AI understanding and fostering responsible digital citizens.

In parallel, the rapid evolution of educational technology presents both opportunities and challenges. AI-powered tools for personalized learning, formative assessment, and immersive simulations are reshaping how students interact with content and each other. However, integrating these technologies requires thoughtful planning, pedagogical alignment, and attention to ethical considerations, including equity, bias, and transparency.

We also explored how pedagogical strategies must evolve alongside these technologies. From constructivist methods to experiential design-based learning, educational models must prioritize active participation, critical thinking, and ethical inquiry. The goal is not only to teach students how AI works but also to enable them to understand its implications, make informed decisions, and participate in shaping its future.

8.2 The Road Ahead for AI Literacy

Looking forward, the road ahead for AI literacy calls for a comprehensive, inclusive, and future-ready vision. AI education must extend beyond technical proficiency to include the human, societal, and ethical dimensions of intelligent technologies. Students must be equipped not only to use AI tools but to question them, challenge them, and ultimately improve them.

This journey will require systemic support—clear policy direction, sustained investment in educator training, and equitable access to digital infrastructure. It also demands innovation in curriculum design, with learning experiences that are interdisciplinary, culturally responsive, and adaptable to diverse learners and learning environments.

The future of AI literacy lies in fostering curiosity, agency, and resilience among students. They should be encouraged to explore AI not just as users, but as creators, collaborators, and ethical leaders. By embracing inquiry, experimentation, and reflection, students can become active participants in the digital age, empowered to shape technology in ways that align with human values and societal good.

Ultimately, building AI literacy is not just about preparing students for future careers—it's about preparing them to navigate and influence a world increasingly mediated by intelligent systems. As educators, policymakers, and communities work together, the shared goal should be to ensure that every learner has the opportunity to understand, question, and contribute to the evolving AI landscape with confidence and integrity.

REFERENCES

AI4K12. (2020). *AI4K12 Five Big Ideas in Artificial Intelligence*. https://ai4k12.org

Barron, B., & Darling-Hammond, L. (2008). Teaching for meaningful learning: A review of research on inquiry-based and cooperative learning. In *Powerful learning: What we know about teaching for understanding* (pp. 11–70).

Beers, S. Z. (2011). *21st century skills: Preparing students for THEIR future*. National Education Association.

Brown, T. (2009). *Change by design: How design thinking creates new alternatives for business and society*. Harvard Business Press.

Bybee, R. W., Taylor, J. A., Gardner, A., Van Scotter, P., Carlson Powell, J., Westbrook, A., & Landes, N. (2006). *The BSCS 5E instructional model: Origins and effectiveness*. BSCS.

Carroll, M., Goldman, S., Britos, L., Koh, J., Royalty, A., & Hornstein, M. (2010). Destination, imagination and the fires within: Design thinking in a middle school classroom. *International Journal of Art & Design Education*, *29*(1), 37–53.

Edelson, D. C., Gordin, D. N., & Pea, R. D. (1999). Addressing the challenges of inquiry-based learning through technology and curriculum design. *Journal of the Learning Sciences*, *8*(3–4), 391–450.

Grant, S. G., Lee, J., & Swan, K. (2017). *Inquiry-based practice in social studies education: Understanding the inquiry design model*. Routledge.

Grover, S., & Pea, R. (2013). Computational thinking in K–12: A review of the state of the field. *Educational Researcher*, *42*(1), 38–43.

Henriksen, D., Mishra, P., & Fisser, P. (2016). Infusing creativity and technology in 21st-century education: A systemic view for change. *Journal of Educational Technology & Society*, *19*(3), 27–37.

Holmes, W., Bialik, M., & Fadel, C. (2019). *Artificial intelligence in education: Promises and implications for teaching and learning*. Center for Curriculum Redesign.

Kangas, M., Siklander, P., Randolph, J., & Ruokamo, H. (2021). Teachers' engagement and students' learning in Finnish schools implementing AI-integrated, phenomenon-based learning. *Education and Information Technologies*, *26*, 4797–4815.

Krajcik, J., & Blumenfeld, P. (2006). Project-based learning. In Sawyer, R. K. (Ed.), *The Cambridge handbook of the learning sciences* (pp. 317–334). Cambridge University Press.

Liedtka, J. (2015). Perspective: Linking design thinking with innovation outcomes through cognitive bias reduction. *Journal of Product Innovation Management, 32*(6), 925–938.

Long, D., & Magerko, B. (2020). What is AI literacy? Competencies and design considerations. *Proceedings of the 2020 CHI Conference on Human Factors in Computing Systems*, 1–16.

Long, D., & Magerko, B. (2020). What is AI literacy? *ACM Transactions on Human-Computer Interaction, 27*(1), 1–29.

Sheridan, K., Clark, K., & Williams, A. (2021). Designing AI learning through empathy and creativity: A design thinking approach. *Journal of the Learning Sciences, 30*(3), 341–366.

Shute, V. J., Sun, C., & Asbell-Clarke, J. (2017). Demystifying computational thinking. *Educational Research Review, 22*, 142–158.

Thomas, J. W. (2000). *A review of research on project-based learning*. The Autodesk Foundation.

Touretzky, D. S., Gardner-McCune, C., Martin, F., & Seehorn, D. (2019). Envisioning AI for K–12: What should every child know about AI? *Proceedings of the AAAI Conference on Artificial Intelligence, 33*(1), 9795–9799.

UNESCO. (2021). *AI and education: Guidance for policy-makers*. https://unesdoc.unesco.org/ark:/48223/pf0000376709

Wing, J. M. (2006). Computational thinking. *Communications of the ACM, 49*(3), 33–35.

Zawacki-Richter, O., Marín, V. I., Bond, M., & Gouverneur, F. (2019). Systematic review of research on artificial intelligence applications in higher education. *International Journal of Educational Technology in Higher Education, 16*(1), 1–27.

Zion, M., & Mendelovici, R. (2012). Moving from structured to open inquiry: Challenges and limits. *Science Education International, 23*(4), 383–399.

Chapter 8
Towards an Integrated Artificial Intelligence Literacy Framework in Education

Elisha Mupaikwa
https://orcid.org/0000-0002-0313-7139
National University of Science and Technology, Zimbabwe

ABSTRACT

A comprehensive framework for artificial intelligence literacy in education is developed in this chapter. A review of 40 journal papers that were retrieved from Google Scholar is presented here. The publication dates of these papers range from 2010 to 2015. The review demonstrates that many scholars have developed several artificial intelligence literacy frameworks, each of which has been tailored to a certain educational level. This chapter's suggested framework includes the four main components of artificial intelligence literacy: knowing and comprehending AI, applying and utilizing AI, assessing and developing AI, and AI ethics. These also include computation thinking, trans-disciplinary knowledge, data literacy, and algorithm literacy.

INTRODUCTION

In recent decades, there has been a surge in interest in implementing and embracing artificial intelligence in educational institutions among educators, students, and administrators. Researchers have therefore been focusing more on different adoption models and techniques, while others have concentrated on the creation of

DOI: 10.4018/979-8-3373-2297-1.ch008

artificial intelligence technologies to support assessment and evaluations, student management, financial management, and teaching and learning. Because there are few frameworks for evaluating users' AI literacy, especially in the educational sector, evaluating artificial intelligence abilities and competencies in higher education has remained a significant barrier despite the rising interest. Curriculum planners and developers at all educational levels have difficulties as a result of the lack of thorough artificial intelligence literacy. While many universities have adopted information and digital literacy programs into their curricula, research has generally indicated that few have included programs on artificial intelligence. The primary focus of these universities has been on learning management systems. Due to the primary focus of earlier studies on digital literacy, many digital literacy frameworks have been developed, some of which have included artificial intelligence, albeit to a minimal extent. Because of this, the earlier research has not produced a thorough framework for artificial intelligence that is equivalent to the existing frameworks for digital literacy. The various requirements of various educational environments, such as those found in elementary, secondary, and postsecondary education, have not been central to existing frameworks. UNESCO is one body that has created artificial intelligence literacy frameworks, although these frameworks are generalised for applications and do not address the unique requirements of teaching and learning in higher education or educational administration. Thus, it is necessary to suggest a framework for artificial intelligence literacy that might be used at different educational levels, allowing each level to choose the concepts that are appropriate for their particular setting. Thus, the purpose of this chapter is to analyse the literature on artificial intelligence and to create a thorough framework for AI that might be used in higher education.

BACKGROUND

Teaching and learning, curriculum creation, development, and evaluation, student and faculty management, student enrollment, and the overall administration of educational institutions are all areas in which digital technology is now essential. Artificial intelligence (AI) has emerged as one of the digital advancements that researchers and educators are most interested in. The term AI refers to a collection of computer tools that simulate human intelligence in solving problems (Xu et al., 2021). However, research on AI's uses in education has only focused on the creation of new AI advances and the uptake and use of these tools in instruction. From the perspective of adoption, the literature notes that low user literacy has been one of the obstacles to the use of AI in education. Even though some researchers have looked at the different aspects of AI literacy, the majority of them have focused on specific levels of education, and no attempts have been made to create AI literacy frameworks that could be used to evaluate students' proficiency with AI and suggest training courses for AI users across all levels of education. Even while AI tools like ChatGPT and Deepseek are quite popular in mainstream secondary education, research shows that pupils are not aware of the underlying ideas and technologies or the possible ethical concerns surrounding AI (Hwang, Lee and Shin, 2023). As such, teachers across various levels of education have been encouraged to employ a variety of pedagogical strategies to enhance AI literacy among learners. Understanding AI technologies, using them responsibly and effectively, and applying critical thinking to their development and use are all components of the broad idea of AI literacy (Abdelghani et al., 2023; Dong, 2023; Hwang, Lee and Shin, 2023). AI literacy is also defined by Laupichler et al. (2022) and Ng et al. (2021) as the ability to critically comprehend, assess, and use AI technology without the need to independently create AI models. However, some researchers have included the aspects of algorithm literacy and application development in their efforts to develop AI literacy frameworks (Stolpe and Hallström, 2024). AI literacy also entails a range of abilities that allow people to interact and collaborate with AI systems efficiently and use AI tools in a variety of contexts (Long and Magerko, 2020).

Some researchers, among them Laupichler et al. (2022) and Tzirides et al. (2024), have reviewed studies on AI literacy in higher and adult education to identify the major themes and recent research trends, and offer recommendations for research and practice. A comparable review was also carried out more recently by Sperling et al. (2024), but this time the literature's focus was on how teachers' various professional knowledge forms are conceptualised about AI literacy, particularly in the context of teacher education. An emerging trend in AI research in the context of AI literacy is the dominance of AI ethics. This is because new technological developments in AI, such as Generative AI, have impacted several areas of the teaching and learning environment as a result of innovations in virtual assistance, AI-driven technologies for essay scoring and grading, student management, personalised learning, student assessment and essay writing assistants (Dabis and Csáki, 2024). In these applications, however, several ethical issues have emerged, and these include algorithm bias and discrimination, data privacy and security, transparency and explainability and equity and universality (Dabis and Csáki, 2024). In light of these ethical issues, it has also become imperative to consider AI ethics when developing ethical frameworks for AI use in education. While developing or proposing frameworks for AI literacy considerations for existing ones may also be necessary. Among the earlier frameworks that have guided ethical usage and development of AI are the Beijing Frameworks and the AI4People's ethical framework, both comprising the major dimensions: safety, accuracy, reliability, privacy, data governance, transparency and communication and access to facts (Corrigan et al., 2023).

AI literacy has emerged as a crucial literacy skill that all students, regardless of their background, must possess to understand and utilise AI as a tool for learning, working, and living in our digital world, in various educational contexts (Burgsteiner et al., 2016; Kandlhofer et al., 2016; Ng et al., 2021; Steinbauer et al., 2021). For example, among young children, Su et al. (2023) say that AI-powered toys are designed to give young children a fun way to learn and engage with the robots and kits while also imparting coding skills. In a different context, the AI literacy course, which aims to improve pre-service teachers' conceptual and literacy skills, fulfils an important function by giving people the tools they need to use AI effectively. This empowers them to interact with technology with confidence and incorporate AI into their teaching methods (Zhao, Wu, and Luo, 2022). Further, according to Zhao et al. (2022), AI literacy in education for teachers entails having the knowledge, concepts, factual information, and mindset required to understand AI. For instance, by learning more about how AI works, pre-service teachers can consider incorporating it into their lessons to help students grow and can then share what they have learned with their peers. Furthermore, a strong grasp of AI empowers pre-service teachers to take part in crucial AI discussions, use AI to revolutionise instruction, and feel more in control of their lives by enhancing their coping strategies (Guo with Hao, 2021). Even though scholars are very interested in studying AI literacy in education, there don't seem to be many uniform frameworks for evaluating AI literacy. This is because the majority of research appears to have concentrated on the more comprehensive perspective of digital literacy, leading to the creation of various digital literacy frameworks by international organisations like UNESCO and the European Commission. This chapter, therefore, first discusses the various forms of literacies in the digital context. This is then followed by a discussion of the concepts of literacy in the AI environment and AI literacy frameworks. The last section proposes a framework for AI literacy in education.

A COMPARISON OF LITERACY

It was often believed that literacy was the capacity to read and write. The rise of the knowledge-based society in the current digital era suggests that all citizens need to be digitally literate and possess fundamental skills to have a better chance at work with equal possibilities (Bawden, 2008). The phrase has been expanded to encompass new forms of literacy, including digital, information, media, computer, and artificial intelligence (Kong et al., 2021). These various forms of literacy allow students to learn new skills and information in the twenty-first century by using computers and related technology in sophisticated ways (Griffin and Care, 2014; Larson and Miller, 2011). In digital environments, operational proficiency and accessibility are frequently mentioned in early conceptualisations of digital literacy (Audenhove, 2024). More recent digital literacy competence models integrate analytical and critical skills. They provide a longer list of particular competencies and skills (Iordache et al., 2017). These competency models have typically grown more intricate, comprehensive, subtle, and steady over time. Recently, a far more thorough framework covering digital literacy, skills, and preparation was proposed by the DQ Institute (2021), and this model comprises eight dimensions of digital literacy. The eight components of the framework are further broken down into specific items. The first dimension-Digital Identity, comprises of three variables, namely: Digital Citizen Identity, Digital Co-Creator Identity, and Digital Changemaker Identity. The second dimension-Digital Rights comprises three variables, namely: Participatory Rights Management, Intellectual Property Rights Management, and Privacy Management. The third dimension is Digital Literacy and this comprises three variables namely: Data and AI literacy, Content Creation and Computational Literacy and Media and Information Literacy. The fourth dimension- Digital Communication, comprises three variables, namely: Public and Mass Communication, Online Communication and Collaboration, and Digital Footprint Management. The fifth dimension is Digital Emotional Intelligence and this comprises there variables namely: Relationship Management, Self-Awareness and Management, Digital Empathy. The sixth dimension-Digital Security comprise, Personal Cyber Security Management, Network Security Management and Organizational Cyber Security Management. The seventh dimension-Digital Safety, comprises Behavioral Cyber-Risk Management, Content Cyber-Risk Management, Commercial and Community Cyber-Risk Management. The eith dimension is Digital Use and this comprises there variables and these are: Balanced Use of Technology, Healthy Use of Technology and Civic Use of Technology.. These days, AI technology is one of the digital tools that demand a high level of literacy because these abilities are now essential in many fields and sectors (Ng et al., 2021; Touretzky et al., 2019).

ARTIFICIAL INTELLIGENCE LITERACY COMPETENCIES

According to Wang, Li, and Huang (2023), the lack of consensus over suitable definitions of AI literacy may have been influenced by the rich evolution of AI literacy in human society, as well as the change in the demand for AI in human society. Given the complexity of AI literacy, numerous recommendations have been made for the skills non-technical people should acquire. Despite their slight variations, many of the recommended competences) can be divided into three groups: (1) AI mechanisms, (2) AI capabilities, and (3) AI ethics (Ding, Kim, and Allday, 2024. The different definitions that have been proposed, however, all agree that AI literacy encompasses a deeper understanding of artificial intelligence technology and its applications, rather than just basic digital skills. AI literacy in education, according to Jiang (2023), however, is the thorough manifestation of the information and abilities, procedures and techniques, emotional attitudes, and values that students who receive AI education eventually develop. AI literacy, according to Kandlhofer et al. (2016), involves understanding the concepts and processes that underlie AI products and services as well as knowing how to use certain technologies or applications. They proposed seven educational topics—automata, intelligent agents, graphs and data structures, sorting, search-based problem-solving, conventional planning, and machine learning—to bolster this idea. According to Tenberga and Daniela (2024), AI literacy is further defined as the ability to use AI tools, comprehend fundamental AI ideas, critically assess AI systems, and manage ethical concerns associated with AI use. Additionally, the ability to understand, use, monitor, and assess AI applications without necessarily being able to build AI models themselves is referred to as being "AI literate" (Laupichler et al. 2022). A different idea of AI literacy learning in four cognitive domains is presented by Ng et al. (2021). In their description of artificial intelligence, Ng et al. (2021) suggested a set of skills and aptitudes that can be connected to the cognitive domains in Bloom's taxonomy. This method categorises the degrees of organised thinking and reasoning abilities required in diverse learning situations. Each of the six steps of the taxonomy requires students to think more deeply and methodically. It is believed that the stages, as depicted in Figure 1 below, are sequential, meaning that mastering one level is a prerequisite for reaching the next.

Figure 1. Six levels of skills for AI

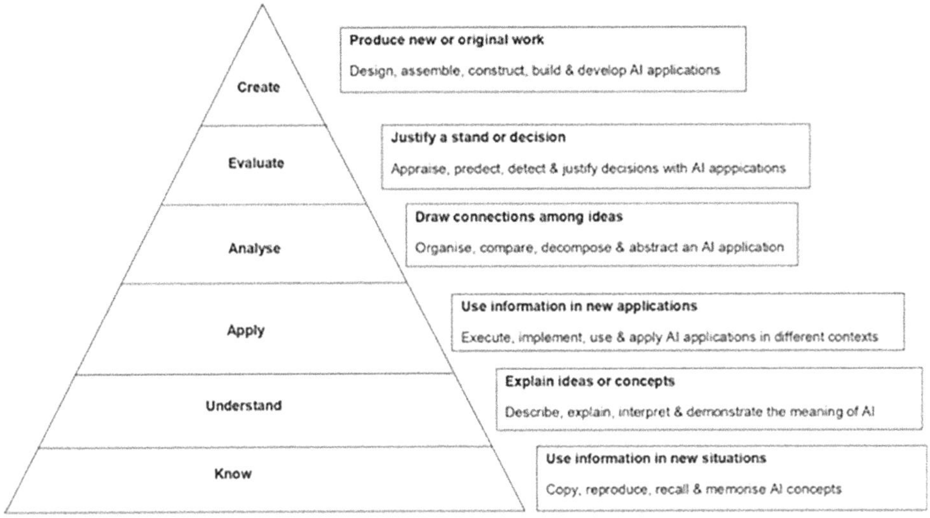

(Ng et al. 2021)

In their study on artificial intelligence levels in junior high schools, Wang, Li, and Huang (2023) further separated artificial intelligence literacy into four dimensions: intelligent social responsibility, practical innovative thinking, intelligent technology application, and artificial intelligence awareness. Figure 2 below illustrates the step-by-step relationship between the four dimensions' required levels.

Figure 2. AI Dimensions

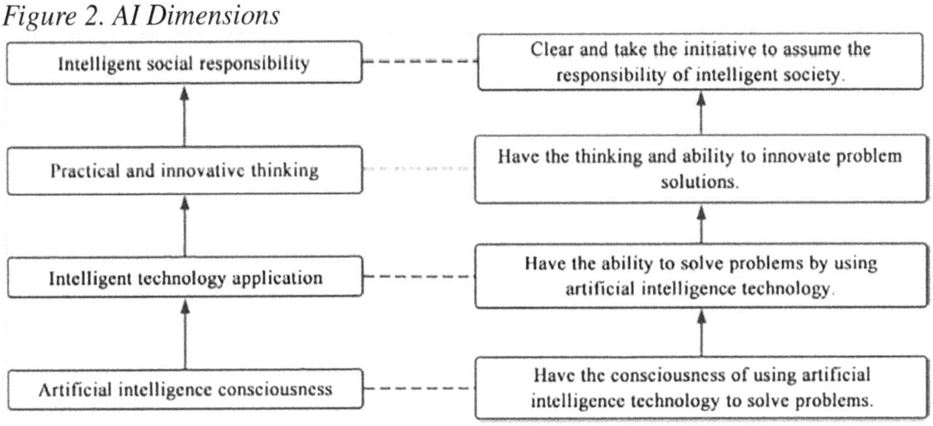

(Wang, Li and Huang, 2023)

The four primary competencies of AI literacy are knowledge of technology, work, human-machine interaction, and learning (Cetindamar et al., 2024). Four elements make up AI literacy, according to Hibbert et al. (2024): understanding AI, applying and using AI, evaluating and analysing AI, and developing AI. According to Ng et al. (2021), there are four elements of AI literacy: applying AI, evaluating and creating AI, comprehending and knowing AI, and AI ethics. The three-competency model of AI literacy developed by Sanusi et al. (2022), cited by Hervieux and Wheatley (2024), for K–12 education includes learning through practice and discovery, team and cooperative involvement, and basic knowledge of AI. The three-competency model developed by Kim et al. (2021), referenced in Hervieux and Wheatley, is based on knowledge (AI definitions and types), competence (using AI tools), and attitude (AI's social impact). Furthermore, Liu and Xie (2021) provide an AI quality cultivation that incorporates the following literacy steps: programming proficiency, computational thinking, and digital literacy. Lastly, academics and educators are particularly concerned about the socio-cultural dimension, which includes the ethical effects of AI on society.

There have been demands to consider the ethical implications of the artefacts created by generative artificial intelligence (GenAI) and its potential to spread misleading information as it has advanced and become more accessible (Lee et al., 2021). Additionally, safety concerns with AI-enhanced systems have become important considerations for non-technical persons. Ding, Kim, and Allday (2024) developed our evaluation based on the three components of AI literacy, drawing from Long and Magerko's (2020) research to identify the core competencies required of non-technical individuals in the field of AI. These abilities fall into the following five primary categories of AI literacy:

i. Knowing the nature of AI,
ii. Acknowledging its potential,
iii. Understanding its underlying mechanisms,
iv. Determining when AI should be used, and
v. Recognizing how the general public views AI.

To address the first aspect of AI literacy, four competences were suggested. These competences focus on identifying AI-enabled technologies, identifying intelligence-related traits, acknowledging that there are multiple ways to build AI, and differentiating between broad and narrow AI. The second component, the ability to identify the benefits and drawbacks of AI as well as the worldwide impacts of AI applications, was composed of two skills. The third facet, which was also the most significant aspect of AI literacy, consisted of nine competencies that mainly focused on people's understanding of the following: how AI makes decisions, how

AI processes and interprets data, how AI physically interacts with the world, how AI senses and collects data, and machine learning steps. One talent was proposed to solve AI ethics and programmability for the fourth and fifth facets (Ding, Kim, and Allday, 2024).

COMPETENCY FRAMEWORKS

Existing literacy frameworks are the most effective way to direct research on AI literacy. There are several AI literacy frameworks tailored to particular industries that address their unique requirements and difficulties. There are some AI literacy frameworks tailored to particular industries that address their unique requirements and difficulties. Karaca et al. (2021), for example, developed a paradigm for AI preparation in the medical field that is based on four pillars: ethics, vision, ability, and cognition. This approach places a strong emphasis on comprehending AI, its real-world applications in healthcare, and being mindful of legal and ethical requirements while using AI and health data. In their technically focused framework for the education sector, Kandlhofer et al. (2016) emphasised the significance of an early introduction to computer science and artificial intelligence concepts as essential components of AI literacy. Ng et al. (2021) proposed a comprehensive framework for AI literacy that addresses several topics, including critical evaluation, effective communication with AI, practical use of AI, understanding AI ideas, and ethical considerations of AI use. A fifth category, "Enabling AI," was added to this paradigm by Southworth et al. (2023), who concentrated on the acquisition of relevant knowledge and abilities to support AI applications and foster multidisciplinary involvement. In contrast, Cetindamar et al. (2022) put out a framework centred on four essential capabilities: learning-related, work-related, technology-related, and human-machine-related. Meanwhile, frameworks such as the "Digital Competence Framework for Citizens" claim that digital competency is a prerequisite for AI literacy (Quille et al., 2022). From media and information literacy to the creation of digital content, problem-solving, and the responsible application of artificial intelligence, digital competency covers a wide variety of abilities. Similarly, the Hochschulforum Digitalisierung (HFD) data literacy paradigm, which encompasses both ethical data management and data-driven decision-making, emphasised the critical significance of data (Schüller, 2022). According to Ng et al. (2021), however, AI literacy is distinct from digital literacy, and their AI literacy TPACK framework should prioritise cognitive learning components of knowledge acquisition, usage, and application in addition to AI ethics considerations.

The fields of computer science and engineering have traditionally served as the foundation for university-level AI literacy frameworks, which reflect the transdisciplinary and interdisciplinary nature of AI. They have included a social and affective component more recently. According to Southworth et al. (2023), this development made it simpler to incorporate programming and statistics into AI literacy, suggesting that AI education ought to be incorporated into all University of Florida curricula rather than just those in the computer science, electrical, and computer engineering departments. In the same way, Kong et al. (2023) argued that focusing solely on the cognitive domain (AI concepts) fails. They proposed using project work to integrate emotional (meaningfulness, impactfulness, creative self-efficacy, and AI self-efficacy) and socio-cultural (ethical awareness) components to guarantee inclusion and comprehensive educational outcomes. Furthermore, Tenorio and Romeike (2023) argued that the current frameworks for AI literacy, which were mostly created from a computer science perspective, would not be enough for students who are not majoring in computer science. In order to democratize AI literacy and enable students of all academic backgrounds to acquire it, they proposed a nine-component AI skills framework (including machine learning, responsible AI, and fundamental AI) that is accessible to students of all technical skill levels. This holistic approach emphasises the need for AI literacy education to adapt to the complex and evolving world of AI in order to guarantee inclusiveness and comprehensive educational outcomes. According to Salhab (2024), there are four key elements of AI literacy. Understanding the fundamental concepts of artificial intelligence (AI), such as its operation, machine learning algorithms, training data, and potential biases and limitations in AI systems, is the first step towards comprehension. Second, people are successfully addressing problems and achieving objectives with AI tools and platforms, which may need coding expertise and the capacity to handle huge datasets. Thirdly, assessment and development entail assessing the reliability and quality of AI systems as well as the ability to create and construct ethical AI systems, which necessitates both technological expertise and knowledge of the moral and societal ramifications of AI. Fourth, AI ethics comprises being aware of the ethical and moral concerns related to AI and making informed decisions regarding its use in different situations while considering aspects such as accountability, openness, equity, and the broader societal impacts of AI.

Several scholars have tried to create artificial intelligence literacy frameworks in educational settings based on the literature. These frameworks have been tailored to meet the requirements of specific educational levels and institutions. Others have concentrated on teaching pre-service teachers, higher education (colleges and universities), and high school education. As a result of these fragmented attempts to create AI literacy frameworks, different and non-standardised AI literacy frameworks have emerged. Teachers' digital and AI skills, including their comprehension, application, evaluation, and ethical handling of AI technologies, are tested by several current digital and AI literacy assessment models. Teachers' knowledge,

new framework for AI literacy makes a strong link between conceptual, procedural, and contextual technological knowledge. According to Stolpe and Hallstrom (2024), the analytical query "What?" identifies technical scientific knowledge because of its content-oriented orientation. Conceptual technological knowledge, such as definitions and theoretical understanding, is what this category represents. Based on computer science and technological scientific knowledge, the framework for AI literacy includes technological scientific knowledge. The following categories of AI literacy knowledge fall under this heading: defining AI, identifying AI, comprehending AI, and comprehending the function of data in AI. Additionally, this category includes knowledge that suggests a specific mode of thinking, such as systems thinking, computational thinking, and design thinking (Stolpe and Hallström ¨om, 2024).

Ng et al. (2021) used Bloom's taxonomy to develop an AI literacy framework, and this framework is shown in Table 1 below:

Table 1. Bloom's taxonomy and AI literacy framework

AI literacy	Definitions
Know and understand AI.	Understand the fundamentals of artificial intelligence and how to use its applications.
Use AI	Using AI concepts, expertise, and applications in many contexts
Evaluate and create AI.	Using AI apps to develop higher-order cognitive abilities (such as assessing, predicting, designing, and evaluating)
AI ethics	Human-centred factors, such as equity, responsibility, openness, morality, and security

In their study of AI literacies and the incorporation of AI into the University of Florida curriculum, Southworth et al. (2023) also put forth a conceptual model that embodied these literacies; Figure 4 below illustrates this model.

Figure 4. University of Florida AI Literacy Framework

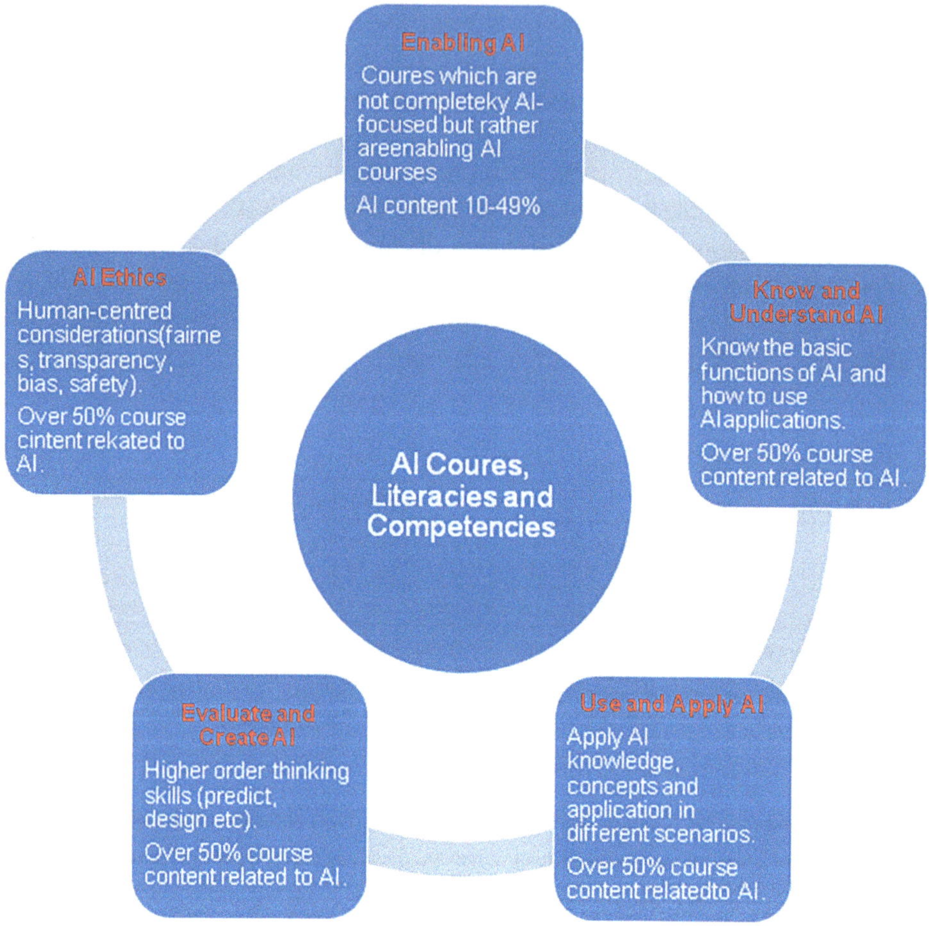

(Southworth et al., 2023)

The foundation of the University of Florida model is based on these four AI literacies, namely:

a) **Knowing and understanding AI:** This entails comprehending the fundamentals of artificial intelligence and its operation. This includes being aware of machine learning techniques, the training data, and the potential biases and limitations of AI systems.

b) **Using and applying AI:** This includes the capacity to solve issues and complete tasks using AI tools and platforms. Programming and coding abilities, as well as the capacity to comprehend and manipulate huge databases, may be required.
c) **Evaluating and creating AI:** This entails having the capacity to evaluate the dependability and quality of AI systems, in addition to designing and developing morally and fairly sound AI systems. This calls for a thorough comprehension of both the ethical and societal ramifications of AI in addition to its technical elements.
d) **AI ethics:** This entails being able to make wise decisions regarding the application of AI in many contexts and comprehending the moral and ethical ramifications of the technology. Fairness, responsibility, transparency, and the possible effects of AI on people and society are all taken into account here. In general, technical expertise and an awareness of the ethical and societal ramifications of AI are necessary to become literate in the field (Yi, 2021). Understanding AI's potential and constraints enables responsible and moral use, which benefits both individuals and society at large (Ng et al., 2021).

TECHNOLOGICAL, PEDAGOGICAL AND CONTENT KNOWLEDGE (TPACK)

Figure 5 below illustrates the Technological, Pedagogical, and Content Knowledge (TPACK), which offers a road map for comprehending how to successfully incorporate AI literacy into the classroom. The affordances and use of domain-specific learning tools, such as hardware and software in AI literacy education, AI-enabled tools, and unplugged learning tools, like role-playing, are covered by technological knowledge. Second, teaching techniques, scaffolding, and feedback on students' learning processes are all part of pedagogical knowledge, which is related to teaching methods and their application to support student AI literacy learning (Janssen et al., 2019). Third, content knowledge refers to the understanding of the topic of AI literacy that particular subjects ought to be taught in the curriculum.

Figure 5. TPACK AI Literacy framework

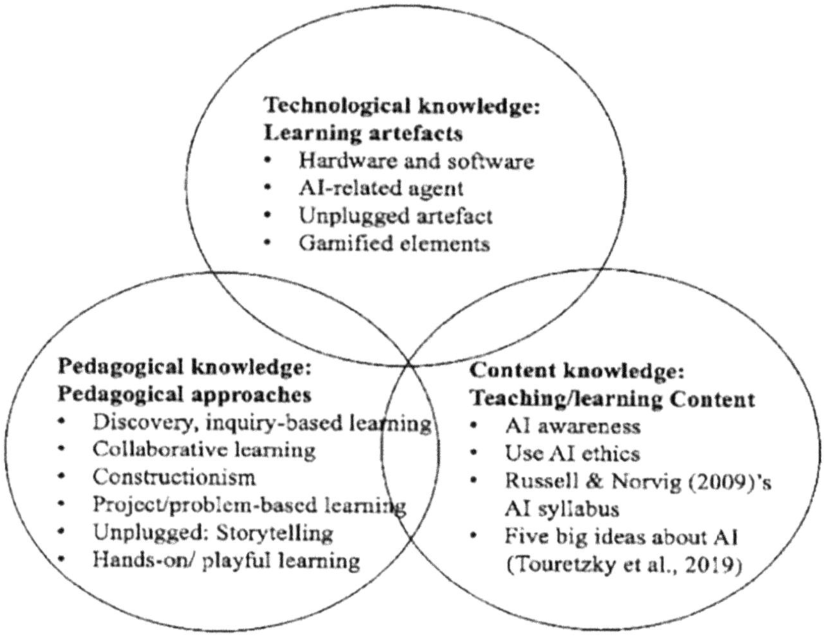

(Janssen et al., 2019)

Technological Knowledge: Given the complexity of AI, it was crucial to use age-appropriate learning resources to help students grasp the concepts of AI and pique their curiosity and drive to learn more about it. Among the artefacts used to learn technological knowledge are:

a) **Hardware-focused artefacts:** Use physical artefacts to learn AI, such as robotics, sensors and Arduino devices.
b) **Software-focused artefacts:** Learn AI by using digital artefacts like simulation and programming that are based on blocks and grammar.
c) **AI-related agents:** Create your machine learning models without knowing any code by using intelligent agents like chatbots, machine learning trainers, and expert systems.
d) **Unplugged:** To learn AI without a computer, use educational activities including role-playing, case studies, lectures, and storytelling.

Pedagogical Knowledge: The pedagogies, which include instructional strategies and approaches, are categorised based on educational levels. Introducing students to the basic ideas of AI and computer science and encouraging them to make the connection between AI applications and the underlying concepts are two goals of secondary school AI literacy instruction. Examples of educational knowledge acquisition include:

a) **Project-/problem-based learning**: Learning strategies that encourage students to work on real-world problems, questions, or challenges to acquire knowledge and skills.
b) **Collaborative learning:** With the help of this methodology, students can learn how to interact with one another, collaborate with peers, and learn how to use smart technologies and artificial intelligence.
c) **Experiential learning:** Through practical experiences and introspection, students can learn by doing and develop a deeper understanding of how to apply classroom ideas and information to real-world scenarios.

Content Knowledge: The following 16 competencies should be acquired by students, according to Long and Magerko (2020): knowledge representations, decision-making, understanding machine learning, recognizing the roles of humans in AI, interdisciplinary skills, distinguishing between general and narrow AI, recognizing AI's strengths and weaknesses, higher-level reasoning of AI, sensors, and ethical concerns behind. The following five "big ideas" of AI, according to Touretzky et al. (2019), have laid a strong basis for future research in advancing AI literacy:

a) **Perceptions:** Computers use sensors to sense their surroundings.
b) **Representation and reasoning:** To reason, agents keep a representation of the world.
c) **Learning:** Computers are capable of learning from vast volumes of data.
d) **Natural interaction:** For intelligent agents to engage with people in a natural way, they need a variety of information.
e) **Societal impact:** AI has the potential to have both beneficial and detrimental effects on society.

Three components make up the conceptual framework for AI literacy as put forth by Kong et al. (2021): the cognitive dimension, which focuses on teaching people the fundamentals of AI and enhancing their ability to use these concepts for assessment and comprehension of the real world; the affective dimension, which emphasizes participant empowerment so they can respond to the pervasive use of AI in their daily lives and at work; and the socio-cultural dimension, which aims to promote the ethical application of AI for sustainable global development. This explanation of the fundamental AI skills that ought to be incorporated into any AI literacy framework was subsequently altered by Kong, Cheung, and Tsang (2024). Figure 6 below illustrates the four dimensions of AI literacy that are described here:

Figure 6. Conceptual AI Literacy Framework

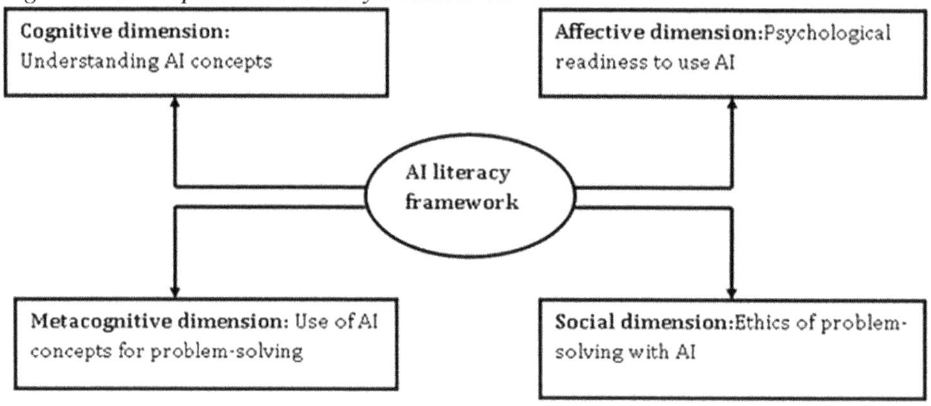

(Cheung and Tsang, 2024)

As seen in Figure 6 above, the components of AI literacy can be categorised into four categories. In the simplest terms, educated persons need to grasp the AI conceptually (Touretzky et al., 2019; Wang et al., 2023; Wong et al., 2020).

The knowledge and concepts of artificial intelligence are constantly recognised as a critical component of AI literacy across the many perspectives presented by authors. Long and Magerko (2020) developed one of the earliest frameworks for AI literacy, highlighting the importance of comprehending the potential of AI algorithms and their uses. The cognitive component of AI literacy is knowing the basic logic of AI algorithms, such as neural networks, supervised learning (e.g., linear regression and the K-nearest neighbor algorithm), and unsupervised learning (e.g., K-means clustering), as well as how these algorithms can be adjusted to address real-world problems (Chiu et al., 2022; Marques et al., 2020; Ng et al., 2022; Zhang et al., 2023). According to Kong, Cheung, and Tsang (2024), the conceptual knowledge of artificial intelligence also includes the advantages and disadvantages of algorithms as well as the kinds of situations for which they might be appropriate and applicable (Ng et al., 2023; Pintrich, 2002). The ability to easily use AI to enhance their skill sets, boost their creativity and productivity, and address real-world issues is a pre-requisite for educated citizens. A crucial stage in applying AI to solve problems is evaluating AI-based solutions that have been developed by oneself or others. In this regard, AI principles are useful, although not essential. To fully utilise AI, educated citizens must be able to address a variety of challenges that require metacognitive processes and transcend conceptual understanding (Ng et al., 2023). Therefore, the metacognitive aspect of AI literacy is the ability to use AI tools for problem-solving. According to Schraw et al. (2006), problem-solving with AI can be summed up in four steps: (1) problem definition; (2) identification of pertinent AI concepts and solutions; (3) selection, planning, and implementation of AI-based solutions; and (4) evaluation of the solutions' outcomes.

PROPOSED ARTIFICIAL INTELLIGENCE LITERACY FRAMEWORK

Based on the research evaluation, educators and students at different educational levels must develop distinct AI literacies due to the disparities in their learning requirements. The suggested framework, which is displayed in Table 2 below, recognises that different learning and teaching requirements exist at different educational levels. While lower-level students use basic AI applications for learning, higher-level students need more sophisticated applications and responsibilities. Teachers' AI literacy is recognised to be guided by the TPACK framework.

Table 2. Proposed AI Literacy Framework

Education level	AI-Dimension	Attributes
Primary	Knowing and Understanding AI	Teachers' Technological Knowledge.
		Teachers' Pedagogical Knowledge.
		Teachers' Content Knowledge.
	Using and Applying AI	Utilise and apply AI concepts, knowledge, and applications to solve problems.
	Data literacy	Utilising data or having the abilities, know-how, and dispositions to actively and creatively use data (interpreting, navigating, gathering, and presenting). Understanding data refers to the abilities, attitudes, and knowledge necessary to intentionally and critically evaluate the function of data through observation, analysis, evaluation, and reflection.
	Digital literacy	Digital rights, digital use, digital security, and digital safety, Digital identity, digital communication, and digital emotional intelligence.

continued on following page

Table 2. Continued

Education level	AI-Dimension	Attributes
	AI Ethics	Moral aspects of information ethics include human-centred considerations, acceptance, adaptation, cooperation, balancing, serving people, enhancing the quality of life, the goal of applying AI, and rules and laws. Principles of AI ethics: transparency, privacy, non-maleficence, beneficence, autonomy, and fairness.
Secondary	Knowing and Understanding AI	Teachers' Technological Knowledge.
		Teachers' Pedagogical Knowledge.
		Teachers' Content Knowledge.
	Using and Applying AI	Utilise and apply AI principles, knowledge, and applications to solve problems and incorporate AI into the curriculum.
	Data literacy	Utilising data or having the abilities, know-how, and dispositions to actively and creatively use data (interpreting, navigating, gathering, and presenting). Understanding data refers to the abilities, attitudes, and knowledge necessary to intentionally and critically evaluate the function of data through observation, analysis, evaluation, and reflection.
	Digital literacy	Digital rights, digital use, digital security, and digital safety, Digital identity, digital communication, and digital emotional intelligence.
	Evaluate and Create AI	Developing and assessing artificial intelligence applications. Cooperation and cooperative activities.
	AI Ethics	Moral aspects of information ethics include human-centred considerations, acceptance, adaptation, cooperation, balancing, serving people, enhancing the quality of life, the goal of applying AI, and rules and laws. Principles of AI ethics: transparency, privacy, non-maleficence, beneficence, autonomy, and fairness.
	Data literacy	Utilising data or having the abilities, know-how, and dispositions to actively and creatively use data (interpreting, navigating, gathering, and presenting). Understanding data refers to the abilities, attitudes, and knowledge necessary to intentionally and critically evaluate the function of data through observation, analysis, evaluation, and reflection.
	Digital literacy	Digital rights, digital use, digital security, and digital safety, Digital identity, digital communication, and digital emotional intelligence.
	Computational thinking	Logical reasoning (classification, prediction, and generation) and problem-solving abilities
	Transdisciplinary and interdisciplinary knowledge	Incorporating ideas and techniques from other fields to improve AI comprehension and use.

continued on following page

Table 2. Continued

Education level	AI-Dimension	Attributes
Higher Education	Knowing and Understanding AI	Teachers' Technological Knowledge.
		Teachers' Pedagogical Knowledge.
		Teachers' Content Knowledge.
	Using and Applying AI	Utilise and apply AI principles, knowledge, and applications to solve problems and incorporate AI into the curriculum.
	Evaluate and Create AI	Developing and assessing artificial intelligence applications. Cooperation and cooperative activities.
	AI Ethics	Moral aspects of information ethics include human-centred considerations, acceptance, adaptation, cooperation, balancing, serving people, enhancing the quality of life, the goal of applying AI, and rules and laws. Principles of AI ethics: transparency, privacy, non-maleficence, beneficence, autonomy, and fairness.
	Data literacy	Utilising data or having the abilities, know-how, and dispositions to actively and creatively use data (interpreting, navigating, gathering, and presenting). Understanding data refers to the abilities, attitudes, and knowledge necessary to intentionally and critically evaluate the function of data through observation, analysis, evaluation, and reflection.
	Digital literacy	Digital rights, digital use, digital security, and digital safety, Digital identity, digital communication, and digital emotional intelligence.
	Algorithm literacy	Understand how algorithms operate, the biases they might have, and how to assess their effects on information produced by artificial intelligence.
	Computational thinking	Logical reasoning (classification, prediction, and generation) and problem-solving abilities
	Transdisciplinary and interdisciplinary knowledge	Incorporating ideas and techniques from other fields to improve AI comprehension and use.

The use of AI across disciplines, which frequently takes place in higher education where interdisciplinary collaboration has become popular in contemporary research, is one of the main findings from the literature study on AI competencies. The literature has also yielded other constructs such as computational thinking, transdisciplinary knowledge, data literacy, and algorithm literacy. As a result, these factors have been included in the main components of AI literacy, which are knowledge and comprehension of AI, application and use of AI, assessment and development of AI, and ethics of AI.

CONCLUSIONS

Research on AI literacy in general and AI literacy in education in particular has produced evidence. According to this review, there aren't any significant differences in AI literacy across different domains. The most common domains of AI literacy are knowing and comprehending AI, applying and using AI, assessing and developing AI, and AI ethics. However, this research has expanded the scope of AI literacy to include the following: computational thinking, data literacy, digital literacy, algorithm literacy, and transdisciplinary and interdisciplinary knowledge.

REFERENCES

Abdelghani, R., Sauz'eon, H., & Oudeyer, P. Y. (2023). Generative AI in the Classroom: Can students remain active learners? http://arxiv.org/abs/2310.03192

Audenhove, L. V. (2024). Data literacy in the new EU DigComp 2.2 framework: How DigComp defines competencies in artificial intelligence, the Internet of Things and data. *Information and Learning Science*, *125*(5/6), 406–436.

Bawden, D. (2008). Origins and concepts of digital literacy. Digital Literacies: Concepts, Policies and Practices, 30, 17–32.

Burgsteiner, H., Kandlhofer, M., & Steinbauer, G. (2016, March). Irobot: Teaching The basics of artificial intelligence in high schools. *Proceedings of the AAAI Conference on Artificial Intelligence*, *30*(1), 4126–4127.

Cetindamar, D., Kitto, K., Wu, M., Zhang, Y., Abedin, B., & Knight, S. (2022). Explicating AI literacy of employees at digital workplaces. *IEEE Transactions on Engineering Management*.

Cetindamar, D., Kirsty, K., Mengjia, W., Yi, Z., Babak, A., & Simon, K. (2024). Explicating AI Literacy of Employees at Digital Workplaces. *IEEE Transactions on Engineering Management*, *71*, 810–823. DOI: 10.1109/TEM.2021.3138503

Chiu, T. K. F., Meng, H., Chai, C. S., King, I., Wong, S., & Yam, Y. (2022). Creation and evaluation of a pre-tertiary artificial intelligence (AI) curriculum. *IEEE Transactions on Education*, *65*(1), 30–39. DOI: 10.1109/TE.2021.3085878

Chiu, T. K., & Sanusi, I. T. (2024). Define, foster, and assess students and Teachers. AI literacy and competency for all: Current status and future research direction. *Computers and Education Open*, 100182.

Chiu, T. K. F., Ahmad, Z., Ismailov, M., & Sanusi, I. S. T. (2024). What are Artificial intelligence literacy and competency? A comprehensive framework to support them. *Computers and Education Open*, *6*, 100171.

Corrigan, C. C., Asakipaam, S. A., Kponyo, J. J., & Luetge, C. (2023).Eds. AI Ethics in Higher Education: Insights from Africa and Beyond. Beyond SpringerBriefs in Ethics.

Dabis, A., & Csáki, C. (2024). AI and ethics: Investigating the first policy responses of higher education institutions to the challenge of generative AI. *Humanities & Social Sciences Communications*. Advance online publication. DOI: 10.1057/s41599-024-03526-z

Ding, L., Kim, S., & Allday, R. A. (2024). Development of an AI literacy Assessment for non-technical individuals: What do teachers know? *Contemporary Educational Technology*, *16*(3), ep512. DOI: 10.30935/cedtech/14619

Dong, C. (2023). How to Build an AI Tutor that Can Adapt to Any Course and Provide Accurate Answers Using a Large Language Model and Retrieval-Augmented Generation. http://arxiv.org/abs/2311.17696

DQ Institute. (2021). World's first global standard for digital literacy, skills and readiness launched by the coalition for digital intelligence: Global Standards for Digital Intelligence. Emerald Publishing Limited. .DOI: 10.1108/ILS-06-2023-0072

El-dosuky, M. A. (2024). *Artificial Intelligence Literacy Framework for K-12 Students*. Elsevier.

Griffin, P., & Care, E. (Eds.). (2014). *Assessment and teaching of 21st century Skills: Methods and approach*. Springer.

Guo, J., & Hao, J. J. (2021). Teachers' role orientation and literacy framework in the age of intelligence. *China Electron Educ*, *2021*(6), 121–127.

Hervieux, S., & Wheatley, A. (2024). *Building an AI Literacy Framework: Perspectives from Instruction Librarians and Current Information Literacy Tools*. Taylor & Francis Group.

Hibbert, M., Altman, E., Shippen, T., & Wright, M. (2024). A Framework for AI Literacy. *EDUCAUSE Review*.

Hwang, Y., Lee, J. H., & Shin, D. (2023). What is prompt literacy? An exploratory Study of language learners' development of new literacy skills using generative AI. /arXiv.2311.05373.DOI: 10.48550

Iordache, E., Mariën, I., & Baelden, D. (2017). Developing digital skills and Competences: A QuickScan analysis of 13 digital literacy models. *Italian Journal of Sociology of Education*, *9*(1), 6–30.

Janssen, C., Segers, E., McQueen, J. M., & Verhoeven, L. (2019). Comparing Effects of instruction on word meaning and word form on early literacy abilities in kindergarten. *Early Education and Development*, *30*(3), 375–399.

Jiang, B. (2023). Course Guide of Artificial Intelligence in Primary and Secondary Schools. *Journal of East China Normal University*, *41*, 121.

Kandlhofer, M., Steinbauer, G., Hirschmugl-Gaisch, S., & Huber, P. (2016). Artificial intelligence and computer science in education: From kindergarten to university. In 2016 IEEE Frontiers in Education Conference (FIE) (pp. 1–9). IEEE.

Karaca, O., Çalışkan, S. A., & Demir, K. (2021). Medical artificial intelligence Readiness scale for medical students (MAIRS-MS)–development, validity and reliability study. *BMC Medical Education*, *21*, 1–9.

Kim, S., Jang, Y., Kim, W., Choi, S., Jung, H., Kim, S., & Kim, H. (2021). Why And What to Teach: AI Curriculum for Elementary School. *Proceedings of the AAAI Conference on Artificial Intelligence*, *35*(17), 15569–15576. DOI: 10.1609/aaai.v35i17.17833

Kong, S. C., Cheung, W. M. Y., & Zhang, G. (2021). Evaluation of an artificial intelligence literacy course for university students with diverse study backgrounds. Computers and Education. Artificial Intelligence, 100026.

Kong, S. C., Man-Yin Cheung, W., & Zhang, G. (2023). Evaluating an Artificial Intelligence literacy program for developing university students' conceptual understanding, literacy, empowerment, and ethical awareness. *Journal of Educational Technology & Society*, *26*(1), 16–30. DOI: 10.30191/ETS.202301_26(1).0002

Kong, S. C., Wang, Q., Huang, R., Li, Y., & Hsu, T. C. (Eds.). (2021). Conference Proceedings (English Paper) of the 25th Global Chinese Conference on Computers in Education (GCCCE 2021). Hong Kong: The Education University of Hong Kong.

Larson, L. C., & Miller, T. N. (2011). 21st-century skills: Prepare students for the Future. *Kappa Delta Pi Record*, *47*(3), 121–123.

Laupichler, M. C., Aster, A., Schirch, J., & Raupach, T. (2022). Artificial Intelligence literacy in higher and adult education: A scoping literature review. *Computers & Education*, *2022*(3), 100101. DOI: 10.1016/j.caeai.2022.100101

Lee, I., Ali, S., Zhang, H., Dipaola, D., & Breazeal, C. (2021). Developing middle School students' AI literacy. In *Proceedings of the 52nd ACM Technical Symposium on Computer Science Education* (pp. 191-197). ACM. DOI: 10.1145/3408877.3432513

Liu, S., & Xie, X. (2021). AI Quality Cultivation and Application Ability Training for Normal University Students. In 2021 7th Annual International Conference on Network and Information Systems for Computers (ICNISC), 116–20. DOI: 10.1109/ICNISC54316.2021.00030

Long, D., & Magerko, B. (2020). What is AI literacy? Competencies and design Considerations. In: *Proceedings of the 2020 CHI Conference on Human Factors in Computing Systems*, (2020): 1–16. DOI: 10.1145/3313831.3376727

Marienko, M. V., Semerikov, S. O., & Markova, O. M. (2023). Artificial intelligence Literacy in secondary education: methodological approaches and challenges. *CTE 2023: 11th Workshop on Cloud Technologies in Education*, Kryvyi Rih, Ukraine.

Marques, L. S., Gresse von Wangenheim, C., & Hauck, J. C. R. (2020). Teaching Machine learning in school: A systematic mapping of the state of the art. *Informatics in Education, 19*(2), 283–321. DOI: 10.15388/infedu.2020.14

Mikalef, P., & Gupta, M. (2021). Artificial Intelligence Capability: Conceptualisation, Measurement Calibration, and Empirical Study on Its Impact on Organisational Creativity and Firm Performance. *Information & Management, 58*(3), 103434. DOI: 10.1016/j.im.2021.103434

Ng, D. T. K., Lee, M., Tan, R. J. Y., Hu, X., Downie, J. S., & Chu, S. K. W. (2023). A review of AI teaching and learning from 2000 to 2020. *Education and Information Technologies, 28*, 8445–8501. DOI: 10.1007/s10639-022-11491-w

Ng, D. T. K., Leung, J. K. L., Chu, K. W. S., & Qiao, M. S. (2021). AI literacy: Definition, teaching, evaluation and ethical issues. *Proceedings of the Association for Information Science and Technology, 58*(1), 504–509.

Ng, D. T. K., Luo, W., Chan, H. M. Y., & Chu, S. K. W. (2022). Using digital story Writing as a pedagogy to develop AI literacy among primary students. Computers & Education: Artificial Intelligence, (3), 1-14. .caeai.2022.100054DOI: 10.1016/j

Ng, D., Tsz, K., Jac, K., Leung, L., Chu, S. K. W., & Qiao, M. S. (2021). Conceptualising AI Literacy: An Exploratory Review. *Computers and Education: Artificial Intelligence*, *2*, 100041. DOI: 10.1016/j.caeai.2021.100041

Ng. D.T.K., Leung, J.K.L., Chu, S.K.W., & Qiao, M.S. (2021). Conceptualizing AI Literacy: an exploratory review. Comput Educ, 2, 100041. .caeai.2021.100041DOI: 10.1016/j

Olari, V. (2023). Introducing artificial intelligence literacy in schools: A review of competence areas, pedagogical approaches, contexts and formats. In Keane, T., Lewin, C., Brinda, T., & Bottino, R. (Eds.), *Towards a collaborative society through creative learning*. Springer. DOI: 10.1007/978-3-031-43393-1_21

Quille, K., Becker, B. A., & Vidal-Meli'a, L. (2022). The European Commission and AI: Guidelines, acts and plans impacting the teaching of AI and teaching with AI. *Proceedings of the 54th ACM technical symposium on computer science education, 2*(1410).

Ren, F., & Ling, L. L. (2024). A Study on the Framework for Measuring Artificial Intelligence Literacy in Junior High School Students. Proceedings of the 2024 5th International Conference on Education, Knowledge and Information Management (ICEKIM 2024). DOI: 10.2991/978-94-6463-502-7_65

Salhab, R. (2024). AI literacy across curriculum design: Investigating college instructors' perspectives. *Online Learning : the Official Journal of the Online Learning Consortium*, *28*(2), 22–47. DOI: 10.24059/olj.v28i2.4426

Schraw, G., Crippen, K. J., & Hartley, K. (2006). Promoting self-regulation in Science education: Metacognition as part of a broader perspective on learning. *Research in Science Education*, (36), 111–139. DOI: 10.1007/s11165-005-3917-8

Southworth, J., Migliaccio, K., Glover, J., Glover, J., Reed, D., McCarty, C., Brendemuhl, J., & Thomas, A. (2023). Developing a model for AI Across the curriculum: Transforming the higher education landscape via innovation in AI literacy. *Computers and Education: Artificial Intelligence*, *4*, 100127.

Sperling, K., Stenberg, C., McGrath, C., Åkerfeldt, A., Heintz, F., & Stenliden, L. (2024). In search of artificial intelligence (AI) literacy in teacher education: A scoping review. *Computers and Education Open*, *6*, 100169. DOI: 10.1016/j.caeo.2024.100169

Steinbauer, G., Kandlhofer, M., Chklovski, T., Heintz, F., & Koenig, S. (2021). A Differentiated discussion about AI education K-12. *KI-Künstliche Intelligenz*, *35*(2), 131–137.

Stolpe, K., & Hallstr¨om, J. (2024). Artificial intelligence literacy for technology education. *Computers and Education Open*, *6*, 100159.

Su, J., Ng, D. T. K., & Chu, S. K. W. (2023). Artificial Intelligence (AI) Literacy in Early Childhood Education: The Challenges and Opportunities. *Computers and Education: Artificial Intelligence*, *4*, 100124.

Tenberga, I., & Daniela, L. (2024). Artificial Intelligence Literacy Competencies for Teachers Through Self-Assessment Tools. *Sustainability*, *2024*(16), 10386. DOI: 10.3390/su162310386

Touretzky, D., Gardner-McCune, C., Martin, F., & Seehorn, D. (2019). Envisioning AI for K-12: What should every child know about AI? *Proceedings of the AAAI Conference on Artificial Intelligence*, *33*(1), 9795–9799.

Tzirides, A. O., Zapata, G., Kastania, N. P., Saini, A. K., Castro, V., Ismael, S. A., You, Y., dos Santos, T. A., Searsmith, D., O'Brien, C., Cope, B., & Kalantzis, M. (2024). Combining human and artificial intelligence for enhanced AI literacy in higher education. *Computers and Education Open*, *6*, 100184.

Wang, B., Rau, P. L. P., & Yuan, T. (2023). Measuring user competence in using Artificial intelligence: Validity and reliability of artificial intelligence literacy scale. *Behaviour & Information Technology*, *42*(9), 1324–1337. DOI: 10.1080/0144929X.2022.2072768

Wang, X. Y., Li, X. M., & Huang, J. Y. (2023). Junior High School Artificial Intelligence Literacy: Connotation, Evaluation and Promotion Strategy. *Open Journal of Social Sciences*, (11), 33–49. DOI: 10.4236/jss.2023.115004

Wong, G. K. W., Ma, X., Dillenbourg, P., & Huan, J. (2020). Broadening artificial intelligence education in K-12: Where to start? *ACM Inroads*, *11*(1), 20–29. DOI: 10.1145/3381884

Yi, Y. (2021). Establishing the concept of AI literacy: Focusing on competence and purpose. Jahr – European Journal of Bioethics, Artificial Intelligence Humanities, 12(2), 353–368. https://doi.org/, 24.DOI: 10.21860/j.12.2.8

Yim, I. H. Y. (2024). A critical review of teaching and learning artificial intelligence (AI) Literacy: Developing an intelligence-based AI literacy framework for primary school education. *Computers and Education: Artificial Intelligence*, *7*, 100319.

Yim, I. H. Y., & Su, J. (2024). Artificial intelligence (AI) learning tools in K-12 Education: A scoping review. *Journal of Computers in Education*, 1–39.

Zhang, H., Lee, I., Ali, S., DiPaola, D., Cheng, Y., & Breazeal, C. (2023). Integrating Ethics and career futures with technical learning to promote AI literacy for middle school students: An exploratory study. *International Journal of Artificial Intelligence in Education*, *33*, 290–324. DOI: 10.1007/s40593-022-00293-3

Zhao, L., Wu, X., & Luo, H. (2022). Developing AI literacy for primary and middle school School teachers in China: Based on a structural equation modelling analysis. *Sustainability*, *14*(21), 1–16. DOI: 10.3390/su142114549

KEY TERMS AND DEFINITIONS

AI Ethics: Guiding principles in the use of AI.

AI Literacy: Various skills in the usage of AI.

AI Literacy Framework: Guidelines that specify skills relevant to the usage of AI.

Algorithm Literacy: The ability to understand how AI algorithms work.

Artificial Intelligence: Digital technologies that simulate human reasoning and actions.

Data Literacy: The ability to explore, understand, and communicate with data in a meaningful way.

Digital Literacy: The confident and critical use of a full range of digital technologies for information, communication and basic problem-solving.

TPACK: Technology integration framework that identifies three types of knowledge instructors need to use AI in teaching and learning.

Compilation of References

Aayog, N. I. T. I. (2018). National Strategy for Artificial Intelligence: #AIForAll. https://niti.gov.in/sites/default/files/2021-07/NationalStrategy-for-AI-Discussion-Paper.pdf

Abbasi, B. N., Wu, Y., & Luo, Z. (2025). Exploring the impact of artificial intelligence on curriculum development in global higher education institutions. *Education and Information Technologies*, *30*(1), 547–581.

Abdelghani, R., Sauz'eon, H., & Oudeyer, P. Y. (2023). Generative AI in the Classroom: Can students remain active learners? http://arxiv.org/abs/2310.03192

AI4K12. (2020). *AI4K12 Five Big Ideas in Artificial Intelligence*. https://ai4k12.org

Akgun, S., & Greenhow, C. (2021). Artificial intelligence in education: Addressing ethical challenges in K-12 settings. *AI and Ethics*, *2*(3), 431–440. DOI: 10.1007/s43681-021-00096-7 PMID: 34790956

Alawneh, Y. J. J., Sleema, H., Salman, F. N., Alshammat, M. F., & Oteer, R. S., & ALrashidi, N. K. N. (2024, April). Adaptive Learning Systems: Revolutionizing Higher Education through AI-Driven Curricula. In *2024 International Conference on Knowledge Engineering and Communication Systems (ICKECS)* (Vol. 1, pp. 1-5). IEEE.

Al-Zahrani, A. M. (2024). Unveiling the shadows: Beyond the hype of AI in education. *Heliyon*, *10*(9), e30696. DOI: 10.1016/j.heliyon.2024.e30696 PMID: 38737255

Amodei, D.. (2016). *Deep speech 2: End-to-end speech recognition in English and Mandarin. International Conference on Machine Learning*, 173–182.

Aravantinos, S., Lavidas, K., Voulgari, I., Papadakis, S., Karalis, T., & Komis, V. (2024). Educational approaches with AI in primary school settings: A systematic review of the literature available in scopus. *Education Sciences*, *14*(7), 744.

Armbrust, M.. (2010). A view of cloud computing. *Communications of the ACM*, *53*(4), 50–58.

Arya, R., & Verma, A. (2024). Role of artificial intelligence in education. *International Journal of Advanced Research in Science. Tongxin Jishu*, *4*(2), 589–594.

Audenhove, L. V. (2024). Data literacy in the new EU DigComp 2.2 framework: How DigComp defines competencies in artificial intelligence, the Internet of Things and data. *Information and Learning Science*, *125*(5/6), 406–436.

Back, T., Fogel, D. B., & Michalewicz, Z. (1997). *Handbook of Evolutionary Computation*. Oxford University Press.

Balcombe, L. (2023). AI Chatbots in Digital Mental Health. *Informatics (MDPI)*, *10*(4), 82. DOI: 10.3390/informatics10040082

Barocas, S., Hardt, M., & Narayanan, A. (2019). Fairness and machine learning. http://fairmlbook.org

Barron, B., & Darling-Hammond, L. (2008). Teaching for meaningful learning: A review of research on inquiry-based and cooperative learning. In *Powerful learning: What we know about teaching for understanding* (pp. 11–70).

Bawden, D. (2008). Origins and concepts of digital literacy. Digital Literacies: Concepts, Policies and Practices, 30, 17–32.

Beers, S. Z. (2011). *21st century skills: Preparing students for THEIR future*. National Education Association.

Bhutoria, A. (2022). Personalized education and Artificial Intelligence in the United States, China, and India: A systematic review using a Human-In-The-Loop model. *Computers and Education: Artificial Intelligence*, *3*, 100068. DOI: 10.1016/j.caeai.2022.100068

Blackwell, S. E., & Heidenreich, T. (2021). Cognitive Behavior Therapy at the Crossroads. *International Journal of Cognitive Therapy*, *14*(1), 1–22. DOI: 10.1007/s41811-021-00104-y PMID: 33584950

Bojarski, M.. (2016). End to end learning for self-driving cars. *arXiv:1604.07316*.

Bolton, R. J., & Hand, D. J. (2002). Statistical fraud detection: A review. *Statistical Science*, *17*(3), 235–255.

Bonsu, E. M., & Baffour-Koduah, D. (2023). From the Consumers' Side: Determining Students' Perception and Intention to Use ChatGPT in Ghanaian Higher Education. Social Science Research Network. https://doi.org/DOI: 10.2139/ssrn.4387107

Bostrom, N. (2014). *Superintelligence: Paths, dangers, strategies*. Oxford University Press.

Brown, T. (2009). *Change by design: How design thinking creates new alternatives for business and society*. Harvard Business Press.

Brynjolfsson, E., & McAfee, A. (1997). *The second machine age: Work, progress, and prosperity in a time of brilliant technologies*. W.W. Norton & Company.

Brynjolfsson, E., & McAfee, A. (2017). *Machine, Platform, Crowd: Harnessing Our Digital Future*. W.W. Norton & Company.

Buchanan, B. G., & Feigenbaum, E. A. (1978). DENDRAL and Meta-DENDRAL: Their applications dimension. *Artificial Intelligence*, *11*(1-2), 5–24.

Budhwar, P., Malik, A., De Silva, M. T. T., & Thevisuthan, P. (2022). Artificial intelligence – challenges and opportunities for international HRM: A review and research agenda. *International Journal of Human Resource Management*, *33*(6), 1065–1097. DOI: 10.1080/09585192.2022.2035161

Bughin, J., Hazan, E., Ramaswamy, S., Chui, M., Allas, T., Dahlström, P., & Trench, M. (2018). *Artificial Intelligence: The Next Digital Frontier?* McKinsey Global Institute.

Burgsteiner, H., Kandlhofer, M., & Steinbauer, G. (2016, March). Irobot: Teaching The basics of artificial intelligence in high schools. *Proceedings of the AAAI Conference on Artificial Intelligence*, *30*(1), 4126–4127.

Bybee, R. W., Taylor, J. A., Gardner, A., Van Scotter, P., Carlson Powell, J., Westbrook, A., & Landes, N. (2006). *The BSCS 5E instructional model: Origins and effectiveness*. BSCS.

Cambra-Fierro, J. J., Blasco, M. F., López-Pérez, M.-E. E., & Trifu, A. (2024). ChatGPT adoption and its influence on faculty well-being: An empirical research in higher education. *Education and Information Technologies*, *30*(2), 1517–1538. DOI: 10.1007/s10639-024-12871-0

Campbell, M., Hoane, A. J., & Hsu, F. H. (2002). Deep Blue. *Artificial Intelligence*, *134*(1-2), 57–83.

Carroll, M., Goldman, S., Britos, L., Koh, J., Royalty, A., & Hornstein, M. (2010). Destination, imagination and the fires within: Design thinking in a middle school classroom. *International Journal of Art & Design Education*, *29*(1), 37–53.

Cetindamar, D., Kirsty, K., Mengjia, W., Yi, Z., Babak, A., & Simon, K. (2024). Explicating AI Literacy of Employees at Digital Workplaces. *IEEE Transactions on Engineering Management*, *71*, 810–823. DOI: 10.1109/TEM.2021.3138503

Cetindamar, D., Kitto, K., Wu, M., Zhang, Y., Abedin, B., & Knight, S. (2022). Explicating AI literacy of employees at digital workplaces. *IEEE Transactions on Engineering Management*.

Chan, C. K. Y., & Hu, W. (2023). Students' voices on generative AI: Perceptions, benefits, and challenges in higher education. *International Journal of Educational Technology in Higher Education*, *20*(1). Advance online publication. DOI: 10.1186/s41239-023-00411-8

Chetlur, S.. (2014). cuDNN: Efficient primitives for deep learning. *arXiv:1410.0759*.

Chiu, T. K. F., Ahmad, Z., Ismailov, M., & Sanusi, I. S. T. (2024). What are Artificial intelligence literacy and competency? A comprehensive framework to support them. *Computers and Education Open*, *6*, 100171.

Chiu, T. K. F., Meng, H., Chai, C. S., King, I., Wong, S., & Yam, Y. (2022). Creation and evaluation of a pre-tertiary artificial intelligence (AI) curriculum. *IEEE Transactions on Education*, *65*(1), 30–39. DOI: 10.1109/TE.2021.3085878

Chiu, T. K., & Sanusi, I. T. (2024). Define, foster, and assess students and Teachers. AI literacy and competency for all: Current status and future research direction. *Computers and Education Open*, 100182.

Chollet, F. (2018). *Deep learning with Python*. Manning Publications.

Clark, A.. (2019). The ethics of AI-generated media. *AI & Society*, *34*(2), 123–135.

Code.org. (n.d.). AI for Oceans. https://code.org/oceans

Cognimates. (n.d.). Cognimates: AI Education for Kids. https://cognimates.me

Corrigan, C. C., Asakipaam, S. A., Kponyo, J. J., & Luetge, C. (2023).Eds. AI Ethics in Higher Education: Insights from Africa and Beyond. Beyond SpringerBriefs in Ethics.

Crawford, J., Allen, K.-A., Pani, B., & Cowling, M. (2024). When artificial intelligence substitutes humans in higher education: The cost of loneliness, student success, and retention. *Studies in Higher Education*, *49*(5), 883–897. DOI: 10.1080/03075079.2024.2326956

Crawford, K. (2021). *Atlas of AI: Power, Politics, and the Planetary Costs of Artificial Intelligence*. Yale University Press.

Dabis, A., & Csáki, C. (2024). AI and ethics: Investigating the first policy responses of higher education institutions to the challenge of generative AI. *Humanities & Social Sciences Communications*. Advance online publication. DOI: 10.1057/s41599-024-03526-z

Davenport, T., & Kalakota, R. (2019). The potential for artificial intelligence in healthcare. *Future Healthcare Journal*, *6*(2), 94–98. DOI: 10.7861/futurehosp.6-2-94 PMID: 31363513

Demartini, C. G., Sciascia, L., Bosso, A., & Manuri, F. (2024). Artificial intelligence bringing improvements to adaptive learning in education: A case study. *Sustainability*, *16*(3), 1347.

Dempster, A. P., Laird, N. M., & Rubin, D. B. (1977). Maximum likelihood from incomplete data via the EM algorithm. *Journal of the Royal Statistical Society. Series B. Methodological*, *39*(1), 1–38.

Diaz, M. (2023). How to use ChatGPT: Everything you need to know. ZDNET. https://www.zdnet.com/article/how-to-use-chatgpt/

Ding, L., Kim, S., & Allday, R. A. (2024). Development of an AI literacy Assessment for non-technical individuals: What do teachers know? *Contemporary Educational Technology*, *16*(3), ep512. DOI: 10.30935/cedtech/14619

Dong, C. (2023). How to Build an AI Tutor that Can Adapt to Any Course and Provide Accurate Answers Using a Large Language Model and Retrieval-Augmented Generation. http://arxiv.org/abs/2311.17696

Dougherty, D., & Eisenberg, M. (2020). Machine learning for kids. https://machinelearningforkids.co.uk

DQ Institute. (2021). World's first global standard for digital literacy, skills and readiness launched by the coalition for digital intelligence: Global Standards for Digital Intelligence. Emerald Publishing Limited. .DOI: 10.1108/ILS-06-2023-0072

Dwivedi, Y. K., Kshetri, N., Hughes, L., Slade, E. L., Jeyaraj, A., Kar, A. K., Baabdullah, A. M., Koohang, A., Raghavan, V., Ahuja, M., Albanna, H., Albashrawi, M. A., Al-Busaidi, A. S., Balakrishnan, J., Barlette, Y., Basu, S., Bose, I., Brooks, L., Buhalis, D., & Wright, R. (2023). Opinion Paper: "So what if ChatGPT wrote it?" Multidisciplinary perspectives on opportunities, challenges and implications of generative conversational AI for research, practice and policy. *International Journal of Information Management*, *71*, 102642. DOI: 10.1016/j.ijinfomgt.2023.102642

Dwork, C. (2008). Differential privacy: A survey of results. In *Theory and Applications of Models of Computation* (pp. 1–19). Springer.

Edelson, D. C., Gordin, D. N., & Pea, R. D. (1999). Addressing the challenges of inquiry-based learning through technology and curriculum design. *Journal of the Learning Sciences*, *8*(3–4), 391–450.

Egara, F. O., & Mosimege, M. (2024). Exploring the integration of artificial intelligence-based ChatGPT into mathematics instruction: Perceptions, challenges, and implications for educators. *Education Sciences*, *14*(7), 742.

Eiben, A. E., & Smith, J. E. (2003). *Introduction to Evolutionary Computing*. Springer.

Ejjami, R. (2024). The future of learning: AI-based curriculum development. *International Journal For Multidisciplinary Research, 6*(4).

Elbanna, S., & Armstrong, L. (2024). Exploring the integration of ChatGPT in education: Adapting for the future. *Management & Sustainability: An Arab Review*, *3*(1), 16–29.

El-dosuky, M. A. (2024). *Artificial Intelligence Literacy Framework for K-12 Students*. Elsevier.

Erebak, S., & Turgut, T. (2021). Anxiety about the speed of technological development: Effects on job insecurity, time estimation, and automation level preference. *The Journal of High Technology Management Research*, *32*(2), 100419. DOI: 10.1016/j.hitech.2021.100419

Esteva, A.. (2017). Dermatologist-level classification of skin cancer with deep neural networks. *Nature*, *542*(7639), 115–118. PMID: 28117445

Eubanks, V. (2018). *Automating Inequality: How High-Tech Tools Profile, Police, and Punish the Poor*. St. Martin's Press.

European Commission. (2021). Proposal for a Regulation laying down harmonised rules on artificial intelligence (Artificial Intelligence Act). https://eur-lex.europa.eu/legal-content/EN/TXT/?uri=CELEX%3A52021PC0206

Fagherazzi, G., Fischer, A., Ismael, M., & Despotovic, V. (2021). Voice for Health: The Use of Vocal Biomarkers from Research to Clinical Practice. *Digital Biomarkers*, *5*(1), 78–88. DOI: 10.1159/000515346 PMID: 34056518

Fahmi, M. A., & Cahyono, B. Y. (2021). EFL students' perception on the use of grammarly and teacher feedback. [Journal of English Educators Society]. *JEES*, *6*(1), 18–25. DOI: 10.21070/jees.v6i1.849

Feigenbaum, E. A. (1980). *Knowledge engineering: The applied side of artificial intelligence*. Stanford University.

Ferrucci, D.. (2010). Building Watson: An overview of the DeepQA project. *AI Magazine*, *31*(3), 59–79.

Flanagan, O., Chan, A., Roop, P., & Sundram, F. (2021). Using Acoustic Speech Patterns From Smartphones to Investigate Mood Disorders: Scoping Review. *JMIR mHealth and uHealth*, *9*(9), e24352. DOI: 10.2196/24352 PMID: 34533465

Floridi, L., Cowls, J., Beltrametti, M., Chatila, R., Chazerand, P., Dignum, V., & Vayena, E. (2018). AI4People—An ethical framework for a good AI society. *Minds and Machines*, *28*(4), 689–707. PMID: 30930541

Floridi, L., Cowls, J., Beltrametti, M., Chatila, R., Chazerand, P., Dignum, V., & Vayena, E. (2018). AI4People—An ethical framework for a good AI society: Opportunities, risks, principles, and recommendations. *Minds and Machines*, *28*(4), 689–707. DOI: 10.1007/s11023-018-9482-5 PMID: 30930541

Fundi, M., Sanusi, I. T., Oyelere, S. S., & Ayere, M. (2024). Advancing AI education: Assessing Kenyan in-service teachers' preparedness for integrating artificial intelligence in competence-based curriculum. *Computers in Human Behavior Reports*, *14*, 100412.

Giarratano, J., & Riley, G. (2005). *Expert Systems: Principles and Programming*. Cengage Learning.

Gilson, A., Safranek, C. W., Huang, T., Socrates, V., Chi, L., & Taylor, R. A.. (2023). How does ChatGPT perform on the United States Medical Licensing Examination? The implications of large language models for medical education and knowledge assessment. *JMIR Medical Education*, *9*, e45312. DOI: 10.2196/45312 PMID: 36753318

Goertzel, B. (2007). *Artificial general intelligence*. Springer.

González-López, Óscar. R., Buenadicha-Mateos, M., & Sánchez-Hernández, M. I. (2021). Overwhelmed by Technostress? Sensitive Archetypes and Effects in Times of Forced Digitalization. *International Journal of Environmental Research and Public Health*, *18*(8), 4216. DOI: 10.3390/ijerph18084216 PMID: 33923407

Goodfellow, I., Bengio, Y., & Courville, A. (2016). *Deep learning*. MIT Press.

Goodfellow, I., Pouget-Abadie, J., Mirza, M., Xu, B., Warde-Farley, D., Ozair, S., & Bengio, Y. (2014). Generative adversarial networks. *Advances in Neural Information Processing Systems*, *27*, 2672–2680.

Google. (2018). Teachable Machine. https://teachablemachine.withgoogle.com

Graham, S., Depp, C., Lee, E. E., Nebeker, C., Tu, X., Kim, H.-C., & Jeste, D. V. (2019). Artificial Intelligence for Mental Health and Mental Illnesses: An Overview. *Current Psychiatry Reports*, *21*(11). Advance online publication. DOI: 10.1007/s11920-019-1094-0 PMID: 31701320

Grant, S. G., Lee, J., & Swan, K. (2017). *Inquiry-based practice in social studies education: Understanding the inquiry design model*. Routledge.

Graves, A., Wayne, G., & Danihelka, I. (2016). Neural Turing machines. *Nature*, *538*(7626), 471–476. PMID: 27732574

Griffin, P., & Care, E. (Eds.). (2014). *Assessment and teaching of 21st century Skills: Methods and approach*. Springer.

Grover, S., & Pea, R. (2013). Computational thinking in K–12: A review of the state of the field. *Educational Researcher*, *42*(1), 38–43.

Guo, J., & Hao, J. J. (2021). Teachers' role orientation and literacy framework in the age of intelligence. *China Electron Educ*, *2021*(6), 121–127.

Halili, S. H. (2019). Technological advancements in education and their implications. *International Journal of Emerging Technologies in Learning*, *14*(5), 36–46. DOI: 10.3991/ijet.v14i05.9357

Hastie, T., Tibshirani, R., & Friedman, J. (2009). *The elements of statistical learning*. Springer.

He, P., Shin, N., Kaldaras, L., & Krajcik, J. (2024). Integrating artificial intelligence into learning progression-based learning systems to support student knowledge-in-Use: Opportunities and challenges. *Handbook of Research on Science Learning Progressions*, 461-487.

Henriksen, D., Mishra, P., & Fisser, P. (2016). Infusing creativity and technology in 21st-century education: A systemic view for change. *Journal of Educational Technology & Society*, *19*(3), 27–37.

Hervieux, S., & Wheatley, A. (2024). *Building an AI Literacy Framework: Perspectives from Instruction Librarians and Current Information Literacy Tools*. Taylor & Francis Group.

Hibbert, M., Altman, E., Shippen, T., & Wright, M. (2024). A Framework for AI Literacy. *EDUCAUSE Review*.

Hinton, G. E., Osindero, S., & Teh, Y. W. (2006). A fast learning algorithm for deep belief nets. *Neural Computation*, *18*(7), 1527–1554. PMID: 16764513

Holmes, W., Bialik, M., & Fadel, C. (2019). *Artificial intelligence in education: Promises and implications for teaching and learning*. Center for Curriculum Redesign.

Huang, A.. (2020). AI and creativity: Music, video, and art generation. *Proceedings of the International Conference on Artificial Creativity.*

Hwang, Y., Lee, J. H., & Shin, D. (2023). What is prompt literacy? An exploratory Study of language learners' development of new literacy skills using generative AI. /arXiv.2311.05373.DOI: 10.48550

IBM. (2020). AI Education. https://www.ibm.com/skills/ai-education

Iordache, E., Mariën, I., & Baelden, D. (2017). Developing digital skills and Competences: A QuickScan analysis of 13 digital literacy models. *Italian Journal of Sociology of Education*, *9*(1), 6–30.

ISTE & IBM. (2020). AI + Ethics Curriculum Guide. https://cdn.iste.org/www-root/Libraries/Documents%20%26%20Files/AI_Ethics_Curriculum_Guide.pdf

Iweuno, B. N., Orekha, P., Ojediran, O., Imohimi, E., & Adu-Twum, H. T. (2024). Leveraging Artificial Intelligence for an inclusive and diversified curriculum. *World Journal of Advanced Research and Reviews*, *23*(2), 1579–1590.

Jackson, P. (1999). *Introduction to Expert Systems* (3rd ed.). Addison Wesley.

Janssen, C., Segers, E., McQueen, J. M., & Verhoeven, L. (2019). Comparing Effects of instruction on word meaning and word form on early literacy abilities in kindergarten. *Early Education and Development*, *30*(3), 375–399.

Jauregui-Correa, J. C., & Sen, M. (2024). Revolutionizing Engineering Education: Adapting Curricula to Address Artificial Intelligence Challenges and Opportunities. *Asean Journal of Engineering Education*, *8*(1), 64–69.

Jiang, B. (2023). Course Guide of Artificial Intelligence in Primary and Secondary Schools. *Journal of East China Normal University*, *41*, 121.

Johinke, R., Cummings, R., DiLauro, F., Johinke, R., Cummings, R., &DiLaurao, F. (2023). Reclaiming the technology of higher education for teaching digital writing in a post—pandemic world. Journal of University Teaching & Learning Practice, 20(2), 01. https://doi.org/DOI: 10.53761/1.20.02.01

Jordan, M. I., & Mitchell, T. M. (2015). Machine learning: Trends, perspectives, and prospects. *Science*, *349*(6245), 255–260. PMID: 26185243

Joseph, O. B., & Uzondu, N. C. (2024). Integrating AI and Machine Learning in STEM education: Challenges and opportunities. *Computer Science & IT Research Journal, 5*(8), 1732–1750.

Jouppi, N. P.. (2017). In-datacenter performance analysis of a tensor processing unit. *Proceedings of the 44th International Symposium on Computer Architecture*, 1–12.

Jurafsky, D., & Martin, J. H. (2020). *Speech and language processing* (3rd ed.). Draft., https://web.stanford.edu/~jurafsky/slp3/

Kamalov, F., Santandreu Calonge, D., & Gurrib, I. (2023). New Era of Artificial Intelligence in Education: Towards a Sustainable Multifaceted Revolution. *Sustainability, 15*(16), 12451. DOI: 10.3390/su151612451

Kandlhofer, M., Steinbauer, G., Hirschmugl-Gaisch, S., & Huber, P. (2016). Artificial intelligence and computer science in education: From kindergarten to university. In 2016 IEEE Frontiers in Education Conference (FIE) (pp. 1–9). IEEE.

Kangas, M., Siklander, P., Randolph, J., & Ruokamo, H. (2021). Teachers' engagement and students' learning in Finnish schools implementing AI-integrated, phenomenon-based learning. *Education and Information Technologies, 26*, 4797–4815.

Karaca, O., Çalışkan, S. A., & Demir, K. (2021). Medical artificial intelligence Readiness scale for medical students (MAIRS-MS)–development, validity and reliability study. *BMC Medical Education, 21*, 1–9.

Karataş, F., Eriçok, B., & Tanrikulu, L. (2025). Reshaping curriculum adaptation in the age of artificial intelligence: Mapping teachers' AI-driven curriculum adaptation patterns. *British Educational Research Journal, 51*(1), 154–180.

Kayal, A. (2024). Transformative Pedagogy: A Comprehensive Framework for AI Integration in Education. In *Explainable AI for Education: Recent Trends and Challenges* (pp. 247–270). Springer Nature Switzerland.

Khurana, D., Koli, A., Khatter, K., & Singh, S. (2022). Natural language processing: State of the art, current trends and challenges. *Multimedia Tools and Applications, 82*(3), 3713–3744. DOI: 10.1007/s11042-022-13428-4 PMID: 35855771

Kim, S., Jang, Y., Kim, W., Choi, S., Jung, H., Kim, S., & Kim, H. (2021). Why And What to Teach: AI Curriculum for Elementary School. *Proceedings of the AAAI Conference on Artificial Intelligence, 35*(17), 15569–15576. DOI: 10.1609/aaai.v35i17.17833

Kohnke, L., Rudolph, R., & Li, Y. (2023). ChatGPT as a Tool for Improving Learning Practices. Journal of Educational Technology.

Kong, S. C., Cheung, W. M. Y., & Zhang, G. (2021). Evaluation of an artificial intelligence literacy course for university students with diverse study backgrounds. Computers and Education. Artificial Intelligence, 100026.

Kong, S. C., Wang, Q., Huang, R., Li, Y., & Hsu, T. C. (Eds.). (2021). Conference Proceedings (English Paper) of the 25th Global Chinese Conference on Computers in Education (GCCCE 2021). Hong Kong: The Education University of Hong Kong.

Kong, S. C., Man-Yin Cheung, W., & Zhang, G. (2023). Evaluating an Artificial Intelligence literacy program for developing university students' conceptual understanding, literacy, empowerment, and ethical awareness. *Journal of Educational Technology & Society*, *26*(1), 16–30. DOI: 10.30191/ETS.202301_26(1).0002

Kostka, I., & Toncelli, R. (2023). Exploring Applications of ChatGPT to English Language Teaching: Opportunities, Challenges, and Recommendations. Teaching English as a Second Language-EJ. https://doi.org/DOI: 10.55593/ej.27107int

Kotsis, K. T. (2024). Integration of artificial intelligence in science teaching in primary education: Applications for teachers. *European Journal of Contemporary Education and E-Learning*, *2*(3), 27–43.

Krajcik, J., & Blumenfeld, P. (2006). Project-based learning. In Sawyer, R. K. (Ed.), *The Cambridge handbook of the learning sciences* (pp. 317–334). Cambridge University Press.

Krizhevsky, A., Sutskever, I., & Hinton, G. E. (2012). ImageNet classification with deep convolutional neural networks. *Advances in Neural Information Processing Systems*, *25*, 1097–1105.

Labadze, L., Grigolia, M., & Machaidze, L. (2023). Role of AI chatbots in education: Systematic literature review. *International Journal of Educational Technology in Higher Education*, *20*(1). Advance online publication. DOI: 10.1186/s41239-023-00426-1

Lake, B. M., Ullman, T. D., Tenenbaum, J. B., & Gershman, S. J. (2017). Building machines that learn and think like people. *Behavioral and Brain Sciences*, *40*, e253. PMID: 27881212

Lam, R., & Moorhouse, B. L. (2022). Using digital portfolios to develop students' writing. https://doi.org/DOI: 10.4324/9781003295860

Lane, N. D.. (2016). DeepX: A software accelerator for low-power deep learning inference on mobile devices. *Proceedings of the 15th International Conference on Information Processing in Sensor Networks*, 1–12.

Larson, L. C., & Miller, T. N. (2011). 21st-century skills: Prepare students for the Future. *Kappa Delta Pi Record*, *47*(3), 121–123.

Laupichler, M. C., Aster, A., Schirch, J., & Raupach, T. (2022). Artificial Intelligence literacy in higher and adult education: A scoping literature review. *Computers & Education*, *2022*(3), 100101. DOI: 10.1016/j.caeai.2022.100101

LeCun, Y., Bengio, Y., & Hinton, G. (2015). Deep learning. *Nature*, *521*(7553), 436–444. PMID: 26017442

LeCun, Y., Bottou, L., Bengio, Y., & Haffner, P. (1998). Gradient-based learning applied to document recognition. *Proceedings of the IEEE*, *86*(11), 2278–2324.

Lee, I., Ali, S., Zhang, H., Dipaola, D., & Breazeal, C. (2021). Developing middle School students' AI literacy. In *Proceedings of the 52nd ACM Technical Symposium on Computer Science Education* (pp. 191-197). ACM. DOI: 10.1145/3408877.3432513

Lee, S., & Song, K. S. (2024). Teachers' and students' perceptions of AI-generated concept explanations: Implications for integrating generative AI in computer science education. *Computers and Education: Artificial Intelligence*, *7*, 100283.

Liedtka, J. (2015). Perspective: Linking design thinking with innovation outcomes through cognitive bias reduction. *Journal of Product Innovation Management*, *32*(6), 925–938.

Lin, H., & Chen, Q. (2024). Artificial intelligence (AI)-integrated educational applications and college students' creativity and academic emotions: Students and teachers' perceptions and attitudes. *BMC Psychology*, *12*(1), 487. PMID: 39285268

Lišnić, B., Zaharija, G., & Mladenović, S. (2025). Integration of Artificial Intelligence in K-12: Analysis of a Three-Year Pilot Study. *AI*, *6*(3), 49.

Liu, S., & Xie, X. (2021). AI Quality Cultivation and Application Ability Training for Normal University Students. In 2021 7th Annual International Conference on Network and Information Systems for Computers (ICNISC), 116–20. DOI: 10.1109/ICNISC54316.2021.00030

Lloyd, S. (2000). Ultimate physical limits to computation. *Nature*, *406*(6799), 1047–1054. PMID: 10984064

Long, D., & Magerko, B. (2020). What is AI literacy? *ACM Transactions on Human-Computer Interaction*, *27*(1), 1–29.

Long, D., & Magerko, B. (2020). What is AI literacy? Competencies and design Considerations. In: *Proceedings of the 2020 CHI Conference on Human Factors in Computing Systems*, (2020): 1–16. DOI: 10.1145/3313831.3376727

Long, D., & Magerko, B. (2020). What is AI literacy? Competencies and design considerations. *Proceedings of the 2020 CHI Conference on Human Factors in Computing Systems*, 1–16.

Long, D., & Magerko, B. (2020). What is AI Literacy? Competencies and Design Considerations. *Proceedings of the ACM CHI Conference*.

Luckin, R. (2018). *Machine learning and human intelligence: The future of education for the 21st century*. UCL Institute of Education Press.

Luckin, R., Cukurova, M., Kent, C., & du Boulay, B. (2022). Empowering educators to be AI-ready. *Computers and Education: Artificial Intelligence*, *3*, 100076. DOI: 10.1016/j.caeai.2022.100076

Makhambetova, A., Zhiyenbayeva, N., & Ergesheva, E. (2021). Personalized Learning Strategy as a Tool to Improve Academic Performance and Motivation of Students. *International Journal of Web-Based Learning and Teaching Technologies*, *16*(6), 1–17. DOI: 10.4018/ijwltt.286743

Malik, A. S., Acharya, S., & Humane, S. (2024). Exploring the Impact of Security Technologies on Mental Health: A Comprehensive Review. *Cureus*. Advance online publication. DOI: 10.7759/cureus.53664 PMID: 38455776

Marienko, M. V., Semerikov, S. O., & Markova, O. M. (2023). Artificial intelligence Literacy in secondary education: methodological approaches and challenges. *CTE 2023: 11th Workshop on Cloud Technologies in Education*, Kryvyi Rih, Ukraine.

Marques, L. S., Gresse von Wangenheim, C., & Hauck, J. C. R. (2020). Teaching Machine learning in school: A systematic mapping of the state of the art. *Informatics in Education*, *19*(2), 283–321. DOI: 10.15388/infedu.2020.14

Mayasari, N., Sastraatmadja, A. H. M., Suparman, T., Mutiara, I. I., & Maqfirah, P. A. V. (2024). Effectiveness of Using Artificial Intelligence Learning Tools and Customized Curriculum on Improving Students' Critical Thinking Skills in Indonesia. *The Eastasouth Journal of Learning and Educations*, *2*(02), 111–118.

McCarthy, J., Minsky, M. L., Rochester, N., & Shannon, C. E. (1956). *A proposal for the Dartmouth summer research project on artificial intelligence*. Dartmouth College.

McCarthy, J., Minsky, M., Rochester, N., & Shannon, C. E. (1956). A proposal for the Dartmouth Summer Research Project on Artificial Intelligence. *AI Magazine*, *27*(4), 12–14.

McCulloch, W. S., & Pitts, W. (1943). A logical calculus of the ideas immanent in nervous activity. *The Bulletin of Mathematical Biophysics*, *5*(4), 115–133.

McDermott, D. (1987). A critique of pure reason. *Computational Intelligence*, *3*(3), 151–160.

Mehrabi, N., Morstatter, F., Saxena, N., Lerman, K., & Galstyan, A. (2021). A survey on bias and fairness in machine learning. *ACM Computing Surveys*, *54*(6), 1–35.

Menekse, M. (2023). Envisioning the Future of Learning and Teaching Engineering in the Artificial Intelligence Era: Opportunities and Challenges. *Journal of Engineering Education*. Advance online publication. DOI: 10.1002/jee.20539

Microsoft. (n.d.). MakeCode for micro:bit. https://makecode.microbit.org

Mikalef, P., & Gupta, M. (2021). Artificial Intelligence Capability: Conceptualisation, Measurement Calibration, and Empirical Study on Its Impact on Organisational Creativity and Firm Performance. *Information & Management*, *58*(3), 103434. DOI: 10.1016/j.im.2021.103434

Molnar, A. (2024). Prescription Digital Therapeutics: Assertions. *Health Affairs*, *43*(6), 897–897. DOI: 10.1377/hlthaff.2024.00152 PMID: 38830162

Mosly, I. (2024). Artificial intelligence's opportunities and challenges in engineering curricular design: A combined review and focus group study. *Societies (Basel, Switzerland)*, *14*(6), 89.

Naeem, S., Qureshi, M. A., & Butt, A. M. (2025). AI Integration Into Course Content Development. In *AI Applications for English Language Learning* (pp. 93–120). IGI Global Scientific Publishing.

Nakshine, V. S., Thute, P., Khatib, M. N., & Sarkar, B. (2022). Increased Screen Time as a Cause of Declining Physical, Psychological Health, and Sleep Patterns: A Literary Review. *Cureus*. Advance online publication. DOI: 10.7759/cureus.30051 PMID: 36381869

Ng, D. T. K., Luo, W., Chan, H. M. Y., & Chu, S. K. W. (2022). Using digital story Writing as a pedagogy to develop AI literacy among primary students. Computers & Education: Artificial Intelligence, (3), 1-14. .caeai.2022.100054DOI: 10.1016/j

Ng, A. (2021). *AI for Everyone: Demystifying Artificial Intelligence*. Coursera.

Ng, D. T. K., Lee, M., Tan, R. J. Y., Hu, X., Downie, J. S., & Chu, S. K. W. (2023). A review of AI teaching and learning from 2000 to 2020. *Education and Information Technologies*, *28*, 8445–8501. DOI: 10.1007/s10639-022-11491-w

Ng, D. T. K., Leung, J. K. L., Chu, K. W. S., & Qiao, M. S. (2021). AI literacy: Definition, teaching, evaluation and ethical issues. *Proceedings of the Association for Information Science and Technology, 58*(1), 504–509.

Ng, D., Tsz, K., Jac, K., Leung, L., Chu, S. K. W., & Qiao, M. S. (2021). Conceptualising AI Literacy: An Exploratory Review. *Computers and Education: Artificial Intelligence, 2*, 100041. DOI: 10.1016/j.caeai.2021.100041

Nilsson, N. J. (1984). *Shakey the robot.* SRI International.

Nilsson, N. J. (2014). *Principles of artificial intelligence.* Morgan Kaufmann.

OECD. (2019). OECD principles on artificial intelligence. https://www.oecd.org/going-digital/ai/principles/

Okada, A., Sherborne, T., Panselinas, G., & Kolionis, G. (2025). Fostering transversal skills through open schooling supported by the CARE-KNOW-DO pedagogical model and the UNESCO AI competencies framework. *International Journal of Artificial Intelligence in Education*, •••, 1–46.

Olari, V. (2023). Introducing artificial intelligence literacy in schools: A review of competence areas, pedagogical approaches, contexts and formats. In Keane, T., Lewin, C., Brinda, T., & Bottino, R. (Eds.), *Towards a collaborative society through creative learning*. Springer. DOI: 10.1007/978-3-031-43393-1_21

Olatunde-Aiyedun, T. G. (2024). Artificial intelligence (AI) in education: Integration of AI into science education curriculum in Nigerian universities. *International Journal of Artificial Intelligence for Digital, 1*(1).

OpenAI (2022, November 30). "ChatGPT: Optimizing Language Models for Dialogue". Archived from the original on November 30, 2022.

Peake, J. M., Kerr, G., & Sullivan, J. P. (2018). A Critical Review of Consumer Wearables, Mobile Applications, and Equipment for Providing Biofeedback, Monitoring Stress, and Sleep in Physically Active Populations. *Frontiers in Physiology, 9*. Advance online publication. DOI: 10.3389/fphys.2018.00743 PMID: 30002629

Pearl, J. (1988). *Probabilistic reasoning in intelligent systems: Networks of plausible inference*. Morgan Kaufmann.

Prajapati, M. A. B. (2024). ARTIFICIALLY INTELLIGENT IN EDUCATION:"REDEFINING LEARNING IN THE 21ST CENTURY". *Journal of Educational Technology, v1., 12818287*.DOI: <ALIGNMENT.qj></ALIGNMENT>10.5281/zenodo

PTSD Help - a Randomized Controlled Trial of a PTSD Mobile Health App. (2019). *Case Medical Research*. https://doi.org/DOI: 10.31525/ct1-nct03862703

Quille, K., Becker, B. A., & Vidal-Meli'a, L. (2022). The European Commission and AI: Guidelines, acts and plans impacting the teaching of AI and teaching with AI. *Proceedings of the 54th ACM technical symposium on computer science education, 2*(1410).

Reaktor & University of Helsinki. (2019). Elements of AI. https://www.elementsofai.com

Ren, F., & Ling, L. L. (2024). A Study on the Framework for Measuring Artificial Intelligence Literacy in Junior High School Students. Proceedings of the 2024 5th International Conference on Education, Knowledge and Information Management (ICEKIM 2024). DOI: 10.2991/978-94-6463-502-7_65

Rodrigues, R. S. (n.d.). *Sarcopenia e atrofia cerebral como preditores de prognóstico funcional em pacientes com aneurisma cerebral.* https://doi.org/DOI: 10.11606/t.5.2024.tde-18062025-095403

Rodway, P., & Schepman, A. (2023). The impact of adopting AI educational technologies on projected course satisfaction in university students. *Computers and Education: Artificial Intelligence*, *5*, 100150. DOI: 10.1016/j.caeai.2023.100150

Rosenblatt, F. (1958). The perceptron: A probabilistic model for information storage and organization in the brain. *Psychological Review*, *65*(6), 386–408. PMID: 13602029

Rumelhart, D. E., Hinton, G. E., & Williams, R. J. (1986). Learning representations by back-propagating errors. *Nature*, *323*(6088), 533–536.

Russell, S., & Norvig, P. (2021). *Artificial intelligence: A modern approach* (4th ed.). Pearson.

Salgado Granda, B. A., Inzhivotkina, Y., & Ugarte Fajardo, J. (2024). *Educational Innovation: Exploring the Potential of Generative Artificial Intelligence in Cognitive Schema Building*. Edutec, Revista Electrónica de Tecnología Educativa., DOI: 10.21556/edutec.2024.89.3251

Salhab, R. (2024). AI literacy across curriculum design: Investigating college instructors' perspectives. *Online Learning : the Official Journal of the Online Learning Consortium*, *28*(2), 22–47. DOI: 10.24059/olj.v28i2.4426

Salter, S., Sivarajah, U., & Kumar, V. (2023). Exploring ChatGPT's Influence on Critical Thinking and Problem-Solving in Education. *Educational Technology Review*.

Sammut, C., & Webb, G. I. (Eds.). (2017). *Encyclopedia of machine learning and data mining*. Springer.

Schapire, R. E. (1990). The strength of weak learnability. *Machine Learning*, *5*(2), 197–227.

Schraw, G., Crippen, K. J., & Hartley, K. (2006). Promoting self-regulation in Science education: Metacognition as part of a broader perspective on learning. *Research in Science Education*, (36), 111–139. DOI: 10.1007/s11165-005-3917-8

Sculley, D., Holt, G., Golovin, D., Davydov, E., Phillips, T., Ebner, D., . . . Dennison, D. (2015). Hidden technical debt in machine learning systems. In Advances in Neural Information Processing Systems, 28.

Seo, K., Tang, J., Roll, I., Fels, S., & Yoon, D. (2021). The impact of artificial intelligence on learner–instructor interaction in online learning. *International Journal of Educational Technology in Higher Education*, *18*(1). Advance online publication. DOI: 10.1186/s41239-021-00292-9 PMID: 34778540

Shahzad, M. F., Xu, S., Lim, W. M., Yang, X., & Khan, Q. R. (2024). Artificial intelligence and social media on academic performance and mental well-being: Student perceptions of positive impact in the age of smart learning. *Heliyon*, *10*(8), e29523. DOI: 10.1016/j.heliyon.2024.e29523 PMID: 38665566

Sheng, V. S., Provost, F., & Ipeirotis, P. G. (2008). Get another label? Improving data quality and data mining using multiple, noisy labelers. *Proceedings of the 14th ACM SIGKDD International Conference on Knowledge Discovery and Data Mining*, 614–622.

Sheridan, K., Clark, K., & Williams, A. (2021). Designing AI learning through empathy and creativity: A design thinking approach. *Journal of the Learning Sciences*, *30*(3), 341–366.

Shi, L., Ding, A. C., & Choi, I. (2024). Investigating teachers' use of an AI-Enabled system and their perceptions of AI integration in science classrooms: A case study. *Education Sciences*, *14*(11), 1187.

Shortliffe, E. H. (1976). *Computer-based medical consultations: MYCIN*. Elsevier.

Shute, V. J., Sun, C., & Asbell-Clarke, J. (2017). Demystifying computational thinking. *Educational Research Review*, *22*, 142–158.

Siciliano, B., & Khatib, O. (2016). *Springer handbook of robotics*. Springer.

Siciliano, B., & Khatib, O. (Eds.). (2016). *Springer Handbook of Robotics* (2nd ed.). Springer.

Silver, D.. (2016). Mastering the game of Go with deep neural networks and tree search. *Nature*, *529*(7587), 484–489. PMID: 26819042

Simon, H. A., & Newell, A. (1956). The logic theory machine: A complex information processing system. *I.R.E. Transactions on Information Theory*, *2*(3), 61–79.

Southworth, J., Migliaccio, K., Glover, J., Glover, J., Reed, D., McCarty, C., Brendemuhl, J., & Thomas, A. (2023). Developing a model for AI Across the curriculum: Transforming the higher education landscape via innovation in AI literacy. *Computers and Education: Artificial Intelligence*, *4*, 100127.

Sperling, K., Stenberg, C., McGrath, C., Åkerfeldt, A., Heintz, F., & Stenliden, L. (2024). In search of artificial intelligence (AI) literacy in teacher education: A scoping review. *Computers and Education Open*, *6*, 100169. DOI: 10.1016/j.caeo.2024.100169

State Council of China. (2017). A Next Generation Artificial Intelligence Development Plan. https://www.gov.cn/zhengce/content/2017-07/20/content_5211996.htm

Steinbauer, G., Kandlhofer, M., Chklovski, T., Heintz, F., & Koenig, S. (2021). A Differentiated discussion about AI education K-12. *KI-Künstliche Intelligenz*, *35*(2), 131–137.

Stolpe, K., & Hallstr¨om, J. (2024). Artificial intelligence literacy for technology education. *Computers and Education Open*, *6*, 100159.

Strickland, E. (2019). IBM Watson, heal thyself: How IBM overpromised and underdelivered on AI health care. *IEEE Spectrum*, *56*(4), 24–31. DOI: 10.1109/mspec.2019.8678513

Strielkowski, W., Grebennikova, V., Lisovskiy, A., Rakhimova, G., & Vasileva, T. (2024). AI-driven adaptive learning for sustainable educational transformation. *Sustainable Development*.

Su, J., Ng, D. T. K., & Chu, S. K. W. (2023). Artificial Intelligence (AI) Literacy in Early Childhood Education: The Challenges and Opportunities. *Computers and Education: Artificial Intelligence*, *4*, 100124.

Szegedy, C.. (2015). Going deeper with convolutions. *Proceedings of the IEEE Conference on Computer Vision and Pattern Recognition*, 1–9.

Szeliski, R. (2022). *Computer vision: Algorithms and applications* (2nd ed.). Springer.

Talkspace receives NIH grants to conduct telepsychiatry research. (2021a). *Mental Health Weekly, 31*(3), 8–8. https://doi.org/DOI: 10.1002/mhw.32648

Tanweer, M., & Ismail, A. (2024). Generative AI in curriculum development: A framework for adaptive, customized, and personalized learning. In *Impacts of Generative AI on Creativity in Higher Education* (pp. 193–226). IGI Global.

Tariq, M. U. (2024). Empowering student entrepreneurs: From idea to execution. In Cantafio, G., & Munna, A. (Eds.), *Empowering students and elevating universities with innovation centers* (pp. 83–111). IGI Global., DOI: 10.4018/979-8-3693-1467-8.ch005

Tariq, M. U. (2025). AI and the Ethical Crossroads: Navigating Privacy, Personhood, and Autonomy in the Digital Age. In Chakraborty, S. (Ed.), *Human Values, Ethics, and Dignity in the Age of Artificial Intelligence* (pp. 49–72). IGI Global Scientific Publishing., DOI: 10.4018/979-8-3693-9035-1.ch003

Tariq, M. U. (2025). *AI-Driven Learning and Engagement in Higher Education*. IGI Global., DOI: 10.4018/979-8-3693-4074-5

Tariq, M. U. (2025). Bridging Cultures and Languages: Innovative Literacy Strategies for Inclusive and Engaged Classrooms. In Tussey, J., & Haas, L. (Eds.), *Supporting Cultural Differences Through Literacy Education* (pp. 257–282). IGI Global Scientific Publishing., DOI: 10.4018/979-8-3693-9271-3.ch010

Tariq, M. U. (2025). Revitalizing Pedagogy: Integrating Indigenous Knowledge and Practices Into Higher Education Disciplines. In Kgari-Masondo, M. (Ed.), *Indigenous Teaching Disciplines and Perspectives for Higher Education* (pp. 379–400). IGI Global Scientific Publishing., DOI: 10.4018/979-8-3693-9296-6.ch018

Tatar, C., Jiang, S., Rosé, C. P., & Chao, J. (2024). Exploring teachers' views and confidence in the integration of an artificial intelligence curriculum into their classrooms: A case study of curricular co-design program. *International Journal of Artificial Intelligence in Education*, •••, 1–34.

Tegmark, M. (2017). *Life 3.0: Being Human in the Age of Artificial Intelligence*. Knopf.

Tenberga, I., & Daniela, L. (2024). Artificial Intelligence Literacy Competencies for Teachers Through Self-Assessment Tools. *Sustainability*, *2024*(16), 10386. DOI: 10.3390/su162310386

Teng, H. (2023). The Ethical Implications of AI in Education: A Critical Review of ChatGPT's Impact on Learning. *International Journal for Educational Integrity*.

The White House. (2023). Executive Order on the Safe, Secure, and Trustworthy Development and Use of Artificial Intelligence. https://www.whitehouse.gov/briefing-room/presidential-actions/2023/10/30/executive-order-on-the-safe-secure-and-trustworthy-development-and-use-of-artificial-intelligence/

Thomas, J. W. (2000). *A review of research on project-based learning*. The Autodesk Foundation.

Tolentino, R., Baradaran, A., Gore, G., Pluye, P., & Abbasgholizadeh-Rahimi, S. (2024). Curriculum frameworks and educational programs in AI for medical students, residents, and practicing physicians: Scoping review. *JMIR Medical Education*, *10*(1), e54793. PMID: 39023999

Tononi, G. (2004). An information integration theory of consciousness. *BMC Neuroscience*, *5*(1), 42. PMID: 15522121

Topol, E. (2019). *Deep Medicine: How Artificial Intelligence Can Make Healthcare Human Again*. Basic Books.

Touretzky, D. S., Gardner-McCune, C., Martin, F., & Seehorn, D. (2019). Envisioning AI for K–12: What should every child know about AI? *Proceedings of the AAAI Conference on Artificial Intelligence*, *33*(1), 9795–9799.

Touretzky, D., Gardner-McCune, C., Martin, F., & Seehorn, D. (2019). Envisioning AI for K-12: What should every child know about AI? *Proceedings of the AAAI Conference on Artificial Intelligence*, *33*(1), 9795–9799.

Turing, A. M. (1950). Computing machinery and intelligence. *Mind*, *59*(236), 433–460.

Tutun, S., Johnson, M. E., Ahmed, A., Albizri, A., Irgil, S., Yesilkaya, I., Ucar, E. N., Sengun, T., & Harfouche, A. (2022). An AI-based Decision Support System for Predicting Mental Health Disorders. *Information Systems Frontiers*, *25*(3), 1261–1276. DOI: 10.1007/s10796-022-10282-5 PMID: 35669335

Tzirides, A. O., Zapata, G., Kastania, N. P., Saini, A. K., Castro, V., Ismael, S. A., You, Y., dos Santos, T. A., Searsmith, D., O'Brien, C., Cope, B., & Kalantzis, M. (2024). Combining human and artificial intelligence for enhanced AI literacy in higher education. *Computers and Education Open*, *6*, 100184.

Uban, A.-S., Chulvi, B., & Rosso, P. (2021). An emotion and cognitive based analysis of mental health disorders from social media data. *Future Generation Computer Systems*, *124*, 480–494. DOI: 10.1016/j.future.2021.05.032

UNESCO. (2021). *AI and education: Guidance for policy-makers*. https://unesdoc.unesco.org/ark:/48223/pf0000376709

UNESCO. (2021). AI and Education: Guidance for Policy-Makers. United Nations. https://unesdoc.unesco.org/ark:/48223/pf0000376709

UNESCO. (2021). Recommendation on the ethics of artificial intelligence. https://unesdoc.unesco.org/ark:/48223/pf0000379922

UNESCO. (2021a). Recommendation on the ethics of artificial intelligence. https://unesdoc.unesco.org/ark:/48223/pf0000381137

UNESCO. (2021b). AI Competency Framework for Students. https://unesdoc.unesco.org/ark:/48223/pf0000379868

Vapnik, V. (1995). *The nature of statistical learning theory*. Springer.

Vaswani, A., Shazeer, N., Parmar, N., Uszkoreit, J., Jones, L., Gomez, A. N., & Polosukhin, I. (2017). Attention is all you need. *Advances in Neural Information Processing Systems*, *30*, 5998–6008.

Velander, J., Taiye, M. A., Otero, N., & Milrad, M. (2024). Artificial Intelligence in K-12 Education: Eliciting and reflecting on Swedish teachers' understanding of AI and its implications for teaching & learning. *Education and Information Technologies*, *29*(4), 4085–4105.

Wan, E. (2021). "I'm like a wise little person": Notes on the Metal Performance of Woebot the Mental Health Chatbot. *Theatre Journal*, *73*(3), E-21–E-30. DOI: 10.1353/tj.2021.0068

Wang, B., Rau, P. L. P., & Yuan, T. (2023). Measuring user competence in using Artificial intelligence: Validity and reliability of artificial intelligence literacy scale. *Behaviour & Information Technology*, *42*(9), 1324–1337. DOI: 10.1080/0144929X.2022.2072768

Wang, X. Y., Li, X. M., & Huang, J. Y. (2023). Junior High School Artificial Intelligence Literacy: Connotation, Evaluation and Promotion Strategy. *Open Journal of Social Sciences*, (11), 33–49. DOI: 10.4236/jss.2023.115004

Weizenbaum, J. (1966). ELIZA—A computer program for the study of natural language communication between man and machine. *Communications of the ACM*, *9*(1), 36–45.

West, D. M., & Allen, J. R. (2018). *How Artificial Intelligence is Transforming the World*. Brookings Institution.

Wing, J. M. (2006). Computational thinking. *Communications of the ACM*, *49*(3), 33–35.

Wong, G. K. W., Ma, X., Dillenbourg, P., & Huan, J. (2020). Broadening artificial intelligence education in K-12: Where to start? *ACM Inroads*, *11*(1), 20–29. DOI: 10.1145/3381884

Xie, B., Sarin, P., Wolf, J., Garcia, R. C., Delaney, V., Sieh, I., & Lee, V. R. (2024, March). Co-designing AI education curriculum with cross-disciplinary high school teachers. *Proceedings of the AAAI Conference on Artificial Intelligence, 38*(21), 23146–23154.

Xie, T., Pentina, I., & Hancock, T. (2023). Friend, mentor, lover: Does chatbot engagement lead to psychological dependence? *Journal of Service Management, 34*(4), 806–828. DOI: 10.1108/josm-02-2022-0072

Yadav, S. (2025). Advancing Education With AI-Driven Education for Diverse Learners: Integrating AI Into Pedagogical Practices. In *Integrating AI Into Pedagogical Education* (pp. 49-80). IGI Global Scientific Publishing.

Yi, Y. (2021). Establishing the concept of AI literacy: Focusing on competence and purpose. Jahr – European Journal of Bioethics, Artificial Intelligence Humanities, 12(2), 353–368. https://doi.org/, 24.DOI: 10.21860/j.12.2.8

Yılmaz, Ö. (2024). Personalised learning and artificial intelligence in science education: Current state and future perspectives. *Educational Technology Quarterly, 2024*(3), 255–274.

Yim, I. H. Y. (2024). A critical review of teaching and learning artificial intelligence (AI) Literacy: Developing an intelligence-based AI literacy framework for primary school education. *Computers and Education: Artificial Intelligence, 7*, 100319.

Yim, I. H. Y., & Su, J. (2024). Artificial intelligence (AI) learning tools in K-12 Education: A scoping review. *Journal of Computers in Education*, 1–39.

Yue, M., Jong, M. S. Y., & Ng, D. T. K. (2024). Understanding K–12 teachers' technological pedagogical content knowledge readiness and attitudes toward artificial intelligence education. *Education and Information Technologies*, 1–32.

Zanella, A.. (2014). Internet of things for smart cities. *IEEE Internet of Things Journal, 1*(1), 22–32.

Zawacki-Richter, O., Marín, V. I., Bond, M., & Gouverneur, F. (2019). Systematic review of research on artificial intelligence applications in higher education – where are the educators? *International Journal of Educational Technology in Higher Education, 16*(1). Advance online publication. DOI: 10.1186/s41239-019-0171-0

Zawacki-Richter, O., Marín, V. I., Bond, M., & Gouverneur, F. (2019). Systematic review of research on artificial intelligence applications in higher education. *International Journal of Educational Technology in Higher Education, 16*(1), 1–27.

Zhai, C., Wibowo, S., & Li, L. D. (2024). The effects of over-reliance on AI dialogue systems on students' cognitive abilities: A systematic review. *Smart Learning Environments, 11*(1). Advance online publication. DOI: 10.1186/s40561-024-00316-7

Zhang, H., Lee, I., Ali, S., DiPaola, D., Cheng, Y., & Breazeal, C. (2023). Integrating Ethics and career futures with technical learning to promote AI literacy for middle school students: An exploratory study. *International Journal of Artificial Intelligence in Education, 33*, 290–324. DOI: 10.1007/s40593-022-00293-3

Zhang, T., Schoene, A. M., Ji, S., & Ananiadou, S. (2022). Natural language processing applied to mental illness detection: A narrative review. *NPJ Digital Medicine, 5*(1). Advance online publication. DOI: 10.1038/s41746-022-00589-7 PMID: 35396451

Zhang, Y., Sheng, Q. Z., Alhazmi, A., & Li, C. (2021). Clean and reliable: Data cleaning and preprocessing in machine learning. *IEEE Access : Practical Innovations, Open Solutions, 9*, 140008–140021. DOI: 10.1109/ACCESS.2021.3118676

Zhao, L., Wu, X., & Luo, H. (2022). Developing AI literacy for primary and middle school School teachers in China: Based on a structural equation modelling analysis. *Sustainability, 14*(21), 1–16. DOI: 10.3390/su142114549

Zion, M., & Mendelovici, R. (2012). Moving from structured to open inquiry: Challenges and limits. *Science Education International, 23*(4), 383–399.

Zuboff, S. (2019). *The Age of Surveillance Capitalism: The Fight for a Human Future at the New Frontier of Power*. PublicAffairs.

About the Contributors

Jitendra Pandey is working at Middle East College since Last 15 years Currently Faculty, Department of Computing and Electronics Engineering. PhD research is completed in Artificial Intelligence Domain from India (Waiting for award). Senior Member IEEE Fellow Member British Computer Society Fellow Member, Higher Education Academy UK since 2012. Published Books on topic "Artificial Intelligence on FinTech". Management book on topic "Shadow Leadership". Another book in pipeline on topic "Artificial Intelligence in Logistics". Editor, International Journal of Advanced Studies in Computer Sciences and Engineering, Member of International Association of Engineers (IAENG), Editorial Member of MEC Journal of Big Data and Smart City Presented Guest Lectures in Colleges / Schools on various topics. Chaired session in IEEE conference in Oman, Romania and India. Keynote speaker for various conferences. Successfully Organized many International conferences in Last 15 years. Received research funds from Ministry of Higher Education and Research and innovation Oman for working on National Projects.

***

Raghuvaran A P is an academician and consultant with a demonstrated history of working in a recruitment industry for a while and then education and consultancy. Skilled in Ideation, Data Analytics, AI tools for Analytics, Operation Research, Team Building, and Knowledge Management. Strong education professional with a MBA focused in HR & Systems from Sri Krishna College of Engineering and Technology, along with a UGC NET qualification, and Engineering from Bannari Amman Institute of Technology. Also, a keynote speaker in the areas of: career goal setting, team-building, AI & technology tools, and personality development. Off late, outbound training, corporate consultancy and training, and curriculum content creation have become dominant areas of interest.

Tejaskumar Bhatt is an Assistant Professor, Ph.D. (Computer/IT Engineering) and is currently serving as an Assistant Professor in the Faculty of Engineering and Technology, B.Tech (Computer Science & Engineering) at GLS University, Ahmedabad, since 2023. He holds a Ph.D. in Computer/IT Engineering from Gujarat Technological University, Ahmedabad, India. With over 16 years of academic and research experience, he has made significant contributions in the field of computer engineering. Dr. Bhatt began his academic journey with a Diploma in Computer Engineering in 2003, followed by a B.E. in Computer Engineering in 2007, and an M.E. in Computer Science and Engineering in 2013. Prior to his current role, he worked (2008 - 2023) as an Assistant Professor in the Department of Computer Engineering at Sardar Vallabhbhai Patel Institute of Technology (SVIT), Vasad, Gujarat. He is actively involved in guiding research and is currently supervising two Ph.D. scholars and five M.E. students. Dr. Bhatt has published over 17 research papers in peer-reviewed international journals and conferences, and holds two published patents. He has also successfully completed nine NPTEL certifications across various computer science subjects. In addition to his academic duties, Dr. Bhatt is a member of the editorial board and serves as a reviewer for journals and conferences, including those organized by Ganpat University, Gujarat. He has been invited as an expert speaker in subjects like Operating Systems and Cyber Security at BIT-Varnama and has actively organized and participated in Faculty Development Programs (FDPs) and Short-Term Training (STT) programs. His research interests include Network Security, Cloud Computing, Mobile Ad-hoc Networks (MANET), Wireless Communication, and Smart Grid technology. He has taught a wide range of subjects, such as Operating Systems, Computer Networks, Cyber Security, Digital Forensics, Computer Information Security, Theory of Computation, Microprocessors, Computer Architecture, and Mobile Computing. Dr. Bhatt has also taken on various leadership roles and been an active member and coordinator for several committees and initiatives such iPlacement, Admission, Mock GUJCET Examination, IIT Bombay Spoken Tutorial, Postgraduate Section, Career Advancement Cell, ISTE Student and Faculty Chapters, Departmental Sports Activities, and Social Media. Outside of academics, he is a certified cricket umpire and officiates matches under the Baroda Cricket Association (BCA), Vadodara.

Amruta Amol Bhawarthi is associated with the Department of Vishwakarma Institute of Technology Pune, Maharashtra, India.

A Prabhu Chakkaravarthy was born on 18th February 1985 in Tamilnadu, India. He received his Ph.D. in Computer Science and Engineering from Sathyabama Institute of Science and Technology, Chennai, India. He is graduated from Anna University, Chennai in 2007 with the Bachelor of Technology degree in Computer

Science and Engineering. He received the Master of Technology degree in Computer Science and Engineering from Sathyabama University, Chennai in 2012 with Distinction. He is currently working as an Assistant Professor in Networking and Communications, SRM Institute of Science and Technology, Kattankulathur, Chennai, India. He has published more than 70 research papers in national, international conferences, journals including 8 in Science Citation Indexed journals with 120 citations. He has published 10 patents, 2 patents granted. His research interests include IoT, Artificial Intelligence, Deep Learning, Data Science, Signal Processing and Image Processing.

Deepika Lalit Falak is associated with the department of Artificial Intelligence and Data Science at the PES Modern College of engineering, Shivajinagar, Pune.

J.Dhanalakshmi received B.E. Degree in Computer Science and Engineering from St. Joseph's College of Engineering, Anna University, Chennai, India, in the year 2015. She did her M.E. Degree in Computer Science and Engineering from Jeppiaar SRR Engineering College, Tamilnadu, India, in 2017 respectively. She is working as Assistant Professor in SRm Institute of Sciecena and Technology, Chennai. She had secured 31st university rank in Anna University. She is currently pursuing her Doctor of Philosophy in the Department of Computer Science and Engineering at B.S. Abdur Rahman Crescent Institute of Science and Technology, Chennai, India. She has published 3 papers in International Journals, 5 papers in International IEEE Conferences, 6 papers in Indian Social Science Congress, 2 papers in Springer Book Series and Book Chapter. Her current research interests are Energy Analytics, Machine Learning, Deep Learning, Data Science and Internet of Things.

Aakanksha Jain is an academician and researcher. She is currently working as an Assistant Professor, specializing in computer science and engineering domains. Her research interests primarily lie in image processing, where she has contributed through projects and scholarly work. She has taught subjects including Design and Analysis of Algorithms, Data Structures, and Image Processing, guiding students in both theoretical and practical aspects. With a passion for research and innovation, she continues to explore emerging areas in computing and technology.

Shweta Anand Joshi is associated with the department of information technology of Trinity Academy of Engineering Yewalewadi Pune.

Jaya K is working as Assistant Professor of English, Department of Humanities, Bannari Amman Institute of Technology, Sathyamangalam holding nine years of experience in teaching and mentoring students. She possesses a strong academic background, having earned a doctoral degree in English Literature at Bishop Heber College, Trichy. In addition to her teaching responsibilities, she is an active member of the academic communities, such as ELT@I and ELTIF. She has presented more than six of her research papers at various conferences and published nearly twelve papers in National and International Conferences. She has acted as a resource person in an International Conference and attended two events as a Guest Speaker. She has contributed her service as one of the editorial members in an International Journal "Language, Education and Culture Research".

Darshita Kalyani is a experienced and passionate IT educator. She holds a PhD in Computer Science with a specialization in Software Engineering, combining 19 years of teaching expertise with a strong research background. Her doctoral work focused on advancing methods in software management, quality assurance, and process improvement, and she continues to integrate these insights into curriculum design and student mentoring. She is currently working as an Assistant Professor, specializing in computer science domain. She has taught many subjects like cloud computing, big data technologies (Hadoop, Hive, PySpark), software development, and mobile app frameworks like Flutter, Human Computer Interaction, PHP Framework, UML, Software Engineering, Data Analysis and Visualization (using R), MongoDB, MYSQL etc.

Jatin C. Modh is a dedicated academic and researcher in the field of Computer Science, with a specialized focus on Natural Language Processing (NLP), Machine Translation, and Indic Language Technologies. He holds a Ph.D. in Computer Science from Gujarat Technological University, Ahmedabad (2017–2022), and an MCA (Master of Computer Applications) from Indira Gandhi National Open University, New Delhi (2004). Over the years, Dr. Modh has significantly contributed to the advancement of computational linguistics, particularly in the domain of Gujarati language processing. His research has consistently aimed at bridging linguistic gaps through technology, focusing on the development of tools and techniques for translating and analyzing Gujarati idioms and text structures in English. Dr. Modh has authored and co-authored multiple peer-reviewed publications in reputed international journals and conferences.

Sundarapandiyan Natarajan, Professor and Director, is an accomplished academic and industry professional with over 20 years of experience. He is currently working as Professor and Director, ASBM, Coimbatore. Holding an MBA, M.Sc (IT), and Ph.D. in Management with HRM, he has made significant contributions to education, both locally and internationally. Having worked in the IT industry in the USA, he later served as Principal of Olympia College in

Malaysia, where he championed faculty development and implemented advanced teaching methodologies. Currently, he is an External Examination Board member for Brittany University, France. Also research supervisor for the University of Gloucestershire (UK). Dr. Natarajan's dedication to education has earned him several accolades, including the Founder's Award from Raffles Education Group and a Certificate of Commendation from the Prime Minister of Malaysia for his work with the Malaysian Government Education Development Programs. He has published more than 60 research and review articles and books in reputed national and internationals journals. His passion for Research, teaching, coaching, and mentoring young entrepreneurs continues to inspire many.

Madhumati Nilesh Pol is associated with the Computer College of Vishwakarm Institute Of technology, Pune.

Muhammad Usman Tariq has more than 16+ year's experience in industry and academia. He has authored more than 200+ research articles, 110+ case studies, 150+ book chapters and several books other than 4 patents. He is founder and CEO of The Case HQ, a unique repository for courses, narrative and video case studies. He has been working as a consultant and trainer for industries representing six sigma, quality, health and safety, environmental systems, project management, and information security standards. His work has encompassed sectors in aviation, manufacturing, food, hospitality, education, finance, research, software and transportation. He has diverse and significant experience working with accreditation agencies of ABET, ACBSP, AACSB, WASC, CAA, EFQM and NCEAC. Additionally, Dr. Tariq has operational experience in incubators, research labs, government research projects, private sector startups, program creation and management at various industrial and academic levels. He is Certified Higher Education Teacher from Harvard University, USA, Certified Online Educator from HMBSU, Certified Six Sigma Master Black Belt and has been awarded PFHEA, SFSEDA, SMIEEE, and CMBE.

Robee Roshna Zia is an undergraduate student at Middle East College in Muscat, Oman, pursuing a degree in Business Administration – General Management. They have a strong academic background in English Language and Literature and a deep interest in educational equity and the role of AI in learning. Their research focuses on the impact of AI tools like ChatGPT on students' academic practices, including ethical use, study habits, and critical thinking. They are passionate about promoting access to education, especially for women in conflict-affected regions.

Index

A

C

D

E

G

I

M

N

O

P

R

S

T

www.ingramcontent.com/pod-product-compliance
Ingram Content Group UK Ltd.
Pitfield, Milton Keynes, MK11 3LW, UK
UKHW051039091026
15624UKWH00011B/552

9 798337 322971